# CAREER
# THEORY
## AND
# PRACTICE

# CAREER THEORY AND PRACTICE

## Learning Through Case Studies

■

## JANE L. SWANSON
## NADYA A. FOUAD

**SAGE** Publications
*International Educational and Professional Publisher*
Thousand Oaks   London   New Delhi

*For information:*

SAGE Publications, Inc.
2455 Teller Road
Thousand Oaks, California 91320
E-mail: order@sagepub.com

SAGE Publications Ltd.
6 Bonhill Street
London EC2A 4PU
United Kingdom

SAGE Publications India Pvt. Ltd.
M-32 Market
Greater Kailash I
New Delhi 110048 India

Printed in the United States of America

**Library of Congress Cataloging-in-Publication Data**

Swanson, Jane Laurel.
   Career theory and practice: Learning through case studies / by
Jane L. Swanson and Nadya A. Fouad.
      p. cm.
   Includes bibliographical references and index.

   ISBN 0-7619-1142-1 (acid-free paper)
   ISBN 0-7619-1143-X (acid-free paper)
   1. Career development—Case studies. 2. Vocational guidance Case
studies. I. Fouad, Nadya A. II. Title.
   HF5381 .S937 1999
   158.6—dc21

                              99-6008

                      05   8   7

| | |
|---|---|
| *Acquiring Editor:* | Kassie Gavrilis |
| *Production Editor:* | Wendy Westgate |
| *Editorial Assistant:* | Nevair Kabakian |
| *Typesetter/Designer:* | Danielle Dillahunt |
| *Cover Designer:* | Ravi Balasuriya |

# Contents

# List of Tables

# List of Figures

# List of Additional Cases

# *Preface*

A few years ago, we were sitting at lunch talking about the past year and some of our experiences teaching vocational psychology or career development classes. We had just been to an excellent conference that examined the relationship between career theory and practice, and we were both eager to try to pass on some of this excitement to our students. We lamented that we could not possibly transmit the energy generated by practitioners and academicians talking together and began examining the strategies we had used in the past to engage our students. When we realized that we both had been using cases to make the theories "come to life," the idea for this book was born.

One of the major goals of teaching a vocational psychology class, whether at the master's level or the doctoral level, is to assist students in grasping the complexity of individuals' lives. Work-related issues have always been a source of interest to us personally, from the role that culture plays in the work decisions that people make, to the rich processes underlying career counseling, to the role that interests play in career decision making, to the very personally relevant issues of work and family balance. So our task is to show students how critical work issues are to clients and how work and career concerns affect all other areas of an individual's life. In short, we must convince students that they need to be competent in understanding all areas of an individual's life to be competent practitioners.

We have both done that in our classes by encouraging students to tell their career stories and to listen to the career stories of others. To assist with this storytelling, we were able to find cases in outlets such as the *Career Development Quarterly,* and we used the career histories of our friends and relatives. But we were not able to find a sufficient number of cases directly linked to theoretical perspectives, and we felt that was a critical missing piece. We wanted our students to see why we were insisting on covering career development theories: that their theoretical perspective influences the way they conceptualize a case, their use of assessment, their interventions, and their counseling goals.

We were not interested in recreating the very comprehensive books on career theories available (e.g., Brown & Brooks, 1996; Osipow & Fitzgerald, 1996). By the same token, we did not merely want a collection of cases. Rather, we wrote this book with the very ambitious goal of tying theory and practice together. We wanted to augment the theoretical introductions that students receive from their instructors and course texts with a perspective of the use of that theory in career counseling. And we hoped to do so in a way that engages students' attention and that helps students see the importance of career counseling.

The organization of the book reflects these aims. Each chapter is organized around a major theory or approach. We give a brief overview of each theory or perspective. We do not intend this review to be the reader's only introduction to the theory, but we also want to ensure that students have an understanding of the language of the theory and the major concepts. We then apply each theory to the case of "Leslie." The idea for Leslie originated in an actual client, but Leslie as presented in Chapter 2 is a composite of many clients we have had over the years.

Finally, we invite students to reflect about how they would use each theoretical perspective to approach three additional cases. The cases we have chosen for this section of the book are occasionally the histories of real individuals, with some minor modifications to protect their privacy. In other places, we developed the cases based on clients and friends, and occasionally, they are total figments of our imaginations. We were very concerned that the cases reflect the diverse populations and issues a career counselor may face. Thus, we attempted to incorporate diversity in gender, age, race, sexual orientation, and social class in our cases—at least as much as is possible with a brief snapshot of an individual's career history. We had a tremendous amount of fun developing the cases. We hope you enjoy reading them and thinking about them.

# *Acknowledgments*

We express deep gratitude to the career development scholars who provided feedback on an earlier draft of the entire manuscript: Nancy Betz, Helen Farmer, Lenore Harmon, and Mary Heppner. In addition, we appreciate the feedback offered by experts in each specific theoretical perspective represented by chapters in the book: Gary Gottfredson and John Holland (Chapter 3), James Rounds and Howard Tinsley (Chapter 4), David Blustein and Mark Savickas (Chapter 5), John Krumboltz and Linda Subich (Chapter 6), Steve Brown and Robert Lent (Chapter 7), Linda Forrest (Chapter 8), and Rosie Bingham (Chapter 9).

We thank the following organizations for providing the materials and scoring of assessment instruments: Consulting Psychologists Press, University Career Services at Southern Illinois University, and Vocational Psychology Research at the University of Minnesota.

Thanks, too, to Jeffrey Prince, John Westefeld, and Chris Finn for feedback on case materials and to Dr. Sarah Johnston-Rodriquez and students in her two career development classes in summer 1998 at the University of Wisconsin–Milwaukee for feedback on use of the book.

Finally, we thank "Leslie" for inspiration.

*To our families, for their love and support:*
*Bill, Merit, and Robert (JS)*
*Bob, Nick, Andrew, and Patrick (NF)*

# O N E

# *Introduction*

Ruth has been out of the paid workforce for 8 years. Her youngest son recently started public school, and she would like to find a job. Ruth has a degree in medical technology and worked in a hospital lab for 5 years before her first child was born. In her geographic area, the job market for medical technologists is poor, so she'd like to consider some other job possibilities. She doesn't know what other options are available.

Harry has worked in the human resources department of a large company for over 20 years. He had been satisfied with his job and had received good performance evaluations. However, he was recently assigned new job responsibilities that he doesn't feel adequately trained to do. Last week, he received a negative report from his supervisor, and he's worried that he might lose his job. Harry has been depressed and angry, and his wife is concerned that he's drinking too much.

Joel is a high school junior who doesn't have any idea what he will do after graduating. His parents want him to go to college, believing that a college education will provide him with opportunities they did not have. However, Joel's grades have been mediocre and he really doesn't want to go to college anyway. His guidance counselor tells him that he needs to make a decision soon.

Imagine that any one of these people has come to you for counseling. What impressions do you have of each one? What do you think about his or her career concerns? What additional information would you like to know? How might you begin to address the concerns these people have expressed?

Think back to a time when you had career or work-related concerns, such as an unsatisfying job, an inability to find work, or uncertainty about which career direction to choose. How did these concerns affect other aspects of your life? How did you resolve the concerns?

Each of these situations represents a struggle with some work- or career-related concern. Because work plays a central role in most people's lives, successful pursuit of work activities is crucial to psychological well-being. Furthermore, vocational issues and mental health issues affect one another in individuals' lives (Betz & Corning, 1993; Blustein & Spengler, 1995; Spokane, 1989; Spokane & Fretz, 1993). It is important for counselors to understand the crucial impact of vocational issues and to assist individuals in the choice and implementation of their career-related goals so that people's lives are enriched.

## PURPOSE OF THE BOOK

The purpose of this book is to provide the reader with hands-on, practical examples of how to apply career development theories to career counseling clients. We view the book as a bridge between career theory and career practice. We intend the book to be used in conjunction with other materials that describe career development theories in depth, so the theoretical material in each chapter is presented as a review rather than a comprehensive treatment. We assume that the reader will either use the casebook as a supplement or read other sources for further information about the theory in question (see Appendix A for a listing).

We organized the book to facilitate the integration of theory and practice. In the next chapter, we will introduce "Leslie," the primary case example we will use throughout the remainder of the book. Then, we will consider Leslie from a new theoretical perspective in each subsequent chapter, to demonstrate how theories can inform the way in which counselors view and work with their clients. In addition to Leslie, other cases will be presented in each chapter to offer the reader more opportunities to practice the application of theory to individual clients.

We bring our own experiences as practitioners, researchers, and teachers to bear on how we approached the writing of this book. As practitioners, we believe that the theoretical orientation one adopts has significant impact on how client issues are conceptualized and treated. As researchers, we know that the ethical delivery of career counseling must be based on sound empirical findings. Finally, as instructors, we are committed to helping students make connections between theory, research, and practice in ways that are ultimately in the service of clients. We have attempted to incorporate all of our experiences into the structure of this book by choosing theories that have received empirical support, by highlighting how the theoretical propositions influence views of clients, and by providing considerable case information for analysis and discussion.

We also wanted to incorporate our commitment to integrating contextual issues in conceptualizations of clients' concerns. We both have spent our careers conducting research and teaching students about the need to consider a client's gender, ethnicity, socioeconomic status, sexual orientation, and disability status when helping that client to make career decisions. We think this is critical to ethical practice, and readers will note our perspective in several ways. We integrate considerations of gender and culture in each chapter, we devote a chapter to each (Chapters 8 and 9), and we include cases that represent the diversity of clients who seek counseling.

We wrote the book with two types of readers in mind. The first type is a student in a graduate-level course, such as theories of vocational psychology or practicum in career counseling, who is learning about theories of career development and how to apply these theories to clients. The second type of reader is an established counseling practitioner who wants additional resources to strengthen his or her delivery of career services or who is expanding the focus of his or her work to include career issues.

In this chapter, we focus on the role of theory in career counseling, beginning with a definition of theory and a description of types of career development theories. We then describe the theories selected for this casebook and discuss how to use theories, particularly as a means to develop hypotheses about clients. Next, we present some models of conducting career counseling, including a discussion of how career and personal issues might interact in individuals' lives. Finally, we discuss the role of assessment in career counseling.

## DEFINITION AND TYPES OF THEORIES

A theory is a series of connected hypothetical statements designed to explain a particular behavior or set of behaviors. We have, for example, theories to explain how people solve problems (e.g., Heppner, Reeder, & Larsen, 1983), to predict causes of stress in the workplace (e.g., Long, Kahn, & Schutz, 1992), or to describe how humans develop socially and psychologically (Erikson, 1968). Theories serve a very important purpose in psychology and in counseling; they help psychologists and counselors to conceptualize human behavior. In essence, theories guide us in making sense of very complex sets of information about how humans behave, to help us understand them and to predict their behavior in the future.

One useful way to envision the role of a theory is to view it as a road map (Krumboltz, 1994). Both maps and theories are representations of reality designed for a particular purpose to help guide the user's understanding of a terrain. Motorists use road maps to facilitate traveling from point A to point B; counselors use career theories to help them explain a client's vocational behavior. Krumboltz notes that maps and theories can be useful for one purpose and not for another. Vocational theories, for example, are useful to help understand career choices but might be less useful in other situations.

Krumboltz (1994) also notes that theories designed to explain and predict complex human behavior must, of necessity, omit some aspects of behavior, distort other aspects to highlight them, and depict some unobservable conditions as reality. Thus, a vocational theory may include some variables that help explain career choices but may omit behavior related to interpersonal relationships. The theory may label some behavior to bring attention to it. The theory of work adjustment (Dawis & Lofquist, 1984), for example, has a number of unique identifiers for work-related behavior to highlight those aspects of behavior the theory is designed to explain. Other theories in this book have developed labels to highlight behavior leading to a career choice rather than to highlight behavior in a work setting. None of the theories explains all work-related behaviors, and in this way, theories distort the reality of the very complicated behavior related to making career decisions prior to and following the entry into the world of work. And all theories make some assumptions about internal conditions that are not observable. Super (Super, Savickas, & Super, 1996), for example, assumes that vocational choice is the implementation of the self-concept; this is not directly observable, yet it is a central tenet of his theory.

The theories discussed in this book are attempts to explain some career-related behavior. Each theory overlaps with the others in some ways, but each has distinct constructs. The behavior that theorists seek to explain reflects their values and often stems from their own experiences. In some ways, however, each theory may be viewed as attempting to explain different aspects of the proverbial elephant; depending on the theorist's vantage point, different aspects of behavior will be emphasized.

Recently, there have been attempts to examine ways that vocational theories may converge, thus integrating all the major vocational theories into one that would explain larger portions of career-related behavior in a more comprehensive fashion. A major conference was held in 1992 (Savickas & Lent, 1994) to examine the feasibility of such an undertaking. Although the conference did not result in a unified theory of vocational behavior, the conference organizers did note that "career psychology is well served by a diversity of theoretical positions. Yet it would seem that this diversity would be complemented by . . . [unifying] our diverse fragments of knowledge" (Lent & Savickas, 1994, p. 269). In other words, although there is considerable overlap among the major vocational theories discussed in this book, they each explain some unique work-related behaviors and thus are useful guides for counselors. Without a theoretical framework to guide us, we would find it very difficult to make sense of the information clients might bring to us about their work-related problems. To return to the map analogy used earlier, we consult a road map before we leave on a trip to know the best way to get to our destination; without a map, we may wander aimlessly. So a good theory helps us to represent reality, understand behavior, and assist clients in understanding their behavior.

Theories of vocational behavior have been divided into categories in various ways, depending on the perspective of those doing the dividing. Osipow and Fitzgerald (1996) propose five categories. The first category consists of trait-and-factor (or person-environment fit) theories that emphasize a match between an individual's traits and the factors inherent in the world of work, and the second category includes the sociological approaches that assume that the greatest influence on vocational choice is luck or chance. The third category has to do with developmental approaches that focus on how an individual's self-concept becomes a vocational concept, and the fourth represents personality approaches that assume that individuals choose careers consonant with their personality types. Finally, the fifth category comprises the behavioral approaches. In this book, we have included trait-and-factor theories (Chapter 3, Holland; Chapter 4, theory of work adjustment), developmental theories (Chapter 5, Super and Gottfredson), and behavioral theory (Chapter 6, Krumboltz's social learning theory).

Hackett, Lent, and Greenhaus (1991) divide theories into dominant and emerging perspectives. The dominant perspectives, those with long histories of scholarship and recognition, include the developmental approach outlined by Donald Super (Chapter 5 in this book), Holland's theory of vocational types (Chapter 3), and the trait-and-factor tradition. Hackett et al. include Dawis and Lofquist's theory of work adjustment (Chapter 4) in the latter category. Emerging perspectives include social learning theory (Chapter 6), contextual-developmental theories, and research focusing on women's career development (Chapter 8) and the role of culture (Chapter 9) in career development. Social cognitive career theory (Chapter 7) is also considered an emerging perspective.

## SELECTION OF THEORIES IN THIS BOOK

We chose seven different theoretical approaches for inclusion in this book. Four of the theories are well established: Holland's typological theory of persons and environments, Dawis and Lofquist's theory of work adjustment, developmental theories (most notably, Super's life span, life space approach), and Krumboltz's social learning theory. A fifth theory, social cognitive career theory, is relatively newer but already has made a substantial impact on the way in which career choice and development are viewed. We chose to include two additional approaches—feminist and gender-aware perspectives, and culturally appropriate career counseling—because they reflect the growing recognition of the critical impact of context on career behavior. Fitzgerald and Betz (1994), in fact, note that one of the unifying themes of all major career development theories is their lack of attention to the cultural context in which most clients live and thus that the theories are applicable to a narrow group of the population. We have included approaches that focus on issues related to gender and to race and ethnicity to present approaches that specifically address these contextual factors.

Our decision to include the two chapters related to gender and race and ethnicity does not imply, however, that we consider them "separate" topics. Nor does their placement near the end of the book reflect their relatively lesser importance. In fact, we contemplated placing them before the more well-established theories to highlight their importance. However, we felt it was important to begin with the established theories so that discussions of contextual issues would occur within a fully grounded understanding of career development theories. Moreover, we also decided to integrate gender and multicultural issues as well as other contextual issues throughout the book, in an effort to bring them to the center of discussions about vocational behavior. We would like readers to contemplate contextual factors such as gender and race each time they evaluate a different theoretical perspective or conceptualize a new client.

A danger in presenting each theory separately is that we might foster a polarization of the theories, as well as the implication that one must choose a specific theory and not deviate from that choice. Nothing could be further from the truth. What we hope will become evident throughout the book is that each theory has some unique and useful perspectives to offer our consideration of Leslie, the primary case described in Chapter 2. Moreover, each theory may be particularly useful for a specific type of client, as evidenced by the additional cases provided in each chapter. Despite the organizational structure, we encourage the reader to think integratively across the theoretical perspectives, and we will provide some assistance in doing so in the final summary chapter (Chapter 10). There, we will model how we as counselors might approach a case from an integrated theoretical approach, and we will summarize how each theoretical perspective added to our understanding of Leslie.

## CLARIFYING DISTINCTIONS BETWEEN THEORIES AND THEORETICAL ORIENTATIONS

We have introduced several slightly different sets of terminology, which may cause some confusion: *theoretical orientation, career development theories,* and *career counseling theories.* The term *theoretical orientation* is most frequently used to describe one's general philosophical stance about the nature of personality and of therapeutic change, such as humanistic, cognitive-behavioral, or family systems. One's theoretical orientation interacts with one's view of career development and of career counseling, although this interaction is rarely discussed because of the manner in which we often compartmentalize career counseling and personal counseling, or career issues and personal issues within counseling. We will revisit the issue of "career versus personal" in a later section.

Our discussion about career-related theories has, thus far, focused on theories of career *development* rather than on theories of career *counseling;* yet they are not identical. Theories of career *development* were devised to explain vocational behavior, such as initial career choice, work adjustment, or life span career progress. The goal of theories of career *counseling,* on the other hand, is to provide counselors with direction for how to work with clients; these theories are more akin to theoretical orientation as defined earlier.

The distinction between theories of career development and career counseling is an important one. In fact, Osipow (1996) contends that we have no career counseling theory, although he acknowledges that Krumboltz's (1996) learning theory of career counseling may be the first. There have been, however, several models for conducting career counseling, which we will discuss later in this chapter (Gysbers, Heppner, & Johnston, 1998; Spokane, 1991). Moreover, there have been some efforts to apply psychotherapy theoretical orientations to career counseling, such as psychodynamic career counseling (Watkins & Savickas, 1990) and person-centered career counseling (Bozarth & Fisher, 1990), as well as efforts to more explicitly link career development theories to career counseling (Savickas & Walsh, 1996).

So a counselor might describe her general therapeutic theoretical orientation as cognitive-behavioral, her view of career development as guided by Holland's typological theory, and her work with clients as following Spokane's model of career counseling, with additional attention to the client's cultural context. These descriptors do not contradict one another, because they all influence how this particular counselor views her clients and affect her in-session behavior with clients. Counselors develop their theoretical affinities through exposure to different perspectives and through their own clinical experience.

We advocate that career development theories can be used in career counseling to help practitioners determine the most appropriate and effective tools to help clients. This is an ideal situation, however, and one met with some skepticism by practitioners and researchers alike. Lucas (1996) for example, points out that "counselors insist on relevance, [and the theory-driven research published in] journals [does] not provide it" (p. 82).

The biggest concern voiced by practitioners is that career development theories explain some pieces of vocational behavior, but no client ever walks into an office with just the exact piece explained by the theory. Practitioners contend that some theories do not adequately explain the career behavior of women, racial and ethnic minority clients, or lesbian and gay clients. They find that other theories do not discuss the interface between work and family or that they do not adequately address the myriad problems a client brings to counseling that include both career and personal concerns. This book does not specifically address the split between practitioners and academicians; there still remains the need for practice to inform science in a substantive way (Osipow, 1996). But we are suggesting that a counselor's solid theoretical grounding helps to shape the way the counselor approaches the client and the questions he or she will ask. The counselor's theory will also help to determine the types of assessment tools used in counseling as well as the interventions and techniques employed.

---

## DEVELOPING HYPOTHESES AND A "WORKING MODEL" OF THE CLIENT

Each client who comes for career counseling brings a unique set of personal characteristics and life experiences. Yet a number of common dimensions can guide a counselor's work with clients. The specific dimensions of interest to a particular counselor will be determined by his or her theoretical orientation and the theories of career development and career counseling to which he or she subscribes.

One way in which career development theories influence career counseling is that they suggest hypotheses for further consideration and exploration. Walborn (1996) describes a hypothesis as "an educated hunch that is grounded in theory" (p. 224) or that may emerge from the interaction between the client and counselor. Developing and sharing hypotheses with the client are critical components in any type of counseling or therapy, particularly in career counseling. Regardless of theoretical orientation, counselors have hunches about clients' presenting problems and what might be done to assist them. Moreover, counselors "must be aware of where they are taking the client and, to do so, they must be aware of their hypotheses" (p. 225).

The language we use throughout this book reflects our focus on generating and testing hypotheses, and we strongly encourage the reader to adopt the inquisitive frame of mind that underlies hypothesis generation and hypothesis testing. The structure of the book offers many natural places for the reader to pause and reflect on (a) what is known about a particular client; (b) whether the reader's hypotheses have been confirmed, disconfirmed, or need further elaboration; and (c) additional hypotheses or speculations that the reader might make about a client. For example, in Chapter 2, Leslie's case history is first presented and summarized; then, assessment information is discussed and illustrated. The reader will form some impressions about Leslie based on her career history, so the reader should articulate those impressions before reading the section with Leslie's assessment results. Then, the reader may review the assessment with his or her impressions and hypotheses in mind and search for confirming and disconfirming evidence.

Development of hypotheses begins with the very first exposure to the client, whether in person or through written intake case information, and is an ongoing process throughout counseling. Hypothesis development may need to be an explicitly conscious exercise for new counselors, but it becomes an automatic process as counselors gain experience. It is important for counselors to be aware of and be able to articulate the hypotheses that they form, whether consciously or unconsciously.

Refinement of hypotheses continues throughout counseling. Walborn (1996) suggests a number of benefits of continual development of hypotheses, including helping the counselor remain an active rather than passive listener, keeping counseling sessions focused, providing alternative interpretations of the client's problem, and fostering a collaborative relationship between counselor and client.

Counselors use all sources of available information to generate hypotheses. Moreover, counselors look for consistent themes across several sources of information as well as for inconsistencies between sources. For example, John's highest interest inventory scores are in the artistic area, and he also reports that the course he enjoyed most last semester was art history. However, he is performing poorly in a photography course this semester. These bits of information provide both consistency and inconsistency, resulting in a hypothesis that merits further investigation: John enjoys artistic, flexible, creative environments as a spectator; he doesn't have artistic skills or abilities, nor does he enjoy producing art. How does the counselor then test this hypothesis? The most direct way is to simply offer the hypothesis to John, to see how he reacts and to invite him to gather evidence related to the hypothesis. For example, John's counselor might comment, "You seem to have a strong interest in artistic activities, but perhaps more as an observer or appreciator of art rather than as 'do-er' of art. How does that fit?" The goal is to help John discover something new about himself or to clarify something he already knows and help him to integrate it within his view of himself.

Sometimes, clients already know what the counselor offers as a hypothesis; for example, it may be quite clear to John that he doesn't have strong artistic skills but that he still enjoys learning about art. At other times, clients may not have thought about their interests and activities in quite the same way that the counselor has presented the hypothesis, and further discussion helps them to clarify information about themselves. It therefore becomes very important that the counselor makes it clear that the hypotheses are just that—hunches about the client that await further evidence and verification.

Counselors communicate the hypothetical nature of their statements via several methods. First, counselors use tentative language when offering hypotheses to clients so that they are not perceived as statements of fact. For example, a counselor might say, "I'm wondering if you might prefer selling ideas rather than selling products," or "It seems that you're most comfortable in situations where you clearly know what's expected of you." Second, counselors engage clients in a collaborative effort to develop and examine hypotheses, primarily by paying attention to the development of the counselor-client relationship. If the client feels that he or she is in a comfortable, collaborative relationship, then the client will be more likely to disagree with the counselor if the hypothesis is not accurate. The counselor might ask, "What do *you* think? How does that fit with what you know about yourself?" Finally, counselors need to remind themselves (and their clients) that they are offering hypotheses that are in need of further evidence and to thoroughly search for such evidence: "What other experiences have you had that support your pursuing an artistic career? How else might you 'test out' your interests and skills?"

Walborn (1996) argues that verbal disclosure of a counselor's hypotheses about the client is a necessary, but not sufficient, condition for effective therapy. The way in which hypotheses are shared with the client depends on the stage of counseling, the client himself or herself, the strength of the client-counselor relationship, and perhaps, the theoretical orientation of the counselor. Within the realm of personal-emotional counseling, Walborn (1996) suggests that the presentation of hypotheses differs by schools of therapy. Humanistic approaches use reflection as the major technique because it directs the client's attention to something that the counselor deems important. Explicit disclosure of hypotheses is a fundamental basis of cognitive approaches, and hypotheses are most often related to a client's faulty cognitions. Finally, a variety of methods are used to disclose hypotheses in psychodynamic approaches, such as interpretation and catharsis. These stylistic differences in how hypotheses are offered and explored also may be seen in career counseling. For example, counselors using Krumboltz's social learning theory might use a didactic style, and feminist counselors would be likely to develop a collaborative approach to developing hypotheses with the client.

A final point is that counselors need to judge whether their hypotheses are accurate. First, the counselor must ask himself or herself whether the hypothesis is culture bound. In other words, is the hypothesis appropriate for the client's culture and gender, or is it based on the counselor's own cultural background? Accuracy may be determined by the client's reaction to the hypothesis and by gathering further evidence to test its veridicality. Furthermore, Walborn (1996) suggests that the *process* of developing and sharing a hypothesis actually may be more important than the *content* of the hypothesis. In other words, one outcome of hypothesis testing is that the client learns self-exploration skills, which is important in and of itself.

## CONDUCTING CAREER COUNSELING

Individual career counseling is an "ongoing, face-to-face interaction between counselor and client" (Swanson, 1995, p. 245) in which the focus is on work- or career-related concerns. Career counseling is also defined as "the process of assisting individuals in the development of a life-career with focus on the definition of the worker role and how that role interacts with other life roles" (National Career Development Association, 1997, p. 1), highlighting the importance of placing career issues within the broader context of individuals' lives. Career services may also be delivered to groups, such as in classes or workshops, and career interventions often include activities that do not require a counselor's presence, such as computer-assisted guidance packages. Although these modes of service delivery are useful, in this book, we will focus on individually delivered career counseling in which there is a relationship between counselor and client.

Several authors have developed models of career counseling. To return to our earlier discussion of terminology, these are truly theories of career counseling rather than theories of career development, because their purpose is to outline how counseling might proceed. Although we cannot provide an exhaustive review of each model, we present two models here as an introduction or review. In general, career counseling models are structured around a phase of introduction and relationship building, a phase devoted to exploration of the client's work-related problem, and a phase devoted to helping the client move toward resolution of the problem.

Spokane's model (1991) is one of the most comprehensive career counseling models. His model, as shown in Table 1.1, consists of three major phases: *beginning, activation,* and *completion.* The beginning phase includes three subphases: opening, aspiring, and loosening. The opening subphase is focused on setting the context for counseling; in this phase the client and counselor work together to define the problem. In the second subphase, aspiring, clients rehearse their aspirations and dreams. Career counselors use a variety of techniques to help clients identify areas they want to explore, including fantasy exercises, imagery, or simply asking clients what they have dreamed of doing. The final subphase in the beginning phase is loosening, in which clients identify conflicts and see incongruities between where they are currently and where they would like to be.

The next major phase is the activation phase, in which counselors promote insight and change (Spokane, 1991). The activation phase has three subphases: assessment, inquiry, and commitment. The assessment subphase includes test interpretation, in which the counselor develops hypotheses about the client's concerns and the client gains greater self-awareness. The second subphase is inquiry, in which the client and counselor put together the information from interviews and assessment tools and begin to generate hypotheses. In the final subphase of the activation phase, the commitment subphase, the client reaches a compromise and selects an option.

The final phase of the career intervention process is the completion phase, with subphases of execution and follow-through. In the execution subphase, the client resolves conflicts and moves to implement a career choice. Counselors reinforce appropriate goal-relevant behavior. It may be important for counselors to serve as advocates for clients, to be aware of indigenous support systems that the client can mobilize as a resource. In the follow-through subphase, clients return for periodic contact. Some counselors may never have clients return for follow-through; others will have clients return for a "check-in" on a regular basis.

Gysbers et al. (1998) outline a model of career counseling that has two major phases: (a) *goal or problem identification, clarification, and specification* and (b) *goal or problem resolution.* During the opening subphase of goal or problem identification, the counselor first estab-

TABLE 1.1 Spokane's Model of Career Intervention

| Phase | Beginning | | | Activation | | | Completion | |
|---|---|---|---|---|---|---|---|---|
| Subphase | Opening | Aspiring | Loosening | Assessment | Inquiry | Commitment | Execution | Follow-Through |
| Principal therapeutic task | Establishment of therapeutic context | Client rehearsal of aspirations | Perception of incongruence | Acquisition of cognitive structure | Mobilization of constructive behavior | Management of anxiety | Persistent search | Consolidation of gain |
| Counselor process | Set expectation | Activate hope | Identify conflicts | Generate hypothesis | Test hypothesis | Share hypothesis | Resolve conflicts | Closure |
| Counselor technique | Structure, acceptance | Fantasy | Reflection, clarification | Test, interpretation | Probing, leading | Reassurance | Reinforcement | Periodic recontact |
| Client reaction | Relief | Excitement | Anxiety | Progress, insight | Self-efficacy, control Exploration | Compromise | Withdrawal, adherence | Satisfaction, certainty |

SOURCE: Spokane (1991).

14

lishes a relationship with the client and helps the client to identify and explore his or her initial problems. The next subphase is gathering client information, accomplished through the use of standard formal assessment, as well as through qualitative data gathered from the interview about the client's dreams, hopes, and aspirations. The last subphase of goal identification is understanding and hypothesizing client behavior, in which the counselor forms some hypotheses about the client that will help to guide counseling interventions.

The second major phase, goal or problem resolution, is also characterized by three subphases. In the first subphase, taking action, the counselor uses counseling interventions to assist the client. The second subphase consists of developing career goals and plans of action so that the client may achieve his or her goals and resolve potential barriers. The last subphase is evaluating results and closing the relationship, accomplished when the client's goals are achieved.

As noted in Figure 1.1, at the core of Gysbers et al.'s (1998) model is the *working alliance* between counselor and client, which consists of agreement on the goals and tasks of counseling and formation of a bond between counselor and client (Bordin, 1979). Working alliance is an important component of career counseling in that it creates the atmosphere in which the work of counseling takes place (Meara & Patton, 1994).

These two models provide useful paradigms to help counselors work with clients who have career concerns. Embedded in both of these models is the implicit acknowledgment that individuals bring to counseling a continuum of career-related issues. Clients seek help for career-related problems that are intricately intertwined with their personal lives. A client might, for example, want help getting more information about a career in nursing, then might want help sorting out how training to be a nurse would fit within the responsibilities she has for three children at home. She might decide to seek help responding assertively to demands made by her family; then perhaps she might return to a more information-oriented need of obtaining financial aid. Gysbers et al. (1998) point out that to work effectively with clients, we need to combine skills in career counseling with skills in personal-emotional counseling. They echo Blustein and Spengler's (1995) call for domain-sensitive counseling, which "refers to a way of intervening with clients such that the full array of human experiences is encompassed" (p. 316). In other words, effective career counselors are able to take the client's concerns as the beginning point of therapy and are able to develop interventions in both career and noncareer domains

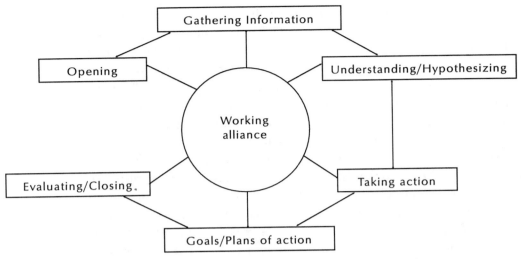

**Figure 1.1.** Gysbers, Heppner, and Johnston's Model of Career Counseling
SOURCE: From Gysbers, Heppner, and Johnston, *Career Counseling: Process, Issues and Techniques.* Copyright © 1998, by Allyn & Bacon. Reprinted with permission.

as is appropriate for the client. In this way, a client's experiences, behaviors, and life roles can be addressed across a variety of contexts.

## INTEGRATING "CAREER" AND "PERSONAL" ASPECTS OF COUNSELING

Because career counseling and personal-emotional counseling developed from different historical traditions and within different specialties of psychology, they are often viewed as independent activities. Haverkamp and Moore (1993) discuss the perceptual dichotomy existing in the profession in which career counseling and personal counseling appear to function as distinct cognitive schemas. They argue that the implicit definition of personal counseling is too broad, consisting of anything not directly related to career; the implicit definition of career counseling, on the other hand, is too narrow, consisting primarily of initial career choices of young adults and neglecting adult work adjustment.

The distinction between career and personal counseling is also maintained by the way that agencies serving these concerns are organized, such as on many college and university campuses. When agencies for career and personal counseling are separated administratively and geographically, presenting issues are unnecessarily differentiated. Counseling often proceeds in one realm (personal or career) without recognition of potential issues in the other realm, and a client might seek both types of services simultaneously (Krumboltz, 1993; Pinkerton, Etzel, Rockwell, Talley, & Moorman, 1990).

Research suggests, however, that it is unwise to view clients with career issues as substantially different from those with personal issues and that they may experience similar levels of psychological distress (Gold & Scanlon, 1993; Lucas, 1992). Moreover, clients might be less satisfied with career counseling when evident personal issues are not addressed in counseling (Phillips, Friedlander, Kost, Specterman, & Robbins, 1988).

A recent trend in the literature is to encourage the integration of personal issues into career counseling. As Hackett (1993) notes, "We are undoubtedly doing our clients a disservice by any attempt to neatly compartmentalize their lives" (p. 110). Betz and Corning (1993) also argue for the inseparability of career and personal issues in counseling, using the variables of gender and race to illustrate the need for a holistic approach.

A related area of literature highlights the connections between career counseling and mental health outcomes. There is increasing recognition that work and mental health are interwoven and that adult vocational needs are complex (Davidson & Gilbert, 1993; Flamer, 1986; Hackett, 1993; Haverkamp & Moore, 1993; Herr, 1989). Brown and Brooks (1985) argue that career counseling with adults may be a viable alternative to stress management and even to personal counseling. Furthermore, they argue that psychologists have overlooked the potential of career counseling, and they encourage practitioners to recognize that the source of psychological symptoms may be in the work situation rather than in intrapsychic factors. They also propose that although all practitioners cannot be skilled career counselors, all should become skilled in recognizing situations in which career counseling is an appropriate intervention.

So how shall we conceptualize the connection between career counseling and personal counseling or between career issues and personal issues? Clearly, career counseling can be very similar to personal counseling, but it can also be very different. Career counseling requires the counselor to use many of the same skills that personal counseling requires, and therefore, the process, at least at times, can be quite similar. Perhaps most important, counselors need to be aware of how career and personal factors are intertwined in their clients' lives and to clearly address the spectrum of issues that clients experience.

## THE USE OF ASSESSMENT
## IN CAREER COUNSELING

Historically, assessment has been an integral part of career counseling. Use of assessment takes a somewhat broader role in career counseling than in counseling for other issues. In personal-emotional counseling, a test is primarily used by the *counselor* to make diagnostic decisions and recommendations. In career counseling, assessment is used primarily for the *client's* benefit, for self-exploration and self-understanding (Duckworth, 1990; Watkins & Campbell, 1990). Because of this expanded role of assessment, it is particularly important that counselors be knowledgeable because they need to explain assessment results to clients accurately, clearly, and in the proper context.

We expect that the reader will have prior exposure and training regarding the use of career assessment or will obtain this information elsewhere. It is beyond the scope of this book to provide the detailed information necessary to use each of these tests in a competent manner. We have chosen to include six different instruments in the primary case (Leslie) to illustrate how a career counselor might use different types of assessment in counseling.

Seligman (1994) discusses benefits and limitations of testing and assessment in career counseling. She suggests that tests are useful for summarizing a person's responses to a set of items or questions, then comparing the responses with those made by other people, thus presenting an objective and standardized picture of a person's behavior. Tests can be used to answer *what* questions (What are the client's primary interests? What difficulties is she having in making a career choice?) and *how* questions (How do the client's interests compare with other women in scientific fields? How do her interests fit with her values?). Tests are less relevant to answering *why* questions (Why is the client having difficulty making a career decision? Why don't her current interests match her past experiences?). The why questions may be sources of further hypotheses about the client to explore in counseling.

The ethical use of psychological assessment requires that counselors be well versed in a variety of topics, including how a test is constructed, norm groups, fairness for female and racial and ethnic minority clients, and strategies for interpretation. Results of career assessment should be considered in the context of all other available information about the client.

Finally, we recognize that the six instruments included in Chapter 2 represent variability in the extent of their development and psychometric characteristics. For example, the Strong Interest Inventory (SII) has a long and rich history, dating back to its first form in 1927, whereas the Skills Confidence Inventory (SCI), developed to complement the SII, is a new addition with less empirical history. Likewise, several of the inventories have been criticized because they have relatively little reliability and validity information or because the evidence available is less supportive than desirable. We chose to use these instruments despite their shortcomings, primarily because they provide ways of operationalizing important constructs in the theories we included in the book. It is critical that counselors choose reliable and valid tests and know the limitations of the instruments that they do choose. We recommend that readers consult sources designed to assist counselors in evaluating assessment instruments, such as the checklists offered by Kapes, Mastie, and Whitfield (1994).

## SUMMARY

We have presented the preceding issues in some detail, because each is crucial to considering how to apply theories of career development to real client issues. We now turn to the primary case of the book, Leslie, in Chapter 2. Then, after considering each of the seven theories in Chapters 3 through 9, we will return in Chapter 10 to some of the ideas presented here in Chapter 1.

# TWO

# The Case of Leslie

Leslie is a 35-year-old Caucasian woman with a bachelor's degree in secondary education. She is seeking career counseling because she is considering quitting her current job as a math teacher in a large suburban high school. Leslie lives in a midsize metropolitan area in the Midwest; she is married with no children.

Leslie reports a considerable amount of dissatisfaction with her current job, particularly related to the stress of many responsibilities and long working hours, as well as the impersonal nature of the school. Leslie reports that her dissatisfaction has been accumulating for several years but that recent events have brought it to the forefront. First, a newly hired principal has instituted administrative tasks that Leslie finds insulting to experienced teachers, such as requiring teachers to keep a weekly log of their activities, submit lesson plans for review, and file quarterly reports on teaching goals. She reports that these activities are "oppressive" and feels quite angry toward the principal. Second, Leslie has had several interactions with parents this year that discouraged her greatly, in which parents showed little involvement in their children's school activities yet expected her to go "above and beyond" her responsibilities as a teacher. This is particularly frustrating because Leslie sees students dealing with increasingly difficult problems at home. She also is frustrated by the lack of intellectual challenge in her job.

21

On the positive side, Leslie reports that she did have an opportunity last year to teach an elective advanced math course, in which her students were more motivated and capable, and that she continues to enjoy the one-to-one aspects of teaching. She feels she is a good teacher, and she values the relationships that she develops with students. She displays considerable enthusiasm when discussing what she likes about teaching.

Leslie is unclear at this point whether or not she will quit her current job and, if so, whether she will be looking for another teaching position or a new career. She wants to explore options to remain in education, whether in a traditional classroom or in some other venue. She also wants to explore new career options outside of teaching. She has thought about a wide range of possible career shifts, such as financial planning, social work, technical writing, and engineering. She is willing to consider pursuing further education if necessary for the career direction that she chooses.

## CAREER AND WORK HISTORY

Leslie grew up in a predominantly white suburban area, where she attended public schools. Leslie excelled in a number of subjects in middle school and high school, including math, science, and social studies. She was a member of the French club, was a math tutor for middle school children, and won first place in the high school science fair during her senior year. She did not actively seek out any positions of leadership within the school but was often viewed as a leader by others, in part because she assumed many organizational responsibilities.

Although her family expected her to go to college, she received little direction from them or her high school guidance counselor in choosing a college or selecting a field of study. She delayed making a decision about attending college until the summer after high school graduation and then decided to enroll at a local community college. She chose the community college because many of her friends were going there, it was close to home, and she was unsure about her motivation to pursue a college education and whether she would be successful.

During her first semester at the community college, she enrolled in general English, math, chemistry, and psychology courses. During this time, she ended a relationship with her high school boyfriend and began dating a college student who was home for Christmas vacation.

The relationship flourished during her second semester, and he encouraged her to join him at the state university 90 miles from home. She finished her first year at the community college and decided to transfer to the state university, in part to join her boyfriend but also because she was disappointed by the lack of challenge in the math and science classes at her community college.

She entered her sophomore year at the university with a number of possible majors in mind but declared herself as "undecided." She enjoyed taking a variety of classes while in college, and she contemplated a number of diverse options—mathematics, engineering, creative writing, psychology, and premedicine—prior to choosing her major. She enjoyed the challenge of her math classes but did not do well in mechanical drawing. She did not enjoy being the only woman in her advanced math classes, particularly because she had some negative experiences with professors who singled out her mistakes. A number of factors detracted from her serious consideration of a degree in mathematics, including lack of encouragement from professors and not wanting to make a commitment to pursue a graduate degree. Her lack of motivation to pursue postbaccalaureate training also precluded her from declaring a major in psychology or premedicine, and she decided not to major in engineering because two professors told her she would have a difficult time combining that career with a family. Leslie finally decided to major in secondary education, with an emphasis in mathematics education, because she could easily combine teaching with raising a family, she could still use her math skills, and it would not require additional schooling beyond a bachelor's degree. In addition, she remembered enjoying her experiences as a math tutor in high school, in which she had feelings of accomplishment when her students understood difficult concepts for the first time.

Leslie had a satisfying student teaching experience in a medium-sized high school in her hometown, and she received positive feedback and excellent evaluations from her supervising teacher. This experience led her to feel excited and confident about her decision to become a teacher.

After graduating from college, Leslie took a teaching position in a small town about 2 hours from the city in which her family lived. Her first year in the position was very stressful, but she also loved being a teacher. As the only math teacher in the school, she taught a diverse range of classes and students, and she enjoyed the challenge of taking sole responsibility for her classes. She also enjoyed being a part of the community. However, she worked every night and weekend to keep up with lesson preparation and grading. She was the youngest teacher in the school and found it difficult to meet people with whom she could socialize outside of work. She also missed being close to her family, and her workload made it difficult for her to see them on weekends. Her relationship with her boyfriend suffered, and they ended the relationship during her second year of teaching.

After 3 years, Leslie found a teaching position in a large school district in the city in which her family lived and looked forward to being closer to them. She soon discovered that her new teaching position, although slightly less stressful, offered fewer rewards than her previous position: Because she was teaching in a larger school system, she was assigned five sections of freshman algebra, which was the least desirable teaching assignment. She found her students to be disinterested, and because they came from a wide geographic area, she no longer felt part of a community. She was also frustrated by the large bureaucratic structure of the school system. She was, however, able to find a greater degree of social support outside of work, including her family and high school friends. She has been in this position for 10 years.

Leslie has a number of interests outside her job, although she does not have much time to pursue any of these interests during the school year due to the time demands of her job. She enjoys several hobbies during the summer, including gardening and other outdoor activities, and teaching swimming lessons at the local YMCA. She also volunteers at the science center, where she maintains the membership records, and she teaches Sunday school at her church.

## FAMILY INFORMATION

Leslie is the second of three children, with an older brother (aged 38) and a younger sister (aged 30). Her brother has a bachelor's degree in electrical engineering and works for a company that designs computer equipment. He was recently promoted to vice president of one of the company's product divisions, in which he coordinates all aspects of a particular product line, from research and development to marketing and sales. He is married to a woman who is a personnel manager for a retail chain; they have two children. Leslie's sister has a bachelor's degree in nursing and has worked at a number of hospitals and home health agencies. She is currently out of the workforce while she cares for two young children; her husband is the district sales manager for a pharmaceutical company.

Leslie's parents are in their early 60s. Her father is a corporate attorney for a midsize manufacturing firm, specializing in product liability and patents. His bachelor's degree was in chemistry, and he worked as a research and development chemist for 10 years before pursuing a law degree. Her mother attended several years of college but left college when she married Leslie's father. She has been involved in community arts organizations, such as volunteering as a docent at the art museum and serving on the board of the symphony orchestra. She did not work outside the home until Leslie's younger sister was in high school. At that time, she found a position with a small business specializing in office interior design, where she continues to work part-time as an administrative assistant.

During college, Leslie's parents stated their support for whatever she chose as a major and provided the financial resources for her college education. Her father strongly encouraged her to major in business, but Leslie found that these were her least favorite classes. Her mother felt that the specific major was not critical as long as she received a good education; she expected that Leslie would not remain in the workforce after marrying and having children. Leslie's family expressed some impatience when it was difficult for her to make a decision about a major; Leslie's brother teased her for "changing her mind so often."

Leslie and her siblings all live within the same metropolitan area as her parents, and they see one another frequently. Leslie has discussed her job dissatisfaction with her family, and they have given her conflicting advice: Her father has renewed his encouragement of Leslie's pursuing a business career, her mother and sister have suggested that now would be a good time for Leslie to have children, and her brother has advised her to quit complaining about such inconsequential aspects of her job.

## MARITAL INFORMATION

Leslie has been married to Joe (39 years old) for 5 years. Joe has an associate's degree from a local community college and is currently a finish carpenter for a residential contractor. He enjoys his work and takes a great deal of pride in his reputation as a highly skilled craftsman; however, he has been thinking about finding a different line of work due to the physical demands and the seasonal fluctuations in available work.

Joe is the older of two sons from a middle-class Hispanic family; both his father and mother are of Mexican descent. Joe's father is a midlevel manager in a hardware store chain. Joe's mother worked as a housekeeper while Joe and his brother were young, but she quit working outside of the home when Joe's father was promoted into management. She has strong connections with the Hispanic community through her involvement in church and neighborhood activities. Joe's brother works as a youth services coordinator, organizing programs at a city-funded community center.

Joe grew up trying to be "American" like the other kids in school. He did not want to acknowledge his Mexican heritage. He refused to speak Spanish at home, he and his parents had great conflicts during his adolescence when he refused to go to church, and he did not include the other adolescents from his Hispanic neighborhood in his circle of friends. His parents were particularly upset when he did not show respect for his grandmother, who came to live with them when he was 15.

Joe graduated from high school with a C average. He did not consider going to college, because he did not enjoy high school and wanted to be working and earning money rather than going to school. The only class he liked was his woodworking class in high school, and he became an apprentice carpenter after graduation. He worked his way up to finish carpenter over a 10-year period. He has worked for the same contractor for the past 7 years.

After the conflicts with his family during and right after high school, Joe increasingly began to appreciate his Mexican heritage. He began to attend community and neighborhood events, although he chose not to live in the same community as his parents. He identifies himself as a Mexican American but has some resistance to the label "Hispanic." He endorses many traditional Hispanic values: a strong emphasis on family, a preference for smooth interpersonal relationships, and respect owed to elders. He is more ambivalent about appropriate roles for men and women in the family. On the one hand, his mother's highest goal was to stay home to care for her family; on the other hand, he realizes that some women want to work and to be more independent.

Joe's first marriage was to a young Hispanic woman who grew up in the same neighborhood. They married at age 22, and his family was very happy that he would stay within their community. His wife, Maria Pilar, worked as a clerk in a small business. The conflicts in their marriage stemmed from her pressuring him to find ways to earn more money. Like his mother, her goal was to have a family and to be a homemaker. Maria was deeply involved in the Hispanic community and the church, and another source of conflict was his resistance to this level of involvement. Their marriage ended 2 years after their son was born. His first wife has since remarried and moved to another Hispanic community.

Leslie and Joe met through a common friend and dated for 6 months before marrying. Leslie's family was not wholly supportive of her decision to marry Joe, although they did not express this directly to Leslie. Joe's family also had concerns about Joe and Leslie's marriage; his mother was concerned that Leslie was too American. Their marriage has been relatively stable: Leslie describes herself as being happy in her marriage. She does, however, express some dissatisfaction with their relationship, primarily due to what she characterizes as their "lack of communication about important issues." Leslie reports that Joe is supportive of her considering a career change, but she feels that he does not understand why she is unhappy with her job and that he seems hesitant about her returning to school.

Joe's 10-year-old son from his first marriage now lives 300 miles away from Leslie and Joe and spends school vacations with them, as well as an occasional long weekend. Leslie wants to have a child, and although Joe has expressed some ambivalence since before they were married, he has been supportive of Leslie's desire. He expects that Leslie would postpone any career decisions if they were to have a child so that she could stay at home full-time until the child was in school. This is consistent with the division of labor that they have assumed, although Leslie is increasingly frustrated that Joe does not contribute more to household responsibilities. Leslie and Joe have had some difficulty related to pregnancy; Leslie had two miscarriages last year. The miscarriages were followed by marital tension and depression, for which Leslie sought individual therapy with a psychologist. Leslie reported that her previous experience with therapy was quite beneficial, although she now wishes that Joe had joined her in therapy.

## LESLIE'S EXPECTATIONS FOR CAREER COUNSELING

Leslie was referred to career counseling by a co-worker who had heard about the availability of career services. She is enthusiastic about career counseling, she is hopeful that the career counselor will help her define her career direction, and she expects to receive information and perhaps advice from the counselor about her "best" career option. She is eager to take the tests that the counselor recommends, stating that she is waiting to hear what the tests will tell her to do.

Leslie feels that she is at a crossroads in her life and is ready to explore her options for her next step. She is evaluating many aspects of her career, family relationships, and marriage. She is looking forward to beginning counseling.

## INITIAL IMPRESSIONS OF LESLIE

Before reading the subsequent section with Leslie's assessment results, use the following questions to formulate your impressions of her:

1. What have you learned about Leslie from the information presented thus far?

2. What general impressions do you have of Leslie? What impressions do you have of her as an employee? As a spouse? As a member of her family of origin?

3. What role do you think Leslie's sex has played in her life and career decisions? What role do you think her culture and socioeconomic status have played? What role do you think her husband's culture and socioeconomic status have played?

4. What more would you like to know about Leslie?

5. What observations or hypotheses do you have about Leslie that the assessment data might clarify? What specifically will you look for in the assessment results?

6. How would you describe her primary career issue(s)? How might you prioritize the direction of counseling? Where would you like to begin in working with Leslie?

## ASSESSMENT INFORMATION

Leslie completed six inventories at the beginning of counseling: the Strong Interest Inventory (SII), the Skills Confidence Inventory (SCI), the Minnesota Importance Questionnaire (MIQ), the Myers-Briggs Type Indicator (MBTI), the Adult Career Concerns Inventory (ACCI), and the Career Beliefs Inventory (CBI). These six inventories were chosen to assess a diversity of components typically considered in career counseling—namely, factors related to career choice *content* (interests, values, and personality) and factors related to career choice *process* (self-efficacy, beliefs, and life-span career issues). Typically, clients would take one or two inventories; in Leslie's case, all six were included to illustrate the types of information that might be assessed as part of career counseling.

## Strong Interest Inventory (SII)

The SII (Harmon, Hansen, Borgen, & Hammer, 1994) is a measure of an individual's vocational and avocational interests. Individuals respond whether they like, dislike, or are indifferent to occupational titles, activities, school subjects, and working with various types of people and whether or not various characteristics are descriptive of them. It is important to note that the SII is not a measure of abilities but, rather, an assessment of an individual's interests.

The SII profile consists of four sets of scales: General Occupational Themes, Basic Interest Scales, Occupational Scales, and Personal Style Scales; each set of scales addresses a different set of questions about the individual. The General Occupational Themes assess an individual's interests in six broad work areas that correspond to Holland's (1997) six vocational personality types, reported in comparison with an individual's same-sex group. The General Occupational Themes are the most global scales and answer questions about work personality: For example, "What am I like? How do I like to work? What types of work environments do I prefer?"

Leslie's SII profile is shown in Appendix B, Figure 1. The profile that she received consists of six pages: a single-page "snapshot" summary of her results on page 1; General Occupational Themes and Basic Interest Scales on page 2; Occupational Scales on pages 3, 4, and 5; and the Personal Style Scales and Administrative Indexes on page 6. Compared with other women, Leslie's SII indicates that she has very high interest in the social theme (helping people), with high interests in the conventional (organization and structure), and the investigative themes (science and analysis). She has average interest in the realistic area (working with things), little interest in the enterprising theme (business oriented, selling), and very little interest in the artistic theme (creative self-expression). Leslie's primary General Occupational Theme code, then, would be social-conventional-investigative, or SCI.

The second set of scales on the SII profile assesses an individual's interests in 25 broad clusters, which may represent vocational or avocational interests, answering the question "What do I like?" The 25 scales are organized in relation to their association with the General Occupational Themes and also indicate the client's level of interest compared with the same-sex group. Leslie's highest Basic Interest Scales, compared with other women, are mathematics (investigative theme), data management (conventional theme), and teaching (social theme), all of which are in the very high range. She also has a high level of interest in religious activities (social theme), science (investigative theme), and social service (social theme). Her lowest Basic Interest Scales are art, applied art, and music/dramatics (all artistic theme), merchandising (enterprising theme), and law/politics (enterprising theme). All of these scores indicate very little interest. The codes for her highest Basic Interest Scales are all social, conventional, or investigative, and the codes for her lowest Basic Interest Scales are artistic, enterprising, or realistic, consistent with the pattern of General Occupational Themes.

The third set of SII scales includes the Occupational Scales, which indicate the similarity of the client's pattern of likes and dislikes to men and women in over 100 occupations, arranged on the profile according to their relation to the six General Occupational Themes. These scales answer the question, "Who am I like?" based on the assumption that similarity to one's co-workers increases job satisfaction. Scores of 40 and above suggest that the client has similar interests to individuals in the particular occupation. Leslie's interests are most similar (scores of 50 or greater) to women who are actuaries, chemists, computer programmers or systems analysts, mathematicians, and mathematics teachers. Her interests are also similar (scores between 40 and 50) to accountants, audiologists, biologists, bookkeepers, credit managers, engineers, medical records technicians, medical technologists, optometrists, pharmacists, physicists, research and development managers, science teachers, special education teachers, and speech pathologists. Her interests are least similar (scores of 0 or below) to women who are artists, art teachers, chefs, florists, interior decorators, medical illustrators, musicians, photographers, public relations directors, and reporters.

The codes associated with Leslie's highest Occupational Scales are primarily conventional or investigative, and the codes associated with her lowest Occupational Scales are primarily artistic and enterprising. Again, the codes for these scales are consistent with the

General Occupational Themes and Basic Interest Scales, with the exception of the social theme. Leslie's interests are moderately similar to only one occupation primarily coded in the social area: special education teachers.

The fourth set of scales is the Personal Style Scales, which assess various aspects of work personality, more specifically addressing the question, "What am I like?" First, is the Work Style Scale, which indicates the client's preferred level of involvement in working with people. Leslie's score is 49, indicating that she has no marked preference for working with people or working alone. Leslie scored 45 on the Learning Environment Scale, which assesses preference for learning by doing versus learning through books and traditional lectures. Leslie's score indicates a slight preference for practical learning over a traditional academic environment. The Leadership Style Scale measures an individual's interest in taking charge of others as a leader. Leslie scored 45 on this scale, showing some interest in working alone rather than assuming a high profile as a leader. The fourth personal style scale is the Risktaking/Adventure Scale, which measures the level of interest an individual has in taking risks and in thrill-seeking activities. Leslie's score is 34 on this scale, indicating that she does not like risk-taking activities.

The sixth page of the SII profile also contains a set of Administrative Indexes, which indicate the way in which the individual has responded to the items. The total responses (TR) indicates the number of items scored, out of a possible 317 items. Although a few items may be omitted without affecting the results, profiles with TR indexes under 300 should not be interpreted. The Infrequent Responses (IR) Index is used to identify invalid or unusual profiles: lower scores (below 5 for females and 7 for males) indicate more unusual responding, but only negative scores should be interpreted as indicating problematic profiles. The remaining eight Administrative Indexes indicate the proportion of preferences that the individual chose for various portions of the SII items: either like-indifferent-dislike, or a forced choice between two options. These indexes may be examined to determine the client's response style in completing the SII across the entire profile as well as within specific sections of items.

Leslie answered all of the SII items (TR index of 317), and she did not respond in an unusual way (IR index of 5). She indicated more dislikes than likes, particularly for items regarding occupations, leisure activities, and types of people. She seemed to be fairly sure about her likes and dislikes, as indicated by very few "indifferent" responses.

## Skills Confidence Inventory (SCI)

Leslie also completed the SCI (Betz, Borgen, & Harmon, 1996) in addition to the SII. The 60-item SCI assesses the level of confidence an individual has in completing tasks associated with the six General Occupational Themes. The overall objective of the instrument is identifying areas for a client to explore. Each scale consists of 10 items, averaged to produce a score between 1 and 5, with 5 indicating very high level of confidence in that area. Leslie has the most confidence in the investigative area, followed by social and conventional (see Appendix B, Figure 2). She has very little confidence in her artistic and realistic skills.

The SCI profile is designed to coordinate with the SII, so the levels of confidence and interest are plotted for each General Occupational Theme. Three scenarios are of particular interest in counseling: Confidence and interest are both high, confidence is higher than interest, or interest is higher than confidence. High confidence and interest in a theme are good areas for further exploration. This is the case for Leslie in the investigative, social, and conventional areas. Leslie has one theme (investigative) in which her interests are slightly lower than her confidence, one theme (social) in which her confidence is slightly lower than her interests, and one theme (conventional) in which interests and confidence are about equal. All three areas are avenues of career exploration, exploring with Leslie whether her interests and confidence could be further developed in these areas. A fourth scenario is represented by Leslie's enterprising and artistic areas, in which her interests and skills confidence are equal but low, suggesting that these areas are "low priority" for further exploration.

## Minnesota Importance Questionnaire (MIQ)

The MIQ (Rounds, Henley, Dawis, Lofquist, & Weiss, 1981) measures 21 work-related needs, grouped into six value categories. An individual's results on the MIQ are presented in two sections. On the first page, intraindividual scores on the 21 needs and six values are plotted relative to one another. The second page consists of comparisons between an individual's need and value profile and reinforcer patterns for various occupations. These two pages provide quite different information: On the first page, an individual is compared only with himself or herself, whereas on the second page, an individual's scores are compared with scores derived from normative occupational groups. An additional type of information is the LCT (logically consistent triads) score, indicating the degree to which the individual responded in a consistent manner across the inventory.

Several points are important in interpreting Leslie's MIQ profile. First, scores on the plotted profile (page 1) are "ipsative" or compared with one's own scores. Leslie's scores represent the relative importance that she gave to the responses. Her "high" scores thus reflect the needs that are most important to her, relative to the other needs measured by the MIQ, and her "low" scores represent the needs that are the least important to her. Second, the least important needs may be those that she is simply indifferent about, or they may represent situations that she wants to avoid. Third, it is important to recall the actual statements to which the client has responded and that underlie the need labels. Referring to these statements (presented on the profile) will help clarify the meaning of the scale labels. For example, a client's score on the scale measuring variety is based on his or her endorsement of the statement, "I could do something different every day." Fourth, it is useful to examine both the 21 individual needs, as well as the 6 higher-level categories, and to determine the degree of consistency or discrepancy between these two levels of scores.

Leslie's MIQ profile is shown in Appendix B, Figure 3. The LCT score for her MIQ profile is 92%, suggesting that her responses were highly consistent across the items. Leslie's highest needs on the MIQ are moral values ("I could do the work without feeling that it is morally wrong"), ability utilization ("I could do something that makes use of my abilities"), achievement ("The job could give me a feeling of accomplishment"), and social service ("I could do things for other people"). Her lowest needs are authority ("I could tell people what to do"), independence ("I could work alone on the job"), and company policies ("The company would administer its policies fairly"). Her highest value categories are achievement and altruism, and her lowest value is status.

The second page of Leslie's MIQ profile consists of 90 occupations arranged alphabetically within six clusters, each containing 15 occupations. Each cluster represents a different pattern of important needs and values, and Leslie's MIQ responses are compared with the patterns of each cluster as well as with individual occupations. Two types of information are presented: a C index, which indicates the degree of correspondence between Leslie's scores and a cluster or occupation, and a predicted level of satisfaction (satisfied, likely satisfied, or not satisfied), based on the strength of the C index. Occupations in the satisfied range are italicized.

Examining the clusters first, four of the six clusters have C index values in the satisfied range (Clusters A, B, C, and F). Leslie's highest C index is for Cluster A (.68), which is characterized by the values of achievement and autonomy and the need of altruism. Cluster C (.60) has the next highest C index and is characterized by the value of achievement and the needs of autonomy and compensation. Cluster A has a large number of occupations that correspond to Leslie's pattern of values and needs: 13 of the 15 occupations have C index values in the satisfied range.

The occupations in Cluster A include counseling psychologist, occupational therapist, speech pathologist, secondary and elementary school teacher, interior designer, architect, and recreation leader. Additional occupations found in Cluster C include real estate sales agent, beauty operator, and caseworker. Occupations with high C indexes are also found in other clusters, including librarian and medical technologist in Cluster F. The lowest C index is for Cluster E, characterized by the value comfort; none of the 15 occupations has a C index value in the satisfied range. The lowest indexes are for occupations such as production assembler, meat cutter, and solderer.

### Myers-Briggs Type Indicator (MBTI)

The MBTI (Myers & McCaulley, 1985) is based on Jung's theory of the preferred ways in which people perceive and process information and make decisions (Kummerow, 1991). Scores are derived on four bipolar dimensions that are then combined to produce one of 16 possible types. The four dimensions are introversion (I) versus extroversion (E), sensing (S) versus intuition (N), thinking (T) versus feeling (F), and judging (J) versus perceiving (P). Interpretation of the MBTI can provide information about two general issues relevant to career counseling: (a) the type of work style that a client prefers or the type of work environment in which a client is most comfortable and (b) the manner in which a client makes decisions and the implications of this decision-making style for the course of career counseling. Discussion of a client's MBTI type thus can introduce an emphasis on work style and decision-making style into career counseling.

To interpret the MBTI with a client, counselors often consider the four dimensions separately as well as the resultant "type." In examining each of the four dimensions, it is important to notice the strength of a client's preferences—that is, how close to the middle or extreme the scores are. If one or more dimensions are not clearly defined, then alternative types might be considered. For example, a client might explore both INFP (introversion-intuitive-feeling-perceiving) and ENFP (extroversion-intuitive-feeling-perceiving) types if his preference for extroversion versus introversion is not clear.

Examining Leslie's MBTI profile (see Appendix B, Figure 4) reveals that she has clear preferences on each of the four dimensions: introversion (vs. extroversion), sensing (vs. intuitive), thinking (vs. feeling), and judging (vs. perceiving). Leslie's introversion score suggests that she prefers to work in privacy and without interruptions, particularly when working on tasks requiring mental concentration, and that she is comfortable working alone. Her sensing score indicates a preference and patience for established routines and an affinity for work tasks that require precision and attention to detail. Leslie's thinking score reveals a logical, analytical method of problem solving and a desire to be treated fairly and to treat others with fairness. Finally, her preference for a judging style of decision making suggests that she enjoys reaching closure and solving problems.

Leslie's scores on the four dimensions result in an ISTJ type. ISTJs are described as "thorough, painstaking, systematic, hard-working, and careful with detail" (Kummerow, 1991, p. 16). As an ISTJ, Leslie is likely to be task oriented, structured, and orderly in her work style and to value a work environment that offers stability and security and that contains other hardworking people who are oriented toward facts and results. She may become impatient when others deviate from the "standard operating procedure."

### Adult Career Concerns Inventory (ACCI)

The ACCI was developed by Super and his colleagues (Super, Thompson, & Lindeman, 1988) to assess issues related to developmental career tasks and stages. The ACCI provides scores on Super's four adult career stages (exploration, establishment, maintenance, and disengagement; see Chapter 5 for more detail), as well as scores for three substages within each stage. A client's scores can be interpreted relative to one another (intraindividually) or by using norms as a point of reference. Scores reflect the amount of concern that a client expresses about various tasks within the stages and substages. The ACCI can be useful in identifying minicycles within maxicycles of

Super's theory, which is of particular interest with a client such as Leslie.

Leslie's ACCI profile (see Appendix B, Figure 5) reveals that her highest stage score is in exploration and that her scores decrease with each subsequent developmental stage (that is, establishment is the second highest score, maintenance is the third highest, and disengagement is her lowest stage score). Thus, her primary career concerns are tasks that are typical of the exploration stage of career development.

Moreover, the substage scales within exploration suggest that she is most concerned about the tasks related to specification, closely followed by crystallization, with lesser concern for implementation. Crystallization includes identifying and developing potential career directions, whereas specification emphasizes choosing a specific occupational direction; these two types of concerns are typical for individuals undergoing career transitions (Super, Savickas, & Super, 1996).

An interesting feature of Leslie's ACCI profile is that, although her maintenance score is relatively low, one substage score is markedly higher than the other two within the stage. The maintenance stage is focused on continuation or further development within one's chosen occupation and position. Leslie expressed concerns related to the innovation substage, which indicates a desire to "do something different or at least to do it differently" within one's established occupation (Super et al., 1996). The innovation substage could be viewed as an "exploration and establishment" minicycle within the maintenance stage.

### Career Beliefs Inventory (CBI)

The CBI (Krumboltz, 1991) was designed to identify irrational and illogical beliefs that individuals use in the process of making a career decision. The 96 items in the CBI form 25 scales. The subscales are further grouped into five general areas: (a) my current career situation, (b) what seems necessary for my happiness, (c) factors that influence my decisions, (d) changes I am willing to make, and (e) effort that I am willing to initiate. A client's responses indicate the level of possible barriers to career decision making that each belief may present. Counselors thus may use the CBI as a tool to help clients pinpoint areas that may be hindering the accomplishment of goals, as well as to aid in identifying cognitive interventions. Scores below 39 in the last column indicate areas for exploration.

Leslie's scores (see Appendix B, Figure 6) suggest the need to examine her desire to excel over others (Scale 8), her need for others' approval (Scale 12), her unwillingness to relocate (Scale 18), her belief that her career path is influenced by others (Scale 10), and her relative unwillingness to take responsibility for her own career decision making (Scale 11). In addition, a counselor may wish to examine Leslie's acceptance of uncertainty (Scale 3), her belief that college is necessary for a good job (Scale 6), her motivation by goals other than achievement (Scale 5), her need for a structured environment (Scale 9), her tendency to compare herself with others (Scale 13), her beliefs that she needs a consistent career path (Scale 17), her lack of satisfaction with her own performance (Scale 19), and her relative lack of willingness to take risks (Scale 21).

Overall, Leslie's career beliefs that appear to be the most problematic for her are in the general area of allowing extraneous factors, primarily other people's opinions, to influence her career decisions. An additional general area a counselor may target is the degree to which she is willing to take risks and accept the uncertainty inherent in the career decision-making process.

### Summary of Leslie's Assessment Information

Leslie has clear interests in the social area, such as teaching, social services, and religious activities, and it is important for her to do things for others and to feel good about what she does. She also has considerable confidence in her ability to do these types of activities, although her interest exceeds her confidence. She enjoys working with people but also values working independently. She is comfortable working alone and frequently prefers it to being with other people. Her favorite part of teaching is the one-to-one interactions with students versus lecturing in front of the entire class.

Her interest in working with people does not include leadership activities, such as managing, persuading, or directing others. She has neither interest nor confidence in enterprising activities.

Leslie appears very comfortable with structure and organization and demonstrates much attention to detail. She is less comfortable when situations are vague or ambiguous and may work to impose structure when none is forthcoming from the situation at hand. She likes developing systems to make her job more efficient.

Leslie also has strong interests in investigative-type activities. She is unfailingly curious and enjoys learning new things. It is important for her to feel that she is accomplishing something, and she enjoys being intellectually challenged. She is confident of her skills as a learner and problem solver. Although she does not have any interest or confidence in artistic activities, she enjoys the creativity involved in solving new problems or figuring out a new way to do a task.

Leslie would appear to be a good candidate for career counseling, and there are many issues that could be profitably addressed in counseling. She is inquisitive and motivated to address her career concerns at this point. Presently, she seems particularly concerned with defining a new direction for herself or creating new opportunities within her original chosen career field. She has some external constraints to her career choices, most notably, difficulty with undertaking a geographic relocation due to family obligations. She also has some internal constraints that the counselor might address, such as the power or influence that she gives to others regarding her career and the way in which she undervalues her own ability and performance. In addition, there might be conflicts due to culture that could benefit from exploration with a counselor.

## WORKING WITH LESLIE'S CASE AND ASSESSMENT INFORMATION

In Chapter 1, we discussed ways in which counselors might use background information and assessment results to develop hypotheses and form a "working model" of the client. Each hypothesis then may be tested by searching for evidence that either confirms or disconfirms the hypothesis, and the working model can be changed to reflect this new evidence. New hypotheses then emerge from the altered model, and the counselor's view of the client is continually refined.

The information presented in this chapter now may be used to develop hypotheses about Leslie. We will present some broad observations about her, followed by specific hypotheses for further investigation.

### Observation 1

There seem to be some discrepancies about social-type activities, values, and personality style. For example, her social General Occupational Theme score is very high, as are several social Basic Interest Scales, yet only one social Occupational Scale is in the "similar" range. She also appears to be fairly introverted, indicating that she often prefers working alone to working with people.

*Hypotheses*

+ Leslie is likely to enjoy social-type activities, particularly those in which she is helping people, but may also find them tiring and stressful. She may need to withdraw from people to rejuvenate and regain her energy.

+ Her interests are dissimilar to other women in social-type occupations (e.g., minister, physical education teacher, parks and recreation coordinator). Members of these occupations are likely to be fairly extroverted, and Leslie's lower scores may reflect her relatively introverted nature.

+ Leslie's interest in social activities could reflect gender stereotyping; she may feel that she "should" like these activities because of gender-role socialization. The General Occupational Theme and Basic Interest Scales, in particular, may be more readily affected by these influences than are the Occupational Scales because of the transparency of the items.

+ Leslie is probably most comfortable when she is in a defined or prescribed role in dealing with others, as is true when she interacts with students as a teacher. She may be less comfortable in less structured interactions.

+ Her interest in social-type activities and in working with people might be limited to specific types of people; she indicated "dislike" to 60% of the items on the Types of People section of the SII.

+ Leslie's interest in the social-type activity of teaching also seems to be fairly circumscribed to mathematics. Mathematics teacher is her highest Occupational Scale directly related to teaching and indicates that she has very similar interests to other math teachers. In contrast, she has low scores on the elementary teacher, foreign language teacher, home economics teacher, and social science teacher Occupational Scales.

### Observation 2

Leslie's low artistic interests are matched by her lack of confidence in these areas, and she has not directly pursued any artistic activities. On the other hand, she does like the creativity that comes with solving problems and designing new methods.

*Hypotheses*

- ◆ Leslie may enjoy artistic activities such as going to concerts or attending museums, but her lack of confidence in her ability to perform artistic activities may have influenced her responses to items on the SII. Alternatively, she may be truly averse to artistic activities.
- ◆ Leslie may feel uncomfortable in artistic environments—those characterized by flexibility, creativity, and self-expression—because they are not as structured as she prefers.
- ◆ Her mother's involvement in artistic organizations and activities is quite different from Leslie's. Leslie may compare herself with her mother and feel that she is not as capable in artistic endeavors.
- ◆ Leslie seems to enjoy creativity as a means to an end—to solve problems or create new ways of doing things—rather than as an end itself.

## Observation 3

Leslie also has low interest and confidence in enterprising activities. Moreover, she ranked as low the MIQ authority item ("telling others what to do"), and her score on the Leadership Style Scale of the SII suggests that she is not comfortable with taking charge or directing others in activities. She has been viewed by others as a leader but has not herself sought out leadership positions. Leslie seems to avoid (as opposed to merely being indifferent to) activities related to leadership or assumption of power or influence. Yet she has taken on administrative duties in her job and volunteer work.

*Hypotheses*

- ◆ Leslie seems to dislike and avoid enterprising-type activities or those that involve active pursuit of leadership roles. Her introverted nature may be antithetical to enterprising activities.
- ◆ Her father may be an enterprising type, with his interests in law and business. Leslie may be disinterested in these activities to set herself apart from her father or because she feels that she cannot match his accomplishments in this area.
- ◆ Leslie has been successful in the administrative responsibilities that she has undertaken. These responsibilities may reflect her conventional interests in structuring and organizing details. Moreover, her administrative duties, like her enjoyment of creativity, may be a means to an end.

◆ Leslie's dissatisfaction with the new principal in her school may be due to her aversion to, or even distrust of, enterprising types. She may feel that he discounts her because she is not like him nor does she value the same things. Leslie may also interpret the new procedures that he has instituted as a sign that he does not respect her ability and experience as a teacher.

### *Observation 4*

Leslie dislikes taking risks, and prefers to "play it safe." Yet she has entered career counseling because she is thinking about changing her career direction, and she seems willing to try new activities and work hard toward goals that are important to her.

### *Hypotheses*

◆ Leslie's dislike of taking risks may be related to her concern about receiving the approval of others. She may be uncomfortable with trying something if there is a possibility that she will fail or will be judged as deficient by someone else.

◆ Her willingness to consider a radical career change, in light of her preference to avoid risk seems to reflect the amount of dissatisfaction she is currently feeling. She may be more willing to take risks than is apparent from her inventory results.

◆ Leslie seems to have a clear sense of what she likes. Equally important, she seems to know what she dislikes. This fact may reduce the perceived risk of exploring a career change.

---

## QUESTIONS FOR DISCUSSION

Review all of the material related to Leslie that has been presented in this chapter, remembering that there are multiple sources of information, including the background and career history, family information, and the results of the six inventories. The questions listed below will guide your review.

1. What other observations do you make from a review of Leslie's background information? From the results of her assessments?
2. What consistent patterns occur within each separate source of information? Across all of the information?

3. What discrepancies do you observe within each source of information? Across all of the information?

4. List specific hypotheses that you have about Leslie.

5. How would you test these hypotheses? How will evidence that you gather confirm or change your working model of Leslie?

6. How is your working model of Leslie shaped by your sex, culture, and socioeconomic background? How is it shaped by her sex, culture, and socioeconomic background?

## CONCEPTUALIZING LESLIE FROM VARIOUS THEORETICAL APPROACHES

The material in this chapter provides sufficiently rich information to begin forming hypotheses about Leslie's career concerns. We now turn in Chapters 3 through 9 to specific theoretical perspectives to working with Leslie. In each chapter, we will add supplementary information about Leslie as appropriate to the specific theory or approach. This additional information is particularly relevant to the "working model" of Leslie that a counselor using a particular theory would be likely to develop.

# THREE

# Holland's Theory of Vocational Personalities and Work Environments

## INTRODUCTORY REVIEW

Theories of person-environment fit, such as Holland's theory and the theory of work adjustment (Dawis & Lofquist, 1984), are considered evolutionary extensions of earlier trait-and-factor counseling (Chartrand, 1991; Rounds & Tracey, 1990), which, in turn, had its roots in a social reform movement at the turn of the 20th century (Parsons, 1909/1989). Person-environment psychology is grounded in the basic assumption that a reciprocal relationship exists between people and their environments; that is, people influence their environments, and environments influence people (Walsh, Price, & Craik, 1992). Perhaps nowhere has this fundamental idea been more thoroughly implemented than in the realm of vocational psychology; in fact, the history of vocational psychology as a scholarly field is intimately intertwined with the evolution of person-environment models applied to career behavior (Swanson & Chu, in press).

Holland's theory of person-environment fit has been an influential force in vocational psychology since its introduction over three decades ago. Part of the theory's appeal is due to the simple and intuitively meaningful premises on which it is based. Holland (1997) describes his theory as answering three fundamental questions. First, what characteristics of persons and environments lead to positive vocational outcomes (such as satisfying career decisions), and what characteristics of persons and environments lead to negative vocational outcomes (such as indecision or dissatisfying decisions)? Second, what characteristics of persons and environments lead to career stability or change over the life span? Third, what are the most effective ways of providing assistance to people with career concerns?

Holland's theory (1997) is based on the underlying premise that career choice is an expression of one's personality and, thus, that members of an occupation have similar personalities and similar histories. He described four working assumptions of his theory. First,  most individuals can be described in terms of their resemblance to six personality types—realistic, investigative, artistic, social, enterprising, or conventional. These types are perhaps best considered as model or theoretical types that describe an individual or with which an individual may be compared. Each personality type has a characteristic set of attitudes and skills to use in response to problems encountered in the environment, and each encompasses preferences for vocational and leisure activities, life goals and values, beliefs about oneself, and problem-solving style (see Table 3.1). An individual is rarely a single "pure" type; rather, individuals are more likely to be a combination of several types, with one type that is dominant and other types that are secondary.

Types develop as a "product of a characteristic interaction among a variety of cultural and personal forces including peers, biological heredity, parents, social class, culture, and the physical environment" (Holland, 1997, p. 2). These experiences lead to an individual's preferring some activities over others; the preferences then develop into strong interests, which lead to related competencies. An individual's interests in conjunction with his or her competencies form a specific "disposition" that allows the individual to "think, perceive, and act in special ways" (Holland, 1997, p. 2).

The second assumption in Holland's theory is that environments can be categorized as one of six model types—again, realistic, investi-

**TABLE 3.1** Characteristics of Holland's Personality and Environmental Typ

| Type | Self-Concept and Values | Potential Competencies | Typical Wo Activities a Environments |
|---|---|---|---|
| Realistic | Emotionally stable, reliable<br>Practical, thrifty, persistent<br>Shy, modest<br>Uncomfortable talking about self<br>Traditional values | Mechanical ability and ingenuity<br>Problem solving with tools, machines<br>Psychomotor skills<br>Physical strength | Job with tangible results<br>Operating heavy equipment<br>Using tools<br>Physical demands<br>Fixing, building, repairing |
| Investigative | Independent, self-motivated<br>Reserved, introspective<br>Analytical, curious<br>Task oriented<br>Original, creative, nonconforming | Scientific ability<br>Analytical skills<br>Mathematical skills<br>Writing skills<br>Perseverance | Ambiguous or abstract tasks<br>Solving problems through thinking<br>Working independently<br>Scientific or laboratory settings<br>Collecting and organizing data |
| Artistic | Independent, nonconforming<br>Self-expressive<br>Intuitive, sensitive, emotional<br>Impulsive<br>Drawn to aesthetic qualities | Creativity, imagination<br>Verbal-linguistic skills<br>Musical ability<br>Artistic ability | Creating artwork or performing<br>Working independently<br>Unstructured, flexible environments that allow self-expression |
| Social | Humanistic, idealistic, ethical<br>Concerned for welfare of others<br>Tactful, cooperative, generous<br>Kind, friendly, cheerful<br>Understanding, insightful | Social and interpersonal skills<br>Verbal ability<br>Teaching skills<br>Ability to empathize with and understand others | Teaching, explaining, guiding<br>Solving problems, leading discussions<br>Educational, social service and mental health organizations |
| Enterprising | Status conscious<br>Ambitious, competitive<br>Sociable, talkative<br>Optimistic, energetic, popular<br>Aggressive, adventuresome | Verbal skills related to speaking, persuading, selling<br>Leadership skills<br>Resilience, high energy, optimism<br>Social and interpersonal skills | Selling, purchasing, leading<br>Managing people and projects<br>Giving speeches and presentations<br>Financial, government and political organizations |
| Conventional | Conscientious, persevering<br>Practical, conservative<br>Orderly, systematic, precise, accurate<br>Careful, controlled | Efficiency, organization<br>Management of systems and data<br>Mathematical skills<br>Attention to detail, perfectionism<br>Operation of office machines | Organizing office procedures<br>Keeping records and filing systems<br>Writing reports, making charts<br>Structured organizations with well-ordered chains of command |

SOURCE: Adapted from Harmon, Hansen, Borgen, and Hammer (1994); Holland (1997); and Sharf (1997).

gative, artistic, social, enterprising, or conventional. The environment's type is determined by the dominant type of the individuals who compose that environment. Because different types of people have varying constellations of skills, abilities, and so on, they prefer to surround themselves with other people who are similar to them: "Where people congregate, they create an environment that reflects the types they most resemble" (Holland, 1997, p. 3). Each environment has a characteristic set of problems and opportunities, as well as requiring differing activities and competencies and offering different rewards (see Table 3.1).

The third assumption of Holland's theory is the heart of the person-environment fit theories—namely, that "people search for environments that will let them exercise their skills and abilities, express their attitudes and values, and take on agreeable problems and roles" (Holland, 1997, p. 4). In a reciprocal manner, environments also search for people, through activities such as social interactions and recruitment and selection practices.

Fourth, personality and environment interact to produce behavior. Knowing an individual's personality type and the type of his or her environment allows us to make predictions about a range of possible outcomes, such as vocational choice, job tenure and turnover, achievement, and satisfaction. Theories of person-environment fit require some mechanism to describe the degree of fit. The mechanism in Holland's (1997) theory is the six types, which can be used to describe either persons or environments, thus allowing a description of how individuals match with their environments.

In addition to the four working assumptions, Holland (1997) also proposed secondary assumptions that outline specific and predictable ways in which the types are interrelated. The first is usually referred to as *calculus:* The six types are arranged in a hexagonal structure, with the distance between types inversely proportional to their theoretical interrelations (see Figure 3.1). That is, types adjacent to one another share more in common than the types that are opposing in the hexagon; for example, realistic types are more like investigative types than they are like social types.

Furthermore, Holland postulated four constructs to describe the relationships between types within people or environments and between people and environments: congruence, differentiation, consistency, and identity. The concept of *congruence* occupies a central role in Holland's theory. Congruence refers to the match between a person and his or her environment, in terms of the six types specified by the

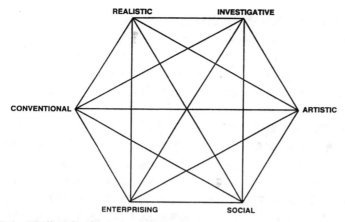

**Figure 3.1.** Holland's Hexagonal Structure
SOURCE: Holland (1997). Reproduced by special permission of the publisher, Psychological Assessment Resources, Inc., from *Making Vocational Choices,* Third Edition, copyright 1973, 1985, 1992, 1997 by Psychological Assessment Resources, Inc. All rights reserved.

theory. An enterprising individual working in an enterprising environment is considered highly congruent, compared with the same individual working within an investigative environment. Congruence is hypothesized to be related to important outcomes, such as job satisfaction and job tenure. As Holland (1997) describes it, "Persons in congruent environments are encouraged to express their favorite behavior repertoires in familiar and congenial settings. In contrast, persons in incongruent environments find that they have behavior repertoires that are out of place and unappreciated" (p. 56).

*Differentiation* pertains to the degree of definition of an individual's interests; interests are considered well differentiated when there is a clear distinction between what an individual likes and dislikes. *Consistency* is a reflection of the "internal coherence" (Spokane, 1996) of an individual's interests in terms of the hexagonal arrangement; an individual with artistic and investigative interests would be considered to be more consistent than an individual with artistic and conventional interests. *Identity* provides "an estimate of the clarity and stability" (Holland, 1997, p. 5) of a person's identity or his or her goals, interests, and talents. Like other constructs in Holland's theory, differentiation, consistency, and identity are used to describe both individuals and environments. Thus, environments as well as people may be characterized by their level of differentiation, consistency, and identity.

These four additional constructs are useful for making predictions about vocational outcomes. More specifically, individuals who are congruent, differentiated, consistent, and high in identity are predicted to be more satisfied and better adjusted than individuals who are incongruent, undifferentiated, inconsistent, and low in identity. For example, a social individual working in a social environment would be happier and more productive than if this same individual were in a realistic environment.

The hexagonal structure (Figure 3.1) in Holland's (1997) theory thus has three functions. First, it defines the amount of consistency in an individual's interests by referencing the relationship of primary, secondary, and tertiary types to one another in the hexagon. Second, in a parallel fashion, it defines the amount of consistency in an environment. Finally, the hexagon defines the amount of congruence between an individual and his or her environment by providing comparisons of the distance between an individual's type and the environment's type.

In summary, Holland's theory places equal emphasis on both an individual and his or her environment. Moreover, the interaction between person and environment is a prime focus of the theory and in predicting an individual's behavior.

## APPLYING HOLLAND'S THEORY TO THE CASE OF LESLIE

### Conceptualizing Leslie's Career History

Leslie's history suggests a stable personality type of social and investigative; she pursued activities in these domains even in childhood. For example, as a child she "played school" with her sister, and in high school she enjoyed her math and science courses and became a math tutor. She has enjoyed working with others through these early activities as well as through her current hobbies of teaching swimming and teaching Sunday school. Her conventional secondary code is reflected in her enjoyment of tasks that require attention to detail and developing systems for managing information. For example, she particularly enjoys organizing her lesson plans and keeping track of her students' progress in her current teaching job, and she chose to be membership coordinator in her volunteer work at the local science center.

It is useful to consider whether Leslie's lack of interest in realistic, enterprising, and artistic activities is because she avoided these areas or because she did not have the opportunities to develop interests in these areas. Holland (1997) suggests that "to some degree, types produce types" (p. 17), primarily because parents engage in activities related to their own types, creating circumstances through which children may develop interests. Leslie's father is a corporate attorney, suggesting that he is an enterprising type, which may have led to his encouraging Leslie to pursue a business career. Her father also may have some interest in investigative activities, as evidenced by his bachelor's degree in chemistry and his work in patents and product liability. Leslie's father, then, ostensibly served as a role model of both enterprising and investigative interests, yet she developed interest in the latter but not the former.

Leslie's mother is an administrative assistant at a small business, which would typically be considered a conventional- or enterprising-type occupation. However, this occupation may not be an accurate reflection of her type because it may have been a choice of convenience rather than an expression of her personality. Moreover, as an interior design firm, the environment of her job actually may have strong artistic elements, which would be consistent with her involvement in artistic volunteer activities, such as being an art museum docent and being active on the symphony board. As with her father, Leslie's mother may have served as a role model for artistic and conventional interests, and Leslie developed interests in one area (conventional) yet not the other (artistic). It would seem, then, that Leslie grew up in an environment in which she was exposed to artistic, enterprising, investigative, and conventional activities. Her brother also developed investigative interests, expressed in his choice of engineering as an occupation, and her sister pursued social and investigative interests in becoming a nurse.

Leslie entered college undecided about her major. She knew that she enjoyed taking advanced math classes and that she had been frustrated by the lack of challenge in those investigative areas in the community college she first attended. Her strategy when she first went to college seemed to be to explore many areas, although most of the options she explored were in the investigative area: engineering, medicine, psychology, and mathematics. There is little information about her social interests in college, either in the coursework she enjoyed or in any outside activities in which she engaged during those years. These two sets of interests—social and investigative—are not wholly consistent in that they are not adjacent to one another on Holland's hexagon. As is true of many individuals with inconsistent interests, Leslie's difficulty with career decision making may have been due to the apparent incompatibility of her social and investigative interests. Leslie's solution was to choose math education, which reflected both types of interests.

The other focal point of Leslie's history from Holland's perspective is evaluation of the environments in which she has been. During her growing up years, her primary environments were her family and various educational settings. Her family represented a heterogeneous environment, with artistic and enterprising elements, as well as investigative and conventional characteristics. Her educational environments were most likely characterized as investigative, particularly in her choice of the more specialized environment that a college math major represented.

## Conceptualizing Leslie's Present Situation

Using Holland's theory to understand Leslie's current career dilemma focuses attention on both her characteristics and the features of her environment. First, Leslie's personality type of social-conventional-investigative (SCI) can be further examined in terms of the constructs of Holland's theory. Her Strong Interest Inventory (SII) profile is well differentiated, with the social interests representing a high peak in her profile and the artistic interests representing a clear low point. However, Leslie's three highest scores (S, C, and I) are all relatively similar to one another and thus show little differentiation. In terms of Holland's hexagonal arrangement of types, Leslie's social, conventional, and investigative interests represent an inconsistent pattern—that is, interests that are not adjacent to one another on the hexagon. These three types are also fairly strong and undifferentiated from one another. Finally, Leslie's vocational identity is fairly clear and stable: She knows where her interests lie, even though they may feel contradictory, and she has maintained these fundamental interests since high school.

An analysis of Leslie's current work environment reveals some important information. In general, high school teachers are likely to be predominantly social types; however, math teachers (conventional-investigative-realistic) and science teachers (investigative-realistic-social) are the colleagues with whom Leslie spends most of her workday. Moreover, her principal is likely to be characterized by social and enterprising interests. From the perspective of person-environment fit, math and science teachers may generally perceive some incongruence in their work environment within a typical high school setting. The particular school in which Leslie works may be characterized as fairly heterogeneous and undifferentiated, because nearly all Holland personality types are represented to varying degrees.

An important question from the perspective of Holland's theory is how much congruence exists between Leslie and her work environment. Leslie's type of social-conventional-investigative would seem to be congruent with the social nature of the high school environment, yet her more immediate environment of her math teacher colleagues presents a more incongruent environment. Furthermore, Leslie may feel somewhere in between the math teachers and the other teachers: She has more social interests than the math teachers, yet more investigative interests than the other teachers, and may feel that she does not really fit with either group. Thus, she may feel unappreciated in her environment.

An additional issue is whether Leslie's current dissatisfaction is related to a shift in her interests, in terms of either absolute or relative strength. That is, she may have increased her interest in social activities relative to her investigative activities, or she may simply want more expression of long-standing social interests.

### Directions and Implications for Career Counseling

Holland's model has been extensively applied in career counseling, most notably in using the six-category typology to categorize individuals in the interpretation of interest inventories such as the Self-Directed Search (SDS; Holland, Powell, & Fritzsche, 1994) or the SII (Harmon, Hansen, Borgen, & Hammer, 1994). In addition, Holland's typology has been used to classify occupational information, college majors, and so on in an attempt to facilitate the matching of individuals and environments.

Holland (1996) attributes the enduring prominence of person-environment fit theories to their focus on two major questions in people's lives: At what kind of work will I be happy? Will I be able to perform the job well? These two questions are relevant to consider in working with Leslie, by exploring the aspects of her current job that are satisfying and dissatisfying and by exploring her performance on the job.

#### Goals of Counseling

From the perspective of Holland's theory, career interventions include using the typology to identify a client's typical mode of interacting with the world of work and using the constructs of differentiation, consistency, and congruence to predict the difficulty of the decision-making process. The typology provides a framework for clients to conceptualize their own vocational personality and see how it may best fit with the world of work. Counseling is intended to "create self understanding and stimulate more insightful and constructive planning" (Holland, 1997, p. 199).

As an initial step, the counselor would listen carefully to Leslie's concerns to clarify how she sees her current situation and why she sought counseling. Clearly, she is unhappy with how she is being treated by her principal, whose behavior might be due to a number of factors, such as poor job performance on her part or poor management style on his part. A goal of counseling with Leslie might be to examine the degree to which her current environment is congruent with her characteristics and to examine other careers or jobs that might provide a better match. In addition, counseling may focus on the inconsistency of her investigative and social interests and the possible shifting of her primary interests in the social and investigative areas.

*Interventions*

Knowing a client's type, in terms of Holland's theory, allows the counselor to make predictions about the manner in which counseling will proceed, such as the amount of interaction with the counselor and the attitude with which the client will approach counseling. How will Leslie behave in counseling as a social-conventional-investigative type? As a social type, Leslie is likely to be verbal and socially skilled, and she is likely to be engaged during counseling sessions. Her secondary conventional type suggests that she will appreciate and work well within structure and will enjoy organizing information about careers. She may prefer the counselor to provide structure and direction within counseling and may feel frustrated if she perceives an insufficient amount of direction. Finally, as an investigative type, Leslie will likely be quite invested in the exploratory activities of career counseling. She will enjoy researching occupations, will ask many questions about the details of her assessment results (including how scores are derived), and will engage in "making sense" of her career history and current dissatisfaction. She is likely to be quite comfortable with following through with assignments between sessions and bringing back new information to discuss with the counselor in the next session. The counselor can thus view Leslie's interest profile and typology as a predictor of her in-session behavior.

Typically, a primary intervention is assessment, both of the client and of his or her environment. A counselor working within Holland's framework would use some assessment tool to determine Leslie's primary, secondary, and tertiary types. Identification of type then would guide further interventions. A counselor working within Holland's theory may have used some alternative assessments to those provided in Chapter 2. First, the counselor would be likely to administer the SDS (Holland et al., 1994) rather than the SII. One unique feature of the SDS is that it elicits a client's vocational daydreams, which then would be classified and coded according to Holland's theory and examined to determine the coherence of her career aspirations. Eliciting Leslie's early vocational daydreams and aspirations may provide a rich source of information, particularly given the messages she received from her family (especially her mother) about the role of work in her life. These aspirations could also be elicited in session and used in conjunction with the SII results.

Second, the counselor may use the Career Attitudes and Strategies Inventory (CASI; Holland & Gottfredson, 1994) to evaluate a range of factors related to Leslie's career situation and her feelings of dissatisfaction. The CASI was designed to address adult career issues and includes scales measuring job satisfaction, work involvement, and family commitment.

As evidenced by the General Occupational Themes of the SII, Leslie's primary type is clearly social. She is interested in helping others, particularly through teaching, and she values her relationships with others. She uses interpersonal skills to solve problems, such as through discussion with others. Conventional types like structured environments and attend well to detail. She may perceive herself as conforming and preferring to follow established rules. As an investigative type, Leslie exhibits intellectual curiosity and likes scientific activities, and she tends to use abstract reasoning to solve problems.

Interpretation of Leslie's SII profile focuses on determining her three-letter Holland code. Her General Occupational Themes indicate a code of social-conventional-investigative, which also is reflected in the Basic Interest Scales. However, examination of the SII Occupational Scales suggests the reverse pattern. Most of her high scores are for investigative occupations, followed by occupations in the conventional area; she has relatively few high scores on social occupations.

The three-letter code resulting from the Occupational Scales portion, determined by the frequency of scales in the "similar" range, is investigative-conventional-social. Following interpretation of the SII, Leslie may consult the *Occupations Finder* (Holland, 1994) or the *Dictionary of Holland Occupational Codes* (Gottfredson & Holland, 1996) to explore occupations with various combinations of her three-letter Holland code, beginning with SCI and ICS.

Leslie's primary codes of social and conventional are frequent types for women; in contrast, her tertiary code of investigative is infrequent for women. One avenue to explore with Leslie is the gender traditionality of her interests. How did her family's expectations shape her interests? What effect did discouragement during college have on her nontraditional (investigative) interests? Would she describe her interests, and her Holland type, as accurately reflecting her authentic self? These questions introduce a gendered context to interpretation of Leslie's SII profile.

Examination of Leslie's Skills Confidence Inventory supports her three-letter code as evidenced on the SII. Leslie indicates a high degree of confidence and a correspondingly high degree of interest in the three areas of social, conventional, and investigative.

Another important focus of counseling is the degree of incongruence that Leslie may experience with her current work environment. The counselor helps her to conceptualize her feeling that she "doesn't fit" in terms of the discrepancy in Holland's typology. This provides Leslie with a framework with which to think about her dissatisfaction that may provide some new clarification and insight.

Holland (1997) recommends using all six themes as part of an analysis of congruence, comparing the relative ordering of types for the individual to the time spent in job tasks or activities related to the six areas. Again, Leslie's highest three codes are social, conventional, and investigative. Leslie engages in many social activities at work, primarily through teaching and through using her interpersonal problem-solving skills in interactions with students and teachers. She also incorporates conventional activities throughout her work day and frequently devises new ways of structuring or organizing her tasks. Investigative activities are reflected in the content matter that she teaches, particularly the higher-level math courses where she engages students in abstract problem solving. The remaining three types—artistic, enterprising, and realistic—all are infrequently occurring tasks in her current job.

Another issue to explore with Leslie in counseling relates to the potential change in her vocational aspirations—in particular, whether her expressed desire to consider other occupations is a by-product of the dissatisfaction she feels with the specific job she currently holds. Holland (1997) notes the reasons underlying stability of aspirations: "People trying to change themselves or their careers receive little environmental support and must overcome the cumulative learning associated with a particular job or self-concept" (p. 12). Individuals may remain in their initial vocational choices because their exploration of alternatives occurs within a circumscribed range and because environmental influences (employers and significant others) discourage change. These issues also could be addressed in counseling with Leslie.

## DISCUSSION QUESTIONS REGARDING LESLIE FROM HOLLAND'S THEORETICAL PERSPECTIVE

1. What specific hypotheses would you develop about Leslie from Holland's theoretical perspective? How does using Holland's theory help you understand Leslie? How might it help Leslie understand herself?

2. How might the inconsistency in Leslie's typology have had an influence on her career decision making in the past? How might it be affecting her current career decision making?

3. What possible reasons might there be for Leslie's similarity to some areas of her mother's and father's interests but not others? What type of influence or encouragement might they have provided her in these areas?

4. How could Leslie find expression for her diverse interests?

5. How might it be helpful for Leslie to conceptualize her current work environment in terms of person-environment congruence? From what does her dissatisfaction stem?

6. What other factors in Leslie's work situation, in addition to congruence, might be related to her dissatisfaction?

7. Leslie can be viewed as existing within multiple environments, such as with her husband, family of origin, and social and leisure activities. To what extent is she congruent with each of these environments? How might this congruence contribute to her overall satisfaction?

8. What types of occupations might offer a more congruent environment for Leslie?

9. What factors in Leslie's life are encouraging her to change occupational directions? What factors are discouraging her from doing so?

## Additional Cases

### Case 1: Allen

Allen is a 36-year-old Asian American man from a traditional Vietnamese family. Allen has lived in the United States since the age of 10, growing up in a primarily white suburb of Atlanta. His father is a successful engineer, but they maintained traditional Vietnamese values; in fact, Allen's mother speaks little English.

Allen did well in high school and attended a large university where he majored in biology. He then entered dental school, following his parents' desires. While in dental school, he married a European American woman, Diane, who was completing an MBA degree. In his second year of graduate school, Allen encountered some problems: He had difficulty with coursework, his wife became pregnant, and Allen's parents were pressuring Diane to quit school and stay home with the baby. Allen was feeling caught between his desire to please his parents and his wife's commitment to her career and her expectations that they have an egalitarian balance of work and family responsibilities.

Allen was interested in his studies, but the emotional turmoil and lack of attention to his work led him to fail his second-year clinical exams, and his adviser recommended that he leave dental school. Diane finished her degree and took a position as a midlevel manager in a large corporation. Allen took a part-time job at a drugstore pharmacy, and took care of their child. Diane's career blossomed, and when she received a significant promotion, Allen's parents began to pressure him to higher achievement and a more traditional role as an Asian male. Allen decided he wanted to become a lawyer. He enjoyed and succeeded in law school, particularly in criminal law. However, neither his parents nor his wife wanted him to become a criminal attorney; his parents did not consider it an appropriate occupation, and his wife didn't like the long hours required. Allen joined a pharmaceutical company as a corporate lawyer, where he has been for 3 years. Allen just told his wife that he is not happy and is quitting his job.

## *Questions for Discussion*

1. What role has congruence played in Allen's career decisions?
2. Examine each of Allen's occupational environments from the perspective of Holland's theory. What would you predict about Allen given this information?
3. Investigative and realistic interests are stereotypic of Asian males, which also corresponded to Allen's initial career choice of dentistry. How might you help Allen determine if these are "true" interests and, if not, would it be appropriate for you to help him choose a more congruent environment?
4. How might you help Allen sort out the expectations he feels from his parents? From Diane? For himself?
5. What unique strengths and assets may Allen have that were unappreciated in his various work environments? How might you help to identify the environment that would be most congruent?

### Case 2: Susan

Susan is a 17-year-old high school junior. She has a 2.5 grade point average, and her favorite classes are drafting and shop. Susan is in a co-op program in which she attends school in the morning and works in the afternoon, which she enjoys because "it's more fun than sitting in class all day." Her father is a building contractor, and her mother is a homemaker.

Susan enjoys athletics and fixing and repairing things. She has no interest in going to college but is not sure what else she might do. She has been talking with her friends and parents about what she might do after graduating from high school. She doesn't know much about the range of job possibilities but thinks she would like to work with her hands. In her co-op program, she's seen the work of welders, tool-and-die makers, mechanics, and assembly line workers. Susan's brother is an electrician, and her older sister stays home with two young children. She also is familiar with the building trades by observing her father's work. Last summer, she asked her father if she could work with him, but he said she was too young. She has asked him again for the upcoming summer and is awaiting his answer.

Susan's parents have given her little guidance about work but do expect her to finish high school and, beyond that, "be happy." She really would like to try something related to building and construction but wonders how difficult it would be as a girl. Although her father has not overtly discouraged her interest in construction, he believes it is an inappropriate choice for her. He is concerned about her physical safety on the job site as well as whether she might be harassed by her co-workers.

Susan doesn't know what to do after high school and feels confused about how to even start choosing a direction. She secretly hopes that her father will hire her after graduation but is afraid to ask him directly about it.

### Questions for Discussion

1. What is Susan's type likely to be, and in what type of environment might she be congruent?
2. How would you use Holland's framework to encourage Susan's exploration? How does Holland's theory assist you in understanding Susan's career dilemma? How might it help you in working with Susan?
3. What interventions might be effective to increase her career exploration and decision making?
4. How might you help Susan address her relationship with her parents, particularly with her father?

### Case 3: Cynthia

Cynthia is a 42-year-old mother of three who is seeking career counseling because she is unhappy in her present job as a purchasing agent for a large furniture company. She took the job a year ago when her own interior design business failed. She started the business 10 years ago when her youngest child started first grade; it had been a dream of hers to own an interior design studio because her friends often told her how nicely decorated her house was. She did quite well in the business for a number of years; however, she developed multiple sclerosis 3 years ago and was increasingly unable to visit clients' homes and engage in the physical activity necessary to keep her business viable.

Cynthia's educational history includes 2 years of college immediately after high school and completion of a certificate program in design. She has taken a few adult education courses at a local community college, primarily to develop new computer skills.

Cynthia's husband died in a car accident 2 years ago. She has managed to save the bulk of an insurance settlement that she received and hopes to keep that money set aside for her inevitable medical expenses. She has been fortunate to have adequate health insurance, but she is concerned about what the future might hold. In addition, her oldest daughter is a sophomore at a state university, and her two younger daughters are planning to attend college if they are financially able to do so. She therefore has a number of practical concerns related to her career, such as maintaining her health insurance, providing for her children, and planning for retirement.

Cynthia took her current job because it was in a similar area, and she believed that she would be able to continue to use her design skills. Unfortunately, in her year on the job, her activities have primarily entailed maintenance of purchasing and client records on the computer, making delivery arrangements, and occasionally dealing with customer complaints. The anticipated promotion to designer does not appear likely in the near future, and although her physical functioning is stabilized, she feels that she should make changes now before her condition deteriorates.

## Questions for Discussion

1. Describe Cynthia's past and current work environments in terms of Holland's theory. In what ways do these environments allow her to express her type?
2. What are some alternate occupations that would allow Cynthia to be in a congruent environment and also accommodate her disability?
3. What have been (and are) the factors involved in Cynthia's original career decision making? How does she balance her practical financial concerns with her dissatisfaction with her current job?
4. How would you incorporate a consideration of her health status into career counseling?

# F O U R

## The Theory of Work Adjustment

The theory of work adjustment (TWA; Dawis & Lofquist, 1984), like Holland's theory, is considered a theory of "person-environment fit." Although these two theories are quite similar in many respects, Holland's theory places greater emphasis on vocational choice, whereas the TWA emphasizes vocational adjustment (Dawis, 1994), thus providing complementary rather than competing views.

The TWA consists of a number of formal propositions and their corollaries that address the process of adjustment to work (Dawis & Lofquist, 1984). These propositions specify aspects of the individual and the work environment that predict job satisfaction and tenure. In other words, the constructs in the TWA would suggest whether an individual would be satisfied on the job and how long he or she may remain in the job. According to the TWA, individuals "inherently seek to achieve and to maintain correspondence with their environments" (Lofquist & Dawis, 1991, p. 18), where correspondence is defined as a "harmonious relationship between the individual and the environment" (p. 22).

As with Holland's theory, the concept of fit or correspondence in the TWA rests on the use of the same dimensions to describe people that are used to describe environments. Holland postulated six types of persons or environments; the TWA takes a different approach. Dawis and Lofquist (1984) describe two sets of common dimensions—namely, an individual's abilities in relation to those required by his or her job and an individual's needs and work values in relation to the rewards available on the job. Both of these are thought to reciprocally interact; in other words, the environment has requirements of the individual (his or her ability to do the job) and the individual has requirements of the environment (the environment's ability to satisfy his or her needs). For example, among the requirements of the occupation of truck driver are that employees are able to drive a truck, load the truck, and keep to a set schedule. Among the requirements of truck drivers are that the job provide them with rewards such as secure employment, independence, and good working conditions.

The TWA stresses the importance of describing the individual's level of *satisfactoriness,* or how well his or her abilities and skills meet what the job or organization requires—literally how satisfactory an employee the individual is. In the preceding example, how well an individual can function as a truck driver is an indication of satisfactoriness. The TWA also stresses the individual's level of *satisfaction,* or how well his or her needs are met by the job. An individual with high security, autonomy, and good working condition needs would be predicted to be satisfied as a truck driver. Satisfactoriness and satisfaction are depicted in Figures 4.1 and 4.2. Figure 4.1 shows the prediction of work adjustment; Figure 4.2 shows the prediction of career choice.

As depicted in Figure 4.1, the individual possesses abilities and the job has ability requirements; if they correspond, the individual is satisfactory. On the basis of their degree of satisfactoriness, employees may be promoted, transferred, or fired, all of which lead to a new job. The path to satisfaction is portrayed at the bottom of Figure 4.1. An individual has values and needs and the job has a reinforcer pattern, or pattern of rewards; if they correspond, an individual is satisfied. Satisfied and satisfactory individuals remain and are retained in the job. If an individual is not satisfied, he or she quits, also leading the individual to seek a new job. A central feature of the TWA is that both satisfaction and satisfactoriness are equally important components in the prediction of work adjustment: "When each party is able to meet the other's requirements—when they are in correspondence—both parties experience and express *satisfaction*" (Dawis, 1996, p. 81).

Despite the dual focus on person and environment, the TWA clearly emphasizes what the person experiences and uses the word *satisfaction* for an individual's satisfaction with his or her job; the word

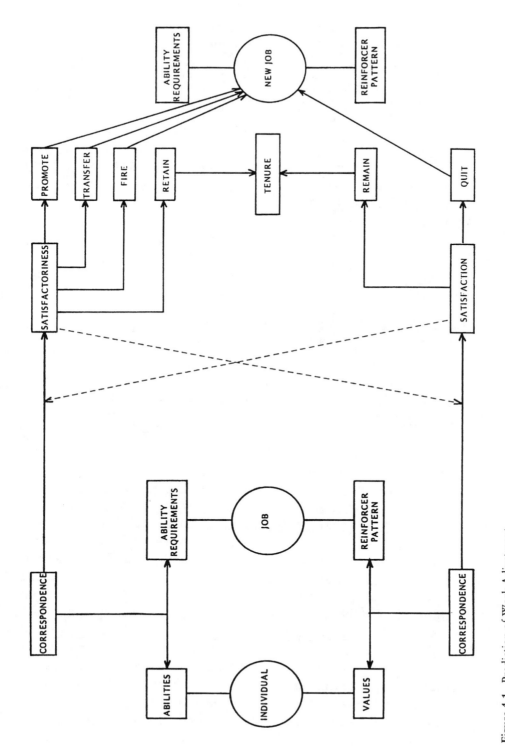

**Figure 4.1.** Prediction of Work Adjustment

SOURCE: Dawis and Lofquist (1984). Used with permission.

63

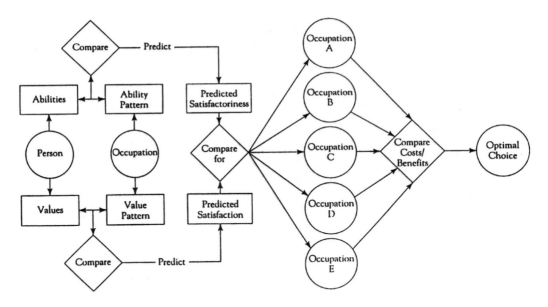

**Figure 4.2.** Using the Theory of Work Adjustment in Career Choice
SOURCE: Dawis (1996). Used with permission.

*satisfactoriness* is used for the individual with whom the work environment is satisfied. Therefore, tenure occurs when an individual is both satisfied and has the abilities to do the job (Dawis, 1996). A further extension of these ideas, which is particularly important for career planning, is that length of time in a job depends on an individual's level of satisfaction and ability to do the job.

The TWA emphasizes the measurement of abilities and values to facilitate the match of an individual to a work environment. Abilities are viewed as "reference dimensions for skills" (Dawis & Lofquist, 1984, p. 233); that is, abilities are seen as general dimensions that underlie groupings of acquired skills. Similarly, values are viewed as representing a grouping of needs. Dawis and Lofquist (1984) define six crucial values—achievement, comfort, status, altruism, safety, and autonomy. On the "environment" side, research underlying the TWA has identified occupational ability patterns and occupational reward patterns to describe a wide variety of occupations. In other words, what abilities does an occupation require of an individual and what needs or values of the individual can the occupation fulfill? In predicting career choice (Figure 4.2), abilities are compared with ability patterns required and values are compared with value patterns supported. Occupations are compared according to how they predict satisfaction and satisfactoriness, and a cost-benefit analysis is conducted to predict the optimal choice for an individual.

Dawis and Lofquist (1984) propose that satisfaction is predicted from the correspondence between an individual's values and the rewards available in the environment. Satisfaction is predicted to be negatively related to the probability of an individual's quitting a job.

An individual's ability to carry out the duties of a job is predicted from the correspondence between his or her abilities and what the environment requires and is negatively related to an individual's being fired from a job. In other words, people are least likely to lose their jobs if they are able to do those jobs successfully. Adjusting to the job and staying in the job for some length of time (job tenure) results from both an individual's level of satisfaction and his or her ability to do the job at a specific time. Moreover, satisfaction and ability to do the job (satisfactoriness) influence the prediction of each other; that an individual is satisfied in a job helps to predict that she or he is able to do the job and vice versa.

The TWA postulates that four personality style variables are important in characterizing how an individual interacts with the environment: celerity, pace, rhythm, and endurance. *Celerity* refers to the speed with which an individual initiates interaction with his or her environment. An individual may have a high celerity—quickly, or perhaps impulsively, acting on the environment—or may have a very low celerity, moving slowly to action. *Pace* indicates the intensity or activity level of one's interaction with the environment. Once the individual acts on the environment, pace indicates the rate of interaction. Individuals may, for example, be viewed as having very high energy; this is an indication of the pace of their interaction with the environment. A high-energy person, however, may have that high energy only when in front of a group of people or may be able to sustain it for only a short period of time. These are indications of his or her rhythm and endurance. *Rhythm* is the pattern of the pace of interaction with the environment (steady, cyclical, or erratic), and *endurance* refers to the sustaining of interaction with the environment. These variables help explain why individuals with similar abilities and values may behave in different ways within a given work environment. Moreover, these constructs can be used to describe environments as well as people, and environments differ from one another in terms of celerity, pace, rhythm, and endurance.

In TWA terms, dissatisfaction serves a central motivational role. Dissatisfaction on the part of either the person or the environment

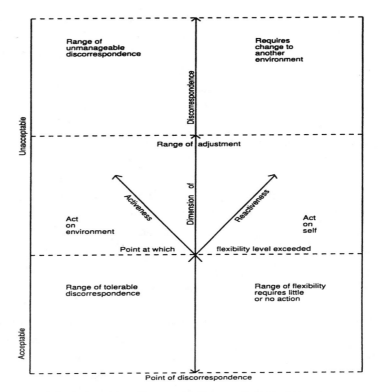

**Figure 4.3.** Relationships Between Adjustment-Style Dimensions
SOURCE: Dawis and Lofquist (1984). Used with permission.

represents disequilibrium in the system and is the impetus for adjustment to occur to restore equilibrium. "Satisfaction motivates 'maintenance' behavior; dissatisfaction motivates adjustment behavior" (Dawis, 1996, p. 87). Figure 4.3 depicts the postulated process of adjustment that occurs when there is discorrespondence between an individual's needs and values and the rewards provided by the job.

The TWA hypothesizes that the stylistic variables of flexibility and perseverance moderate the prediction of satisfaction, satisfactoriness, and work adjustment. The bottom point of the axis in Figure 4.3 indicates zero discorrespondence. Flexibility is the ability to tolerate a mismatch (discorrespondence) between needs and rewards offered by the environment before doing something to make an adjustment. However, at some point, the lack of correspondence between an individual's needs and the environmental rewards is too great, and the individual will move into an adjustment mode. This is shown as the lower horizontal line in Figure 4.3. The individual may strive to adjust himself or herself (reduce level of needs) or may try to adjust the environment (increase rewards). These are depicted as the vectors in Figure 4.3; activeness is acting on the environment, and reactive adjustment is adjusting self. Perseverance is continuing in the job after a mismatch is noted and the individual works to bring it into adjustment, shown as the upper horizontal line. For example, a man who needs autonomy will exhibit flexibility if he is able to tolerate some close supervision. There may be a point, however, when he no longer can tolerate the discrepancy between his need for autonomy and the supervision, and he will try to make an adjustment that reduces the discorrespondence. He will exhibit perseverance if he continues in the environment while he is in adjustment mode. At some point, of course, if he cannot successfully adjust the discorrespondence, he would then be predicted to terminate employment. Flexibility and perseverance are conceptualized as fluctuating constructs; an individual may be flexible and able to tolerate discorrespondence one day, then unable to tolerate it the next, at which point he or she moves into an adjustment mode.

As shown in Figure 4.3, adjustment can occur in two different modes. In the *active mode*, the individual attempts to change the work environment to reduce the amount of discorrespondence by changing the requirements of the environment or the rewards available in the environment. For example, in response to feeling overworked, an employee could ask for a reduction in job assignments or ask for a raise or promotion. In the *reactive mode*, the individual attempts to change himself or herself to reduce discorrespondence by changing his or her work skills or the importance attached to needs. In the previous example, an employee could learn time management skills to increase efficiency or shift priorities so that less focus is placed on work. Thus, adjustment behavior can be aimed at one of four targets: the individual's skills or need requirements and the environment's available ability requirements and rewards.

The concepts of active and reactive modes and of flexibility and perseverance are thus important predictors of what individuals are likely to do if they are dissatisfied (or if the environment is dissatisfied with their behavior). These concepts are also important considerations from a broader perspective: An individual develops a characteristic *adjustment style* over time, which is useful information in career counseling.

Three general stages of development are hypothesized within the TWA. *Differentiation* occurs in the first 20 years, in which abilities, skills, values, needs, and personality style are forming. *Stability* corresponds to the majority of adulthood and is characterized by relative constancy of abilities and values, although specific skills and needs might vary. *Decline* is characterized by physiological changes that alter one's abilities, values, and style. The transitions between the three stages—between differentiation and stability, and between stability and decline—are "the critical points at which adjustment problems are expected to peak" (Dawis, 1996, p. 97).

The TWA is heavily based on an individual differences premise—that is, that individuals differ in their abilities, needs, values, and interests, among other variables. This tradition views people as complex individuals who differ on a number of dimensions and believes that counseling needs to be individualized to allow for the expression of those differences (Dawis, 1994). The individual differences approach suggests that individuals' sex, national origin, sexual orientation, or ethnic background are not reliable bases for determining their abilities and needs.

However, Dawis (1994) notes that an individual's current situation is a product of the opportunities he or she has had to develop work skills and needs. Individuals who have experienced gender or racial discrimination have been restricted in their opportunities for development. The individual differences tradition acknowledges that one's sex or racial or cultural background does not necessarily restrict opportunities, for individuals of all groups and both sexes exist in all occupations. But Dawis (1996) notes that gender and racial and ethnic background "become important when they influence level, ranges, and patterns of work skills and work needs that are or are not developed . . . [a]nd when these person characteristics adversely affect employability" (pp. 95-96).

## APPLYING THE THEORY OF WORK ADJUSTMENT TO THE CASE OF LESLIE

### Conceptualizing Leslie's Career History

The developmental focus of the TWA is on the stages described earlier. Differentiation occurred for Leslie as she began to realize that she had high abilities in math and science and the ability to teach children. She did well in other classes, as well, indicating that her pattern of abilities was high. Leslie placed a high value on achievement, as indicated by her frustration at the lack of challenge in her math classes. She also placed a high value on helping others, such as working as a middle school tutor, and making decisions on her own rather than having others make them for her.

Leslie's needs for challenge and achievement were not rewarded at the community college she entered right after high school. She was frustrated by the lack of challenge in her math classes, in particular, but her social support needs were met. Her achievement needs were more fully satisfied by the university environment, and because she transferred to be with her boyfriend, some of her social needs were met. However, she was dissatisfied by some of the environmental aspects of a math major, such as being the only woman in her courses.

Leslie was a satisfactory employee in her first teaching position. Clearly, the job met some of her needs. Teaching challenged her; it met her achievement needs. She also was able to meet her responsibility needs, because she was able to make decisions in her own classroom. She felt she was able to help others and felt part of the larger community. However, many of her social needs were not met in the smaller town. Although the specific occupation of teaching was a good choice for Leslie, who was both satisfactory and satisfied in the occupation, the overall setting did not provide rewards for her.

### Conceptualizing Leslie's Present Situation

Leslie has been a satisfactory employee in her current job in that she has been in the same school for 10 years. However, she reported some dissatisfaction even before a new principal began to change the rewards in the job. Leslie enjoyed the interaction that teaching allowed her with the children, providing social service rewards. However, she reported that the long hours and the stress of the position frustrated her. The stress she reports may be a result of the lack of correspondence with her environment. This has been exacerbated by the new policies implemented by the principal, which have influenced her ability to get her autonomy and responsibility needs met. In addition, interactions with parents have left her feeling that she is not receiving adequate recognition for her work.

### Directions and Implications for Career Counseling

Career counseling from the perspective of the TWA addresses both the client's satisfaction with the occupation and his or her satisfactoriness. In helping a client make a career choice, TWA counselors assess a client's abilities and needs and evaluate them against the abilities required of and rewards provided by an occupation. As the name implies, however, the TWA is particularly well suited to counseling related to job adjustment. In helping clients with career concerns related to adjustment, counselors evaluate where they are in terms of their threshold of flexibility and evaluate their skills in reactive and active adjustment modes. It is not apparent whether Leslie has sought career counseling for help with a decision to choose a different career or to adjust to her current career. This, in fact, is often typical of midcareer clients seeking career counseling.

### Goals of Counseling

The basic tenets of the TWA have evolved into a broader theory of "person-environment correspondence" counseling (PEC; Lofquist & Dawis, 1991), which argues that many problems that clients bring to counseling can be conceptualized as a lack of fit between an individual and the environment. Lofquist and Dawis suggest that PEC can be applied to diverse counseling situations such as marital counseling, rehabilitation counseling, and stress counseling, as well as to career counseling. Career counseling can serve many purposes, including identifying a career choice, clarifying decision making, helping a client identify opportunities for adjustment, and helping a client decide on various ways to change an environment. However, as Dawis (1996) notes, "The enhancement of self-knowledge is the first goal" (p. 107) regardless of the purpose of career counseling. In fact, in many cases, self-knowledge may be the only goal that can be accomplished.

Fundamentally, person-environment correspondence counseling focuses on the discorrespondence clients experience in the environment. Lofquist and Dawis (1991) outline seven hypotheses that counselors may entertain as they help clients identify the discorrespondence they are experiencing. The first is that there is discorrespondence between the clients' actual abilities and the job requirements; the client's abilities may be too high or too low for the requirements. For example, a nurse may have more abilities than the job requires, or a secretary may not have the computer skills required by the job. The second hypothesis focuses on the client's subjective evaluation of his or her abilities and discorrespondence with the environmental ability requirements. The client's abilities may be perceived as higher or lower than they are in reality, or the environmental requirements may be perceived as more or less difficult than they actually are.

The third hypothesis is that abilities and requirements correspond to each other but that the client has exhibited inadequate performance, which entails discorrespondence with other general environments. In other words, the client may be able to do the job task but is not able to perform tasks in other life roles. In the fourth hypothesis, abilities and requirements correspond, but inadequate performance is a result of need-reward discorrespondence. In this situation, a client's inadequate job performance is not due to his or her lack of abilities but results because the client's needs are not met. The fifth hypothesis concerns the lack of correspondence between the client's needs and rewards; rewards may be higher or lower than needs. This is the situation in which a client's needs are not met by the job environment.

The sixth hypothesis is that the assessed needs are, in fact, arrived at vicariously rather than actually serving as psychological needs. For example, a client's need for variety is derived from imitating others' needs but is not really a strong need for that client. Therefore, when the client is in an occupation that has high rewards for variety, he or she is not really satisfied, because variety is not a true psychological need. Finally, the counselor may test the hypothesis that the client is both satisfactory and satisfied and is coping with problems in other domains. In this case, the client's concerns are less with the work environment than with possible dissatisfaction in other areas of the client's life, such as in a marital relationship.

Goals of counseling may include helping clients adjust to the work environment. Dawis (1996) notes that "counselors typically think of effecting change in the client because it is the client who is immediately accessible. But change can be effected in the work environment as well" (p. 109). Thus, counseling goals may include examination of the possibility that the work environment will be adjusted or how likely it is that the client is able to engage in active adjustment.

### Interventions

Lofquist and Dawis (1991) identify five counseling stages, with specific interventions at each general stage. These stages, or general aims of counseling, delineate specific counselor behaviors at each stage and suggest some indicators of achievement of counseling goals. Setting the groundwork for counseling, clients must come to counseling acknowledging that there is a problem for which they seek professional assistance; they also must be able to communicate. Counselors must be trained in communication and relationship-building skills, have skills in assessment and teaching, have a commitment to individual differences, and be ethical with regard to client differences and confidentiality.

The first stage of counseling involves establishing a working relationship. In this stage, the counselor greets Leslie warmly, uses empathy and active listening skills to encourage her to explain the problem. The counselor also sets the stage for counseling, explains the need for and parameters of length and frequency of interviews. Counselors also set expectations that clients will participate in the assessment process and will complete all homework assignments: "Leslie, the career counseling process that we will go through will include taking a variety of assessment tools to find out more about your abilities and needs. We will spend time talking about the results in here and which occupations best correspond to your needs and abilities. It will also be important for you to do some work outside of the session." Homework for the end of the first session includes completion of a biographical data form and a listing of problem-related incidents that Leslie has encountered in the work environment. Counseling goals are achieved if the ratio of client-counselor talk increases and if Leslie acknowledges the counselor's reflections, completes all assignments, and returns for the second interview.

The second stage of counseling focuses on exploring Leslie's problem. In this stage, the counselor reviews the homework (biographical data form and the problem list) and begins to explore the environments in which Leslie has experienced the most problems. The counselor may say, " Leslie, you have talked about teaching in a smaller school and teaching at your current school. Tell me about some of the problems you have encountered in these." The problems that Leslie identified in her first teaching position included the stress of not feeling competent as a teacher, being concerned about what others thought of her as a teacher, and feeling isolated in the community. The problems she identified in her current position were her frustrations with the new policies imposed by the principal, not having the opportunity to teach advanced classes, discouraging interactions with parents, and student problems.

Once problems are identified, Leslie and her counselor rate them in terms of severity of problems and identify the environment in which each problem occurred. Leslie identified her frustrations with the bureaucratic policies as the least severe and the lack of challenge as the most severe in her current environment. Leslie's ratings are compared with the ratings compiled by the counselor, and the counselor helps her identify the central environment on which counseling will focus—in this case, the high school in which she works. The counselor then asks Leslie to rate environments to identify which environment to target for adjustment. This includes helping her identify the importance of the environment for adjustment as well as the likely motivation of engaging in adjustment. Leslie decided she would try to engage in adjustment behaviors in her role as a teacher. She is given an environmental satisfaction questionnaire for the target environment as homework. Indicators that the counseling goals are met include Leslie's identifying a target environment, completing the homework, and returning for additional interviews.

In the third stage of counseling, the focus is on assessing Leslie's work personality and self-image. The counselor identifies assessments that will be used to help her understand the role that assessment will play in counseling and asks Leslie to provide a self-rating of abilities and needs. Once assessment results are provided to Leslie, the counselor discusses the accuracy, or lack thereof, between Leslie's self-ratings and the assessment results. As an example, the counselor might note, "Leslie, you rated yourself at about the 65th percentile in mathematical reasoning, yet as a math teacher, you have been quite successful in this area." This stage includes the use of interpretation and confrontation skills if needed to help Leslie modify her self-image to be more congruent with assessed dimensions. Counseling goals are met if Leslie completes the self-ratings, takes the assessments, and is able to describe herself congruent with assessment results.

Leslie rates herself on her needs and abilities, and these are compared with her assessed abilities and needs. Leslie's Minnesota Importance Questionnaire (MIQ) indicated that her highest values are achievement, altruism, and autonomy. Her most important rewards are moral values (doing the work without feeling it is morally wrong), ability utilization (doing something that makes use of her abilities), achievement (the job's giving her a feeling of accomplishment), and social service (doing things for others). She also indicated that co-workers (making friends with co-workers), autonomy (planning her work with little supervision), and responsibility (making decisions on her own) are important. Leslie did not take an ability assessment;

therefore, she is inferred to be high in general cognitive ability and verbal ability, because she successfully completed her college degree, and, from her math background, high in numerical ability. However, no information is available on her perceptual or motor abilities. A TWA counselor would have asked Leslie to take an ability assessment, in addition to the other instruments.

The third stage, then, assesses the individual's work abilities and needs; the fourth stage of counseling involves assessment of the environment in similar terms. In this stage, the counselor assesses the ability requirements of the occupation as well as the rewards it provides. This is done through the use of expert ratings, previous research, or interpretation of the information Leslie has provided. The occupational aptitude patterns indicate that Leslie's work environment of teaching has ability requirements of cognitive ability and verbal ability. Rewards available in the environment have been found to be achievement, autonomy, and altruism. The MIQ Correspondence Index indicates that Leslie's pattern of needs may be most reinforced by Cluster A occupations (characterized by values of achievement, autonomy, and altruism). Occupations within Cluster A predicted to satisfy Leslie's needs are counseling psychologist, speech pathologist, occupational therapist, and secondary school teacher.

The counselor then asks Leslie to examine the correspondence between her self-image of abilities and needs and that of the target environment. Leslie identified the discorrespondence between the environment and her needs for achievement, ability utilization, and autonomy. It is critical to understand what a client means in responding to each MIQ statement. Thus, the counselor might ask Leslie, "Tell me what you mean by not doing work that you feel is morally wrong? What might be some examples of times that has occurred?" The counselor asks similar probes about feeling that the job would give Leslie a feeling of accomplishment, make use of her abilities, or allow her to help others. Leslie gives examples of times she felt that she was using her abilities, accomplishing things on the job, and helping others. Leslie also discusses how her needs for responsibility and autonomy are not being met with the new bureaucratic policies implemented by the principal. She acknowledges that the most important priority is to create more correspondence between the environment and her need for achievement and ability utilization.

The counselor then invites Leslie to identify actions to reduce the discorrespondence between herself and the environment, discussing this in terms of personality and adjustment styles. Leslie's personality style appears to be characterized by a fairly steady rhythm and a relatively high level of endurance, both of these inferred from her continuous employment in the same high school. It is more difficult to infer her celerity or pace from her employment history. The counselor uses a personality style checklist to aid in this discussion. In assessing Leslie's adjustment style, the counselor finds that Leslie has chosen reactive adjustment in the past—that is, changing her own expectations and priorities. However, she also has a high level of perseverance, because she has remained in the environment even though she has felt discorrespondent with it. The counselor then identifies actions that Leslie might take, also discussing the consequences of those actions. These actions may include identifying ways that she might change her environment to increase her feelings of accomplishment and ability utilization or ways that she might find other environments to meet those needs. She might also choose to reprioritize to increase the importance of rewards available in the environment, such as security or creativity.

Behaviors that indicate achievement of goals include Leslie's completing the personality style checklist and accurately describing the correspondence between herself and the target environment. Additional behaviors might include Leslie's choosing adjustment style actions and possibly actively exploring alternative jobs or occupations more congruent with her personality dimensions. Finally, it is anticipated that Leslie will report satisfaction after changing her behavior.

The final counseling stage is assessing the effect of counseling on the problem. In this stage, the counselor asks Leslie to summarize the presenting problem and to evaluate the difference between the problem and her current state. For example, "Leslie, over the past several weeks we have evaluated your abilities, needs and interests, and have examined a variety of occupations. Could you go back and recap for me what initially brought you here and how that concern may have changed since our first session?" The counselor asks Leslie to complete an environmental satisfaction questionnaire and compares it with the initial one. Counseling is completed with the invitation to return for follow-up interviews if needed. Counseling goals for this stage are achieved when Leslie can describe the differences in presenting and current states and reports few problems in her current state. Goals are also achieved if her satisfaction with her current environment is significantly higher than in the first stage of counseling.

## DISCUSSION QUESTIONS REGARDING LESLIE FROM A WORK ADJUSTMENT PERSPECTIVE

1. What specific hypotheses would you develop about Leslie from the TWA? How does using the TWA help you understand Leslie? How might it help Leslie understand herself?

2. How would you incorporate the other assessment information that Leslie completed?

3. Leslie did not complete an ability assessment; the counselor inferred abilities from past achievements. What are other ways to assess ability information? Is it important for adults to have their abilities tested?

4. The counselor estimated Leslie's satisfactoriness from the length of her tenure in the same position. However, this information is from one single source—the client herself, who may have underestimated or overestimated her satisfactoriness. What are other ways you could assess satisfactoriness?

5. How might it be helpful for Leslie to conceptualize her current work environment in terms of person-environment correspondence or discorrespondence?

6. How would you incorporate other life issues into counseling? What is the degree of Leslie's correspondence with the other multiple environments in her life? How might these multiple environments interact with one another?

7. Working from the perspective of a TWA counselor, how would you incorporate Leslie's sex and cultural background into counseling?

## ADDITIONAL CASES

### Case 1: Phil

Phil is a 48-year-old Caucasian man who is a foreman in charge of shipping in a small manufacturing company. He sought career counseling at the urging of his wife, who was concerned that he was underemployed; she felt that he could be earning more money than he is in his current job. Phil had attended college briefly during the late 1960s to secure a college deferment for the Vietnam War but did not complete a degree. He had planned to major in accounting, primarily because of his father's encouragement rather than as a reflection of his real interests. He was much more interested in fixing things and was particularly interested in anything related to cars.

While at school he became involved in the antiwar movement, and he and his girlfriend decided to leave school and go to Canada so that he could avoid the draft. While in Canada he worked at a variety of unskilled jobs. He did not want to enter schooling or work at a career, primarily because he was afraid of being sent back to the United States and facing the legal consequences of avoiding the draft. He also was concerned about negative reactions from his family.

By 1975, the war was over, and he and his girlfriend returned to the United States. They got married and had a daughter, and Phil began working as an assembly line worker for a manufacturing company to support his family. He described this first job as "checking his brain at the door," but in reality, he was not overly concerned that the work did not engage him intellectually. He was able to use his abilities in a number of ways outside of work; he was active in chess and bridge clubs and was an avid reader of *Science* and *Scientific American* magazines.

Phil also enjoys building and repairing model trains and has an extensive model train collection that he inherited from his father. Both his father and grandfather had been railroad executives, and his only brother is a civil engineer who designs railroad bridges. Phil's family had a love of railroads in general and of the Burlington Northern railroads in particular. Phil's model railroad collection includes several antique engines; he has developed a small following as an antique model train expert.

Phil's first marriage ended in divorce, and he was left with financial obligations to his first wife and their daughter. He subsequently married again, and he and his second wife have two sons and are expecting a third child. Phil eventually worked his way from entry-level loading dock to foreman of shipping. This was primarily a result of the recognition of his abilities by his supervisors. His tested abilities were uniformly high in all areas, and he placed high value on security, compensation, and achievement. Phil is quite bright and capable of learning, but his lack of formal education has limited his options. His supervisor has told him he cannot expect any more promotions in the company because he would need a baccalaureate degree to be eligible.

Phil is not averse to returning to school to finish his degree, but his credits will not transfer, and he would have to start over again. Meanwhile, he will soon have four children, and his wife is not currently working outside the home. He cannot afford to quit his job to go to school, and he is very unsure what he would major in if he did go back. Overall, Phil is satisfied with his job. He likes feeling he can do the work without a lot of stress, likes the men and one woman he works with, likes the security of belonging to a union, and likes the benefits the company provides. He is dissatisfied with the amount of money he is making, however, and has a vague feeling that he could be doing more.

## Questions for Discussion

1. Given the financial pressures that Phil feels, how does he balance his high need for achievement with his equally high need for security?
2. What are possible other environments that could provide achievement rewards for Phil?
3. How would you evaluate Phil's adjustment style?
4. Phil entered counseling at the urging of his wife. How would you handle this? How would you incorporate Phil's other life roles into counseling?
5. How would you incorporate Phil's avocational interests into counseling?

## Case 2: Jo

Jo is a 32-year-old Caucasian woman who is a midlevel executive working for a large firm that conducts marketing research. She holds a bachelor's degree in economics and an MBA in marketing. She is married to John (a 42-year-old Caucasian man) who works for a similar company in another town; they met while they were attending a professional meeting. They have been married for 7 years and have two small children, ages 2 and 4. The children live primarily with Jo; John comes home each weekend. Jo, then, has primary responsibility for the household and child rearing during the week, but she and John share the tasks on the weekend.

Jo sought career counseling because she was feeling anxious, and resentful of the demands she was juggling at work and at home. She feels that she and John are able to communicate very well; they talk and e-mail each other several times a day, and they maintain time for themselves on the weekends, also feeling that they both make time for their children. But she is frustrated that they live so far apart and that her job is not as rewarding as she hoped. She enjoys some aspects of her work, primarily the opportunity to create new research surveys, and she enjoys working with clients and with her colleagues in the company. She does not feel, however, that she is able to use her skills most effectively and also feels that she does not receive adequate recognition for her work. She has been passed over for promotions, and she is not certain if this was due to her performance, her status as a working mother, or because she is a woman. The last time she was passed over for a promotion, she seriously considered talking to her manager about it but decided against it because she did not want to "rock the boat."

She and John have talked about opening their own marketing research firm; that is one option that she is considering. John's company has no openings at her level, so it is not possible for her to move to join him at his firm. There is no real reason they need to stay in this geographic area, because they have no family obligations or ties other than their current jobs.

## Questions for Discussion

1. What are the rewards in Jo's environments?
2. How would the TWA characterize Jo's satisfactoriness? How would you incorporate this into counseling?
3. What is Jo's adjustment style, and how would you work with her to increase the correspondence with her environment?
4. How would you incorporate the personal issues that Jo is facing into career counseling?
5. How would you incorporate Jo and John's work-family interface into counseling?

## Case 3: Judy

Judy (a 38-year-old Caucasian woman) is a successful attorney who recently became a partner in a medium-sized firm in Denver. Without warning, she tendered her resignation. She sought counseling for depression. She had quit because she was not enjoying her work and she resented the demands made by partners as well as the inordinately long hours. Her therapist suggested she also seek career counseling.

Judy finished her baccalaureate degree in psychology at a small midwestern liberal arts college. She had decided on psychology based on her interest in working with people, particularly children, and because her friends told her she was a good listener. She enjoyed her classes in psychology and volunteered at a crisis line during her sophomore year. She became a resident assistant her junior year and worked in the dorms for two years. She did well in college, and her adviser strongly encouraged her to apply to graduate programs in psychology. She considered that but was dating a young man who did not want her to pursue her doctorate.

She decided to become an attorney because her fiancé was in law school. She thought this would be a good way for them to be in the same geographic location, and she had some interest in the field of law. She was accepted into the same school and excelled. She was particularly interested in litigation, whereas her fiancé was interested in corporate law. She passed the bar exam on the first try, but her fiancé failed three times and finally chose another career. Their relationship ended. She was quite depressed about the termination of her engagement but decided to move to another city to work and, she hoped, meet a new man.

Judy joined the law firm after law school and impressed the attorneys with her diligence and willingness to work extra hours. She soon became the associate that partners vied to have assigned to them. She worked hard and enjoyed some of the work she was assigned, although she also found some of it boring. Eventually, the partners voted to make her partner a year earlier than she had expected. After Judy became a partner, she began to question her activities and values and, in general, became depressed. Although she had dated occasionally, she did not really have any time to devote to a relationship. She also did not have much time to make friends outside the law firm and felt that her life was quite narrowly focused.

## *Questions for Discussion*

1. How would you explain Judy's behavior from the perspective of a TWA counselor?
2. What is the correspondence between Judy's abilities and the job requirements? Between her values and the job rewards?
3. How would you incorporate Judy's depression into counseling through the perspective of the TWA?
4. What is Judy's adjustment style?
5. How would you evaluate Judy's person-environment fit in terms of true needs?

# FIVE

# *Developmental Theories*

Developmental theories include Super's life span, life space approach and Gottfredson's theory of circumscription and compromise. Compared with the person-environment fit theories described in Chapters 3 and 4, Super's and Gottfredson's theories are characterized by viewing career decision making as a process rather than an event and by incorporating developmental concepts into this process.

### *Super's Life Span, Life Space Theory*

The developmental theory of Donald Super has been one of the most influential vocational theories of the 20th century (Borgen, 1991). Super (1953) introduced 10 propositions outlining his theory in his 1952 presidential address to the Division of Counseling Psychology of the American Psychological Association. Those 10 propositions were later expanded to 14 (Super, Savickas, & Super, 1996). Super continued to develop and refine his theory until his death in 1994 and was remarkable for his active scientific investigation of real-life phenomena, its eventual theoretical implications, and the application of his work in counseling (Herr, 1997; Savickas, 1997).

One of the hallmarks of Super's theory is that vocational development is a process of making several decisions, which culminate in vocational choices that represent an implementation of the self-concept. Voca-

83

tional choices are viewed as successive approximations of a good match between the vocational self and the world of work.

Among the basic assumptions underlying the propositions is that development is a process. Three propositions indicate an underlying belief in the differences among people and among occupations. That is, people differ in terms of their abilities, personalities, and values, as well as other variables. Occupations have distinctive combinations of required abilities and personality traits. Differences among individuals translate into suitability for a number of different occupations; that is, individuals may have characteristics appropriate for multiple occupations. Thus, no one occupation is the only possible fit for an individual, nor does only one individual fit a particular occupation.

Six additional propositions discuss development of the self-concept and its implementation in vocational choices. Embedded in these propositions are the notions that self-concepts are formed by vocational preferences and competencies, that these change and evolve over time in interaction with situations, that they are products of social learning, and that they are increasingly stable over the life span. Super proposed five distinct life stages, noting that each has unique developmental tasks. He also suggested that career patterns (the sequence of jobs or occupations held by individuals) are determined by a variety of personal and environmental characteristics. Two propositions discuss the concept of career maturity, which is the readiness of the individual to cope with the demands of the environment. Finally, three propositions deal with the factors involved in work and life satisfaction. For example, work satisfaction is predicted to increase proportionately with self-concept implementation and depends on the importance of and satisfaction with other life roles. Super suggested that individuals hold different roles in their lives that vary in importance across the life span. Individuals may, in fact, find little satisfaction with the worker role but may be fully satisfied with another life role.

The five life stages, or "maxicycles," are growth (ages 4-13), exploration (ages 14-24), establishment (ages 25-44), maintenance (ages 45-65), and disengagement (over age 65). Super characterized the stages as linear and predictable, but not invariant. In other words, he described a series of stages that individuals typically go through but was careful to note that not everyone progresses through these stages in the same manner or at fixed ages. Each transition between stages is characterized by a "minicycle," or a recycling through the stages of growth, reexploration, and reestablishment.

Figure 4.1. The Life-Career Rainbow: Six Life Roles in Schematic Life Space.

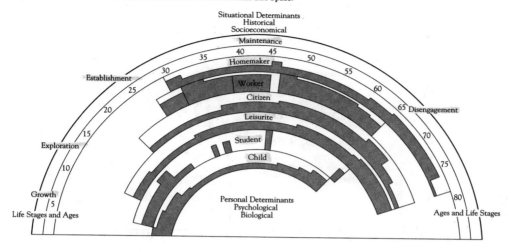

**Figure 5.1.** Super's Life-Career Rainbow
SOURCE: Super, Savickas, & Super (1996). Used with permission.

Within each stage, Super proposed characteristic developmental tasks. Successful mastery of these tasks allows individuals to function effectively in their life roles within that stage and prepares them for the next task. Successful coping with the requirements of each stage depends on the individual's career maturity. Career maturity—or readiness to effectively master the developmental tasks of each stage— involves both attitudinal factors and cognitive factors. Osipow and Fitzgerald (1996) note that "vocational maturity allows the observer to assess the rate and level of an individual's development with respect to career matters" (p. 114). In adults, however, the concept of maturation is less appropriate, and Super et al. (1996) and Savickas (1994) discuss *career adaptability*, defined as "readiness to cope with changing work and work conditions" (Savickas, 1994, p. 58).

Super considered the development of vocational choices within the context of other life roles: "While making a living, people live a life" (Super et al., 1996). He delineated six roles that individuals hold, sometimes concurrently: child, student, homemaker, worker, citizen, and leisurite. Individuals hold multiple roles, and those roles interact. The life-career rainbow schema in Figure 5.1 is a pictorial representation of the intersection of stages and roles and can be used to clarify the various roles for a particular client (Super, 1980). "Life space" corresponds to the roles that one fulfills at various times in life,

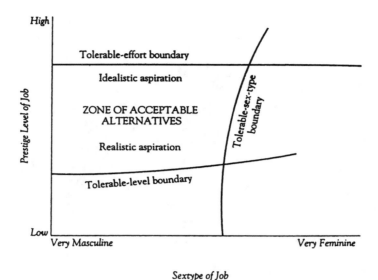

**Figure 5.2.**  Gottfredson's Model of Circumscription and Compromise
SOURCE: Gottfredson (1996).

and "life span" denotes the stages described earlier. An individual "lives in the intersection of the two dimensions" (Super et al., 1996, p. 128).

A fundamental aspect of Super's theory is that vocational choice is an implementation of the self-concept. The self-concept includes the objective view of the self along with the subjective view of the self. The implication for career counselors is that in addition to providing a client with objective information about the self (i.e., interests, values, abilities), counselors also need to integrate a client's subjective view of who he or she is.

### Gottfredson's Theory of Circumscription and Compromise

Gottfredson (1996) developed her theory of circumscription and compromise to explain why individuals' vocational expectations, even when they are children, vary by sex, race, and social class. Gottfredson differs from Super in that she views vocational choice first as an implementation of the social self and only secondarily as an implementation of the psychological self. Inherent in this is the circumscription of psychological variables such as interests or values by social variables such as gender or social class. Gottfredson focuses on cognitive development as children grow in awareness of themselves and their social place in the world and begin to eliminate vocational options that are not compatible with their evolving self-image.

Vocational aspirations are viewed as the product of accessibility (choices that are most realistic) and compatibility (person-environment fit). Circumscription is the process by which children narrow the "zone of acceptable alternatives" by progressive elimination of unacceptable alternatives (see Figure 5.2). Gottfredson's four-stage model of circumscription characterizes children as having an increasing capacity to think abstractly. She also suggests that elimination of alternatives is progressive and irreversible.

In Stage 1 (ages 3-5), children develop an orientation to size and power. They categorize people in simple ways, such as big versus little. Although they do not have firm ideas about sex differences or gender roles, they do recognize observable physical differences between men and women. This recognition increases in Stage 2 (ages 6-8), when children develop an orientation to sex roles. They tend to use dichotomous thinking, characterize their own sex as superior to the other sex, and use sex appropriateness to define their vocational aspirations. In this stage, children construct their tolerable-sextype boundary (see Figure 5.2).

Stage 3 (ages 9-13) entails orientation to social valuation, or sensitivity to prestige and status, whether by their peers or larger society. Children establish their tolerable-level boundary to eliminate occupations that are unacceptably low in prestige and their tolerable-effort boundary to eliminate occupations that are too difficult to attain. Finally, in Stage 4 (ages 14 and older), adolescents develop their orientation to the internal, unique self. Here, interests, values, and abilities are clarified, and occupational exploration occurs within the zone of acceptable alternatives as circumscribed in earlier stages. Stages 1 through 3 are focused on rejecting unacceptable alternatives; Stage 4 is focused on identifying which of the acceptable alternatives are most preferred (Gottfredson, 1996). Stage 4 begins the process of compromise.

Compromise entails the modification of alternatives due to inaccessibility, leading to acceptance of less attractive alternatives. Gottfredson (1996) suggests that sex type, prestige, and field of interest are the three dimensions considered in the process of compromise. She further specified an order of compromise such that sex type is least likely and field of interest most likely to be compromised. She suggests that most individuals will settle for a "good enough" choice rather than the best possible choice.

Gottfredson's theory explicitly addresses the impact of sex-role socialization and other societal factors that influence the development of occupational aspirations. As such, it offers a complementary perspective to Super's theory. On the other hand, Super's theory was designed to span a much broader scope of career behavior than does Gottfredson's theory and thus is a more comprehensive theory of life span career development.

## APPLYING DEVELOPMENTAL THEORIES TO THE CASE OF LESLIE

### Conceptualizing Leslie's Career History

Developmental theorists would view Leslie's case as a series of decisions from childhood through adulthood. We will discuss Leslie's decisions using Super's stages as a framework. We will then discuss developmental career counseling and possible career interventions.

### Childhood

Four tasks are addressed in the growth stage (ages 4-13): becoming concerned about the future, increasing personal control over one's own life, convincing oneself to achieve in school and at work, and acquiring competent work habits and attitudes (Super et al., 1996). Gottfredson (1996) suggests that the ages 6 to 8 are characterized by a child's increasing awareness of gender-appropriate roles and by dichotomous thinking. Children are motivated by choices that they believe are socially appropriate, particularly focusing on sex-typed choices. During ages 9 to 13, children begin to incorporate prestige as a factor in consideration of acceptable alternatives.

Leslie consistently enjoyed school throughout her elementary and junior high years. Many subjects intrigued her, and she enjoyed the attention of good teachers who challenged her and sparked her interest in a variety of activities. She began to excel in math and science in elementary school but struggled during middle school with gender-stereotyped expectations and aspirations about mathematics. For a time, she underplayed her math abilities due to teasing about being an "egghead" by her classmates, particularly boys.

Other influences on her developing self-concept included her mother, who was her primary role model during childhood. Her father, however, was her earliest occupational role model. As she progressed through elementary and middle school, additional role models were teachers, particularly a female math teacher she had in seventh grade. School in general played an important role in Leslie's life, and her teachers provided valuable support and encouragement. Leslie's earliest occupational fantasies involved being a teacher, and "playing school" was a frequent activity for Leslie and her younger sister.

Leslie's parents communicated their expectations to her about achievement, emphasizing that she should do her best. On the other hand, while her parents were happy that Leslie enjoyed and excelled in school, they did not expect work-related achievement to be a central focus in Leslie's life. She was not expected to work throughout her adult life but, rather, to work until she married and had children, a pattern modeled by Leslie's mother and followed by her sister. Thus, she received messages to continue to achieve, but not to place achievement as her top priority.

### Adolescence and Early Adulthood

During the exploration stage (ages 14-24), the primary tasks are crystallizing, specifying, and implementing career choice (Super et al., 1996). Gottfredson proposes that the occupational alternatives adolescents consider are circumscribed by options considered appropriate for their sex and within the range acceptable for their social class and self-perceived abilities.

Leslie experimented with a number of different options, and her difficulty in choosing was related to her ability to see many possible selves due to her wide-ranging interests and talents. Moreover, her indecision may have been exacerbated by the expectations that Leslie experienced from others, particularly her parents, about the importance of the work role in her life: It may have been difficult for her to make plans and be decisive about something that others believed would not be important in her life. In contrast to Leslie's experience, her older brother was coached and encouraged by their parents to carefully consider his career alternatives, beginning in early adolescence. Leslie, on the other hand, received little guidance and direction about the process of planning for the future; consequently, she did not plan her entrance into college and had difficulty negotiating the tasks of the exploration stage. Within her family, then, Leslie experienced messages about career choice that differed by one's sex. As she moved into high school, her natural interest in math, particularly advanced math, carried her through the teasing into a time when she enjoyed being recognized for her ability in math. She tutored other students while in high school and later in college. Thus, excelling at math became a central part of Leslie's developing self-concept. Leslie also developed conscientious study habits, and she took pride in her work.

These messages about career issues relative to gender issues were mirrored by other sources throughout Leslie's adolescence. She continued to receive mixed messages about the appropriate role that a career should play in her life, as well as the appropriateness of her interest in math-related activities and her pursuit of these activities as a career. When she won first place in the science fair during her senior year of high school, her mother's only comment was about the clothing she had worn to the competition.

Leslie's subjective view of herself conformed to traditional sex-role socialization, in that she focused on marriage and family roles as opposed to long-term investment in her work role. She therefore opted out of some career decisions because they were outside of her self-concept. For example, she decided against engineering because of her perceptions of the difficulty of combining work and family, and she decided against math because of her disinterest in pursuing graduate-level education. Math education, on the other hand, represented a compromise between traditional and nontraditional options.

The construct of career maturity, or readiness to make vocational decisions, becomes central in Super's exploration stage. Leslie's difficulty with making a decision about attending college and about her college major may have been related to slightly delayed career maturity; developmentally, she was not as ready to make a decision as she ideally might have been. This delay, in turn, may have been related to the issues just discussed: Leslie had had little experience in making career plans prior to entering college because she was not encouraged or expected to do so. The "unreadiness" also led to some discomfort at not having a decision made, and she found herself comparing her progress in making a decision with her college friends as well as with her brother, who teased her when she had difficulty with decision making. At times, she agonized over the "right" choice of college major and career, and the actual decision point stretched over several semesters as she struggled to keep her options open. Her salient life roles during this period included child and student, although she also was preparing for the homemaker role because she anticipated marrying after college.

Despite the difficulty she experienced in making a decision, Leslie's choice of secondary education seemed to represent a good avenue for implementing her self-concept as it was developed to that point in her life. The salient parts of her self-concept included being good at math and being recognized for her achievements in math and being responsible, conscientious, and caring. Teaching allowed her to express these elements of her identity.

### Conceptualizing Leslie's Present Situation

The establishment stage (ages 25-40) entails entering and becoming established in one's career and work life, and the tasks of this stage include stabilizing, consolidating, and advancing. *Stabilizing* involves settling in and learning what needs to be done to perform one's job adequately. *Consolidating* occurs when an individual feels comfortable that he or she possesses the skills required by the job and feels secure that he or she is performing well in the eyes of supervisors and co-workers. *Advancing* refers to moving up within one's job, assuming greater responsibility at higher pay. Advancing can occur throughout the establishment stage but, typically, is subsequent to stabilizing and consolidating.

Leslie entered teaching with much enthusiasm and experienced the transition into her full-time work role in a manner typical to many young adults; that is, she found it both satisfying and stressful. Despite her success as a teacher, she decided to leave her first position. This decision was primarily based on a discrepancy between her work and nonwork roles. Leslie's feeling that she did not have enough time to spend with her parents and siblings and the termination of the relationship with her boyfriend led her to question her work-nonwork priorities. She hoped that the job change would provide a better balance between roles and therefore that she would feel less stressed and more satisfied. In Super's terms, Leslie spent most of the 3 years in her first job working on the task of stabilizing. Although from an objective perspective she clearly possessed the necessary skills, she did not feel confident that her skills were sufficient to make her a good teacher. She wondered whether the amount of stress she was experiencing resulted from her being inadequate at her job, and there were no other new teachers with whom she could compare her job performance and stress level.

After taking her new (current) job, Leslie was able to get a different perspective on her skills as a teacher, primarily because she noticed that other teachers also seemed to experience a similar level of stress. She thus completed the process of stabilizing and moved on to the tasks related to consolidating in her career. Currently, however, Leslie's dissatisfaction with a number of factors in her job suggests that these tasks may need additional attention and exploration within counseling.

Leslie's current dissatisfaction can be viewed as related to career adaptation—namely, that she is struggling to adapt to changes in her work environment. These changes may be simply too extensive for her to address simultaneously in that she expressed dissatisfaction with the principal, her fellow teachers, the children, and their parents. An alternative hypothesis is that her dissatisfaction with one aspect may have spilled over into other areas and colored her view of the entire work situation. Moreover, a view consonant with developmental theory is that Leslie's dissatisfaction has escalated as her self-concept has become more refined and crystallized. Following this line of thought, the counselor might choose to affirm and validate Leslie's feelings of anger and dissatisfaction, because they may indicate an evolving clarity of who she is and who she wants to become.

Leslie has primarily focused on her student and worker roles. In addition, her role as "child" is still active, and her family of origin continues to be an important influence in her current career situation. Moreover, Leslie is considering a shift in the priority of her life roles by becoming a parent. As with many people in early adulthood, Leslie has focused on entering and establishing her career and now is stopping to examine her decisions to date. Leslie could be viewed as experiencing an additional stage of midlife career renewal (Williams & Savickas, 1990).

In summary, Leslie can be conceptualized as being in the midst of the establishment stage (stabilizing, consolidating, advancing). However, like many individuals who have entered career counseling at this point in their careers, she may be recycling back to a consideration of tasks in the exploration stage (crystallizing, specifying, implementing).

## Directions and Implications
## for Career Counseling

### Goals of Counseling

From Super's framework, the goals of counseling are for clients "to (1) develop and accept an integrated and adequate picture of themselves and their life roles, (2) test the concept against reality, and (3) convert it into reality by making choices that implement the self-concept and lead to job success and satisfaction as well as benefit to society" (Super et al., 1996, pp. 158-159). Super's theory has also been expanded into an explicit model of counseling, named the career development assessment and counseling model (C-DAC; Osborne, Brown, Niles, & Miner, 1997; Super, 1983; Super, Osborne, Walsh, Brown, & Niles, 1992).

The C-DAC model was developed to use concepts from Super's developmental theory to augment trait-and-factor approaches to career counseling. The model incorporates four phases of assessment: (a) life structure and work role salience; (b) career development status and resources; (c) vocational identity, including values, interests, abilities; and (d) occupational self-concepts and life themes. In each of these four phases, assessment can be accomplished either in session with the client or by using inventories developed by Super and his colleagues.

The first step, assessment of life structure and work role salience, begins by exploring the importance of the work role to the client, particularly in relation to the other potential roles in a client's life, such as child, student, homemaker, citizen, and leisurite. "Life structure" refers to the constellation of core and peripheral roles that define an individual's life. The degree to which the work role is salient will influence the weight placed on the three subsequent assessments, because these focus specifically on the work role and identity.

The second focus of assessment is career development status and resources. The counselor needs to determine which developmental tasks are of concern to the client. Identification of the client's concerns is then followed by an assessment of the coping resources that he or she possesses to deal with those concerns. Coping resources are typically viewed as the attitudes and competencies that the client holds for dealing with the specific developmental tasks that he or she is facing.

Third, the assessment of vocational identity represents the "traditional trait-and-factor" portion of the C-DAC model (Super et al., 1996) and includes values, abilities, and interests. The goal of this step is to develop a description of these aspects of the client's vocational identity and then explore how this identity might be expressed in the various roles in the client's life.

The fourth and final step in assessment focuses on occupational self-concepts and life themes. Here, the focus shifts from the "objective" assessment during the previous step to an assessment of the client's subjective self-concept. The C-DAC model recommends two methods: (a) a cross-sectional method that focuses on the client's current self-schema and (b) a longitudinal method that focuses on themes that have developed throughout the client's life.

Following these four steps in assessment, the counselor then develops an "integrative interpretation which narrates the client's life story" (Super et al., 1996, p. 157) and serves as a transition from the assessment phase to the counseling phase. Super (1957) described a process of counseling that alternates between directive and nondirective techniques. For example, the counselor may begin with a nondirective exploration of Leslie's career concerns, followed by a directive setting of topics for further discussion, then nondirective clarification of Leslie's self-concept and life structure, directive discussion of assessment results, and nondirective discussion of her reactions to the assessment. This cyclical approach to career counseling offers a way to "balance attention to the objective and subjective dimensions of self and career" (Super et al., 1996, p. 162).

Consonant with the goals of developmental theory, Leslie's goals include achieving a better view of herself and what is causing her dissatisfaction at work and understanding the ways in which she can juggle the multiple roles of child, worker, and parent. She stated that she wants to make a decision about whether to stay at her current job or move to a new field and that she wants to discuss incorporating possible shifts of roles.

## Assessment of Life Roles and Work Role Salience

The interaction of primary roles in Leslie's life has potential for either creating stress or reducing stress; "multiple roles can enrich life or overburden it" (Super et al., 1996, p. 129). Furthermore, the process of completing a career transition may lead to the evolution of roles and how roles interact in a client's life: Roles may be added or deleted, or ongoing roles may be modified.

The counselor begins with a clarification of roles in Leslie's life and their relative salience at this point. How would she characterize her current balance of roles? How might she construct an ideal balance of roles? How much discrepancy is there between her current balance of roles and her ideal balance? Moreover, Leslie is contemplating adding the role of "parent" to her life, and the interaction of that role with her work role needs to be examined.

Super's life-career rainbow suggests that Leslie is fulfilling a number of different social roles in her life and that she may be reevaluating the relative priority or salience of these roles. An intervention that may help Leslie clarify her life roles is an "interrole assessment" technique (Brown & Brooks, 1991). This technique can be used to identify and clarify the interaction of work roles with other life roles. First, Leslie lists the life roles in which she currently is involved and estimates the amount of time spent in each role. Next, she ranks her life roles using values as the basis for ranking. Finally, Leslie identifies roles that conflict with one another, roles that are compensatory with one another, and roles that complement one another (Brown & Brooks, 1991).

*Assessment of Career Development*
*Status and Resources*

To determine which developmental tasks are of concern to Leslie, the counselor uses results from the Adult Career Concerns Inventory (ACCI; Super, Thompson, & Lindeman, 1988) as a guide. Leslie's highest score of the four stage scales is in exploration, suggesting that her primary career concerns are tasks related to Super's exploration stage. This is particularly useful to note and to address in counseling, because Leslie may be feeling some discrepancy between her age and her expected career stage. That is, she may feel that she should be further along in her career path. Indeed, she expresses that she "should have figured this out by now." Moreover, Leslie's parents and siblings convey their amusement about her still being "undecided about what she wants to do."

The counselor also examines the substage scores on the ACCI for further clues about Leslie's concerns. Her highest scores within the exploration stage are on specification and crystallization, with a relatively lower score on implementation. These scores suggest that Leslie is focused on identifying and choosing a specific occupational direction, confirming what she has expressed to the counselor.

Given the career concerns that Leslie expresses, the counselor then assesses the coping resources available to Leslie. The first type of resource is positive attitudes toward career planning. Leslie is quite enthused about career counseling and feels ready to "make a career choice the right way this time." She is interested in researching different occupations, and her analytical skills should serve her well in this regard.

A second type of coping resource is Leslie's knowledge about herself and about the world of work. Her knowledge about herself appears appropriate to her age and experience, as indicated by her confidence in completing the assessment inventories, her ability to describe the positive and negative aspects of her current job, and her self-description of her strengths and weaknesses. The counselor, however, remains attentive for areas in which Leslie could benefit from additional self-exploration, as well as areas in which Leslie underestimates her abilities and skills. Leslie's knowledge of occupational information also seems quite appropriate to her situation, and she clearly expresses specific occupations about which she would like additional information. Again, the counselor is attentive to misinformation that Leslie might hold or areas in which she needs further information.

The final type of coping resource that the counselor assesses is decision-making skills. Because Leslie reports that she has "not made good decisions in the past," the counselor attempts to make a careful and thorough assessment of her decision-making strategies and skills. The counselor asks Leslie to describe the process that she uses to make decisions, by analyzing several situations in which Leslie has made decisions in the past (e.g., changing jobs, buying a car). One hypothesis that the counselor explores is whether Leslie's decision-making skills are truly inadequate or whether she only believes this to be true because her family has told her so.

### Assessment of Vocational Identity

Vocational identity is the focus of the third step and is described by integrating information about Leslie's interests, values, abilities, and personality from the inventories that she took prior to counseling. She is interested in working with and helping people, as evidenced by her scores on the Strong Interest Inventory (SII) and the Minnesota Importance Questionnaire (MIQ), yet her confidence in social activities does not match her interest; her lack of confidence may be due to her tendency to be introverted in nature. She also is quite comfortable working alone and may, in fact, be perceived by others as preferring to work alone. Leslie is also interested in mathematical and scientific activities, which is supported by her logical and analytical style and her valuing of achievement and the use of her abilities.

The counselor explores how Leslie's vocational identity is expressed in her life, through her work role and other life roles. One area for exploration is whether Leslie wishes to incorporate more social-type activities into her work role or whether she can express those interests in her leisure pursuits.

### Assessment of Occupational Self-Concepts and Life Themes

In the final step of assessment in the C-DAC model, the client's subjective self-concept is explored. The focus in this step is on Leslie's self-schemas—how she "makes sense" of herself and her world. The counselor assesses Leslie's self-concept by listening carefully to how she describes herself, both as she is today and as she has seen herself throughout her life. Leslie seems to view herself as capable and talented, yet she is self-critical and easily discouraged when she compares herself with others. She has internalized her family's perception of her as indecisive as well as their mixed messages about achievement, although she is beginning to examine these beliefs about herself. Leslie feels that she has a lot of offer, if only she could identify the best outlet for her talents.

### Other Interventions

Leslie's focus on tasks related to the exploration stage suggests the use of interventions related to exploratory behavior. The counselor thoroughly examines Leslie's career decisions up to this point in her life. How did she make her earlier career decisions? What factors influenced the process and outcome of her decisions? What other career options had she considered and why? Why were the other options discarded in favor of teaching?

The counselor helps Leslie to explicitly acknowledge and accept her status in the exploration stage. She may benefit from "making meaning" for herself about where she is in the career development process. For example, she may decide that she is "starting over," but this time possessing greater wisdom and self-knowledge and with different questions to answer for herself. The counselor encourages Leslie to see herself as "recycling" through the exploration stage, with a description of the tasks of crystallizing, specifying, and implementing career choice. Super proposed that individuals go through a minicycle during career transitions; Leslie could be conceptualized as in a career transition, although the extent of the transition is not yet clear.

Super et al. (1996) state that "individuals eventually complete the task of specifying an occupational choice by translating the privately experienced occupational self-concept into educational/vocational choices" (p. 132). Leslie's self-concept continues to evolve, becoming more clearly defined with age and with experience. The counselor helps Leslie explore how her current self-concept fits with the career choice that she implemented immediately after college and whether her dissatisfaction with her current job may be related to changes in her self-concept. Have her job responsibilities kept up with her evolving self-concept? Are there opportunities where she is now or in a new teaching-related position, or is a career change indicated?

The construct of career maturity (or career adaptability) is particularly relevant in the exploration stage, and the counselor examines how ready Leslie is to make vocational decisions. The uncertainty of her future pregnancy plans adds another dimension to Leslie's readiness. How is she feeling about making a career decision? Moreover, Leslie's previous experiences with career decision making were associated with some anxiety, related to time pressure, family expectations, the decision-making process itself, or some combination of all of these.

## DISCUSSION QUESTIONS REGARDING LESLIE FROM A DEVELOPMENTAL PERSPECTIVE

1. What specific hypotheses would you develop about Leslie from Super's theory? From Gottfredson's theory? How does using Super's theory or Gottfredson's theory help you understand Leslie? How might it help Leslie understand herself?

2. What are the advantages of viewing Leslie as reentering the exploration stage (minicycle within maxicycle)? What are the disadvantages?

3. How ready is Leslie to make a career decision right now? How does she feel about the prospect of making a decision, particularly of making a job or career change? How might her previous experiences with career decision making influence the process or content of this current decision?

4. Who is likely to influence her decision? How much pressure does she feel now? What types of pressure and from whom?

5. Which life roles seem most salient to Leslie? How can she balance the roles that she desires?

6. How might Leslie describe her self-concept and the narrative of her life? How does she make meaning from the interaction of her various life roles?

7. How has Leslie circumscribed and compromised her occupational aspirations?

---

## ADDITIONAL CASES

### Case 1: Walter

Walter is a 65-year-old Caucasian man who is a manufacturing representative for a large tractor company. He has worked for this company for almost 40 years and worked his way up to his current position of regional manager. Walter plans to retire within a year or two.

Walter married his wife, Martha, while he was in the Army. He had completed 2 years of college but discontinued his education when their first daughter was born. Walter did not pursue any further formal education and expresses regret that he did not complete his degree.

Walter and Martha have four children, all of whom are married and successfully employed. Walter and Martha have nine grandchildren, seven of whom live within a 30-mile radius. Martha has been a traditional homemaker, raising the children and supporting Walter's business activities. She is a very active civic volunteer and maintains a busy schedule.

Walter (and Martha) will be entering retirement with good health and financial security. He is preparing himself for voluntary retirement; however, he would prefer to continue working indefinitely, but Martha has encouraged him to retire so that they can do more traveling. Also, Walter is feeling some unspoken pressure to retire from being vice president of sales so that another individual can be promoted into Walter's position.

Walter typically worked 80 hours per week and spent a good deal of time on the road. Because of this very busy workload, he has not had time to develop many hobbies other than the golf he played as a business activity. His expressed plans for retirement include traveling, playing golf, and learning French. He has also expressed interest in taking college courses, perhaps to finish his degree. Martha has

encouraged Walter to enter counseling because of her worry
that he will not have enough to do and will "be underfoot" at
home. He recently has experienced several anxiety attacks,
initially believed to be minor heart attacks, and his physician
also has encouraged him to pursue counseling.

Another issue facing Walter and Martha is that his
87-year-old mother may need more daily living assistance than
she currently is receiving in her apartment.

## Questions for Discussion

1. How would you conceptualize the salience of roles in Walter's
   life? How might he be experiencing the shifting roles in his life,
   with more emphasis on the grandparent, leisurite, student, and/or
   caretaking roles?
2. What issues would you encourage Walter to consider as he shifts
   into the disengagement phase of his career? How might he use
   the remaining time in his work role to prepare for retirement?
3. In what specific activities could Walter engage to develop alternate
   roles?
4. Are there any unresolved tasks from earlier life-career stages that
   might need to be addressed in counseling?
5. How would you assess Walter's career adaptability?
6. What issues might be occurring between Martha and Walter?
   How might you address these issues?

## Case 2: Maria Josefina

Maria Josefina is an 18-year-old woman of Puerto Rican
descent living in the Southeast. She is the oldest daughter of
six children; her father is a skilled laborer in construction, and
her mother is a homemaker. She has one older brother who
attended a community college to learn how to be an electrician
and is working for the same construction company as their
father. Maria Josefina's family moved from Puerto Rico eight
years ago, when she was 10, her older brother was 12, and her
younger sisters and brothers were 8, 6, 4, and 2. Her family
lives in a middle-class neighborhood that is ethnically diverse,
and they get along well with their neighbors. They primarily
socialize with other Puerto Ricans, however, and often spend
time with members of their extended family in the area.

Maria Josefina feels that she lives in two worlds: school and home, each characterized by different languages, expectations, and relationships. At school, she speaks English and has many friends with whom she enjoys spending time talking about boys and clothes and the future. At home, she speaks Spanish, spends time with her brothers and sisters, and enjoys support and warmth of having her aunts, uncles, grandparents, and cousins around her. They sing, talk, and dance together.

Maria Josefina has done well in school and has been encouraged by her high school teachers and guidance counselors to consider college. She was admitted to several universities with the possibility of attractive financial aid packages. Her parents, however, do not want her to leave home and are encouraging her to attend the same community college that her brother attended. Maria Josefina knows that, as the oldest daughter, she is expected to be home to help her mother, but she would very much like to become a social worker. Her aunt, who is strongly encouraging her to attend one of the universities, has referred her for career counseling.

## Questions for Discussion

1. Conceptualize Maria Josefina from a developmental framework.
2. What developmental tasks has she accomplished? What tasks does she yet have to accomplish?
3. How would you characterize her objective and subjective self-concepts?
4. What are the role interactions she is encountering?
5. How would you help her make a decision?

### Case 3: Deborah and Trish

Deborah (age 33) enters counseling at a community agency specializing in women's issues at the urging of her partner, Trish (age 38). Deborah has been depressed and irritable for the past few months, and Trish is concerned that Deborah is unhappy with their 5-year relationship, although Deborah has denied that this is the case.

Deborah is currently experiencing considerable dissatisfaction in her career. She is a lawyer in the district attorney's office in a medium-sized town in the Southwest. She views her work environment as undesirable for a number of reasons, including the lack of opportunities for advancement and her perception that she cannot disclose her sexual orientation at work. She frequently comes home from work depressed. Deborah recently had an offer from a law firm in San Francisco that was quite attractive; however, she did not accept the position because of the difficulty of relocating.

Trish is an associate professor of biology at a state university. She has successfully established herself and is happy in her profession and work environment. She supported Deborah's application for the San Francisco job but also made it clear that moving to another university might be difficult and would cause a disruption in her career. Trish expresses skepticism that Deborah's depression could be the result of work factors and continues to believe that Deborah is dissatisfied with their relationship.

As is typical in their professions, Deborah and Trish both work many hours and frequently work at home in the evenings and weekends. This dedication to their respective careers was one of the aspects that first attracted them to one another, and they support one another's career advancement. However, lately, Deborah has begun to wonder if there isn't more to life than work and has wished that she and Trish could spend more time together taking trips and just enjoying the weekends. Trish, however, easily gets absorbed in the work she brings home and frequently stays up late at night working on projects.

## Questions for Discussion

1. How might Deborah be conceptualized from the perspective of developmental theories? How might Trish be conceptualized?
2. With what developmental tasks might Deborah be struggling?
3. How could you help Deborah and Trish understand one another's career perspectives? What, if any, discrepancies exist between their respective career stages and issues?
4. How might you address their relationship issues? How might career and relationship concerns be connected for Deborah? For Trish?

# SIX

## Krumboltz's Social Learning Theory of Career Choice and Counseling

Chapters 3 and 4 emphasized how the interaction between the person and the environment shapes the career choice and adjustment process, and Chapter 5 focused on the how individuals' careers develop over time. The theory discussed in this chapter also assumes that individuals interact with their environment in making career choices, but the emphasis in Krumboltz's learning theory of career choice and counseling (Mitchell & Krumboltz, 1996) is on how individuals learn from those interactions. The theory examined here extends Krumboltz's social learning theory of career decision making (Mitchell & Krumboltz, 1990) by incorporating a theory of the origin of career choice with a practical perspective for counselors considering career-related problems. Mitchell and Krumboltz (1996) note that both aspects might be termed the learning theory of career counseling.

The learning theory of career counseling was originally based on an assumption that behavior is best understood as stemming from learned

103

experiences rather than primarily stemming from innate psychic processes. Learning theory assumes that human beings are intelligent problem solvers and that rather than being passively controlled by the environment, individuals strive to control their environment.

Learning theory posits two types of learning. The first is instrumental learning, in which an individual is reinforced or punished for his or her behavior. Behavior is repeated when it is positively reinforced and is likely to decrease if it is punished. For example, an individual who is reinforced for learning and speaking French is likely to continue to learn and speak French, whereas an individual who is ridiculed (punished) for a poor accent is likely to quit taking French classes.

The second type of learning posited by learning theory is associative learning, in which something neutral is paired with an emotionally laden stimulus. The result is that the neutral stimulus becomes positive or negative as a result of the association. An individual could, for example, associate police officers with an enjoyable television program and become interested in activities that may lead to being a police officer. Mitchell and Krumboltz also note that vicarious, or indirect, experiences may be considered associative learning. Vicarious learning is learning from the behavior of others either through direct observation or through a more indirect way, such as observing others' behavior in movies, television, or books.

Mitchell and Krumboltz (1996) outline four factors influencing individuals' career paths. The first of these is individuals' innate genetic endowment and any special abilities they may have inherited. Although social learning theory does not specifically state the extent to which heredity affects human characteristics, it does acknowledge the possibility that heredity plays at least some role in ability differences. Musical, artistic, and athletic abilities (among others) may well have some genetic component. Mitchell and Krumboltz (1996) note that learning experiences clearly interact with innate abilities in such a way that an individual has varying opportunities to develop those abilities to overcome barriers created by innate genetic endowment.

The second factor influencing career paths are environmental conditions and events. These environmental events are often outside the control of the individual and may or may not be planned. Mitchell and Krumboltz (1996) list 12 categories of environmental conditions, such as job opportunities, social policies such as affirmative action, rewards for some occupations, labor laws, physical events, natural resources, technological developments, changes in social organization, family training and resources, educational system, and neighborhood and community influences.

The third and most central factor in social learning theory has to do with learning experiences. These learning experiences may be either instrumental or associative. Instrumental learning includes antecedents, behaviors, and consequences. Antecedents include genetic endowment and environmental conditions; behaviors may be covert (e.g., thoughts) or overt, and consequences may be immediate or delayed. Associative learning (classical conditioning) occurs when two stimuli are paired, so we learn that a smile means approval and a frown, disapproval.

The final factor in career decision making is task approach skills, hypothesized to result as an interaction of innate abilities, environmental conditions, and learning experiences. Task approach skills are those skills that individuals bring to a task, such as their expectations of performance, work habits, cognitive processes, and emotional responses.

Learning theory postulates that the four factors described earlier interact and result in the formation of generalizations, which may be about the self or about the world. Generalizations that individuals make about themselves stem from their own observations about themselves and are termed *self-observation generalizations*. These are generalizations that individuals make about their attitudes, work habits, values, interests, and skill level. Generalizations may be overt or covert and are thought to have a reciprocal nature in that they are the result of learning experiences and, in turn, influence the outcomes of learning experiences. For example, a girl may form a generalization that she is good at baseball from the number of home runs she has and from her knowledge about baseball statistics. In turn, viewing herself as good in baseball leads her to try out for the high school team in which she does well, further influencing her self-observation generalization. Worldview generalizations also result from learning experiences and are the generalizations that individuals make about their environment(s). Worldview generalizations are formed to make sense of the world and to predict outcomes in the environment. In this way, an individual who has experienced racial discrimination begins to predict that discrimination will occur in interactions, and an individual who has been privileged by virtue of his or her socioeconomic status will predict that privilege will be granted in all situations.

Krumboltz (1994) outlines six specific testable propositions from his learning theory of career decision making. The first three suggest that individuals will express preference for an occupation if (a) they have succeeded at tasks they think typical of that occupation, (b) role models have been reinforced for those activities, or (c) someone has spoken positively to them about that career. The remaining three propositions are that individuals will avoid an occupation if (d) they have failed at tasks typical of the occupation, (e) they have observed a role model not being reinforced for those activities, or (f) someone has spoken negatively about the occupation.

Krumboltz also delineates areas that a career counselor must address. Mitchell and Krumboltz (1996) note that career counselors need to contend with four major trends in the world of work. They suggest that people need to expand their capabilities and interests, that they need to prepare for changing work tasks, that they need to be empowered to take action, and that career counselors need to play a major role in dealing with all career problems. In other words, career counselors should help individuals explore new areas in which they may develop skills, as opposed to those areas identified by past interests. Career counselors need to help individuals enter a world of work that is changing rapidly and help them through the process of implementing career decisions as well as making the decisions. Finally, career counselors need to broaden the scope of problems to include implications of career decisions, which suggests the need for career counselors to become competent in a variety of interventions.

Mitchell and Krumboltz (1996) describe the goal of career counseling as learning and the role of career counselors as facilitating that learning. Clients may need to learn not only what their current skills and interests are but also what skills and interests they would like to develop. Mitchell and Krumboltz outline several interventions, such as the use of the Career Beliefs Inventory (CBI), structured interviews, thought listing, in vivo self-monitoring, imagery, simulations, reconstruction of prior events, behavioral inferences and feedback, cognitive restructuring, simple reinforcement, role models, films, and computer-guided programs.

## APPLYING KRUMBOLTZ'S THEORY TO THE CASE OF LESLIE

### Conceptualizing Leslie's Career History

Career counselors using a learning theory model begin by investigating Leslie's career history to examine how her innate abilities, learning experiences, and task approach skills have combined with environmental events to influence her decision making and choices.

The genetic factors that influence Leslie include the fact that she is a white woman who is physically able. She has abilities in a wide variety of areas, particularly in math and science, that may result from some combination of genetic and environmental influences. She has little ability in drawing or in other artistic activities.

Environmental events may be divided into three areas: social factors, educational conditions, and occupational conditions. Social factors that have affected Leslie include being born to a two-parent family in the second half of the 20th century, expanding support and opportunities for women to enter the world of work, and societal discrimination against women in technical careers. As a white woman, Leslie was not exposed to racial stereotyping or restriction of opportunities due to her race. Increased awareness of the roles available to women in the 1960s and 1970s and concerns to promote women's entry into the workforce were environmental forces that may have influenced Leslie's early career choices. By the time Leslie graduated from high school in 1980, it was socially acceptable for women to prepare for a career. However, it was still relatively rare for women to enter technical careers, as evidenced by the low numbers of women in her advanced math classes. In addition, she experienced overt discouragement to enter a technical career from individuals who adopted a prevailing perception that women do not excel in math and science skills.

A second broad area of environmental events relates to education, which includes opportunities for education and training, policies related to education (e.g., admissions policies), and resources for training (or lack thereof). The public school system from which Leslie graduated afforded her the opportunity to take higher-level math and science courses as well as the opportunity to tutor middle school students. However, the same public school did not provide adequate career counseling or advice, nor did it have specific math and science programs to help promote young women's entry into technical careers. Educational conditions include the high expectations that Leslie's family held about her graduating from college and the resources they possessed to support her pursuit of a college degree. Finally, environmental events that affected Leslie's education were the availability of the training opportunities at both the community college and the university that she attended.

Environmental events related to occupational conditions include job opportunities, geographic limitations, economic conditions, and the rewards of various occupations. In Leslie's case, the economy in her region (Midwest) was in a recession, and the number of children in public schools was declining as the birth rate declined in the late 1970s and early 1980s. The availability of teaching positions was low. This led her to accept a job as a math teacher in a small community in which she had no social support systems. However, 3 years later, economic factors influenced greater opportunities in the teaching profession, the economy improved, and a state law granting early retirement benefits to teachers created more job opportunities in her hometown.

The third factor in the learning theory of career decision making is learning experiences, which as discussed earlier, may be associative and instrumental. An example of associative learning related to Leslie's career choice is the positive associations Leslie had with the occupation of teacher when she and her sister played "school" during their childhood.

Leslie had many instrumental learning experiences that shaped her career decisions. Leslie did well in math in elementary and middle school, for which she received verbal reinforcement and recognition and that led her to continue to enroll in math courses in high school and college. She later tutored middle school students, which offered her financial rewards and additional exposure to teachers as role models. She received much praise for her work as a tutor and enjoyed the interaction with the children she tutored. She won her high school science fair, providing further opportunities for reinforcement. Leslie also received recognition for her organizational skills, which led to leadership positions within her high school.

Leslie also experienced occasional negative outcomes related to math and other academic activities. Classmates teased her when she did well in math, and Leslie learned that if she took more math classes, she might incur additional ridicule. She continued to learn this in college classes when her professors singled out her mistakes for ridicule. She learned from observing her mother that although it was acceptable for women to work, women should expect to marry and have a family. She furthermore learned that those family obligations should be a primary focus of her future planning. This led to her decision to not seek additional schooling beyond a baccalaureate degree and to steer away from engineering when her professors told her it would be a difficult career to combine with having a family.

The fourth factor in Leslie's career decision making from a learning theory perspective is task approach skills. These develop from the other factors we have discussed and include her responsiveness to children that led her to receive praise for her work as a tutor and later as a student teacher. She had high organizational skills as well as the ability to pay attention to detail that led to her recognition as a leader in high school. She had high scholastic skills and approached her schoolwork, and eventually her job, in a diligent and serious manner.

The preceding factors led to Leslie's behaviors and beliefs. Leslie's self-observation generalizations developed from her innate abilities, learning experiences, and task approach skills in combination with environmental events. Leslie's first self-observation generalizations may have included, "I am good in school" and "I am good in math." She also may have learned that "I am a woman and should put having a family before a career," followed by "I am not be smart enough to continue studying math at the graduate-school level." Finally, her experiences as a tutor and later as a student teacher may have led her to "I am a good teacher."

Those self-observation generalizations were changed when she moved to her first job as a teacher in a small town. She began to observe herself as working much harder than the other teachers and may have initially concluded that "I am a better teacher than they are." However, she later revised her self-observation to "I am taking too much responsibility for my students" and "I am trying to show that I care more than the other teachers." She began to view her lack of social relationships as a problem and subsequently chose to decrease the amount of time she spent on grading. These self-observation generalizations may have eventually led to her decision to leave the small town to return to her family as a support system.

### Conceptualizing Leslie's Present Situation

Leslie moved back to her hometown, where she continued her teaching career at a large high school. The size of the high school became a problematic environmental condition, because it was much more bureaucratic than her previous school. The school was large enough that many sections of freshman algebra were needed, and she had fewer opportunities to teach advanced math classes. In addition, the recent resignation of the principal led to the school district's hiring a new principal. His policies became an environmental condition that she did not like.

Leslie learned that she enjoyed the direct interactions with students in her classes, forming the self-observation generalizations that she was a good teacher and that she cared about the children. However, she also believed that parents should be involved in their children's education, and she formed the belief that parents did not care about their children if they were less active in their schooling. A conflict emerged when parents whom she judged as not caring asked her to change her teaching style for their children. This was in direct opposition to both of her self-observation generalizations that she cared more than the parents did and that she was doing her best as a teacher.

The positive influences on self-observation generalizations related to teaching began to shift to the negative. Leslie is not being reinforced for tasks related to teaching as often as she was previously. Her principal appears to be reinforcing activities that Leslie does not value, she is listening to parents tell her she is not doing her job well, and she seems to be observing teachers whom she does not value as role models being rewarded for behavior she finds inadequate. At the same time, she most enjoyed her job when she was able to teach an advanced class and when she herself enrolled in continuing education classes. She was highly reinforced by her professors for her strong work ethic and diligence. She has begun to generalize an observation to herself that she enjoys the challenge of learning and that has led her to consider another degree.

However, Leslie is also trying to become pregnant, with the expectation that she will not work while her child is young. This is an expectation her mother modeled and that is communicated by her husband as well. She learned from her family's comments that they view her as having trouble making a decision, and she has begun to view herself as wishy-washy.

The generalizations that Leslie has developed about the world include general notions about a teaching career, women's ability to balance work and family, the role of a mother in her child's early years, and the openness of the educational system to returning students. She appears to have made some tentative conclusions about teaching as an occupation, that it may not offer as much challenge and opportunity for learning as she would like. She also appears to have made some generalizations that mothers are the most important caregivers for their children, particularly in the early years, and that women need to stay out of the workforce to be with their children. In considering careers that require further training, it seems that Leslie views higher education as an open system (rather than merely reserved for late adolescents) and that she further views changing careers as a possible option open to her.

Leslie's task approach skills are consistent with those she developed as an adolescent. She is organized, has a commitment to following through on tasks, and enjoys challenging herself to learn and grow. She appears, however, to be relatively passive about taking opportunities to change her environment. Although Leslie indicates that she is angry with the principal and is frustrated at the lack of opportunities to teach advanced math classes, there is no indication that she has attempted to change those situations.

## Directions and Implications for Career Counseling

### Goals of Counseling

Krumboltz defines the goal of counseling as "to facilitate the learning of skills, interests, beliefs, values, work habits and personal qualities that enable each client to create a satisfying life within a constantly changing work environment" (Krumboltz, 1996, p. 61). Furthermore, he defines the career counselor's role as promoting client learning. In career counseling with Leslie, an overall goal is to empower her to examine the ways that her learning experiences have both facilitated her growth and served as barriers to taking advantage of new opportunities.

Leslie appears to have a history of expecting or allowing others to make decisions for her. She enters counseling hoping that the counselor will tell her the best options for a career; she wants the test to tell her what to do. She has sought the advice of her family and of her husband as to her next step. This is evidenced in her history as well. Her initial decision to go to a community college was influenced by her friends, and she subsequently went to the university to be with her boyfriend. Finally, her decision to major in secondary math education seemed to be more a path of least resistance than a deliberate choice commensurate with her interests. This may be a starting point for career counseling. The counselor might begin, "Leslie, let's start with telling me about your career history. We will then explore ways that you can begin to take charge of your own decisions."

### Assessment

Career counselors using the perspective of social learning theory view assessment as one avenue to help clients explore new learning experiences as well as a way to create new learning experiences (Krumboltz & Jackson, 1993; Mitchell & Krumboltz, 1996). Thus, assessment has two purposes: (a) to make inferences about how clients might match potential educational or occupational environments and (b) to suggest areas for clients to pursue new learning experiences. Mitchell and Krumboltz (1996) discuss assessment of skills, interests, beliefs, values, and personality, although they focus on changeable and learnable aspects of the constructs assessed in these instruments. As Krumboltz and Jackson (1993) note, "Tests might better be viewed as a source of possible ideas for future learning" (p. 394).

Leslie's interests may be viewed, then, as evidence of the learning experiences she has had as well as those she may wish to have. Social learning counselors use the scores to identify interests that may be developed if given the opportunity. Leslie's highest score on the Strong Interest Inventory (SII) is in the social General Occupational Theme, followed by the conventional and investigative General Occupational Themes. These interests reflect the experiences she has had as a math teacher, helping students and enjoying teaching as an activity. She enjoys being organized and being in a structured environment. The results also show, however, interest in the investigative area. She had interest in this area early in her schooling but chose not to pursue further learning experiences. This may be an area for her to pursue further learning experiences. The counselor may encourage her: "Leslie, let's explore ways that you could take advantage of some opportunities to determine if this is an area in which you may want to gain more experience." She may do this through classes, through talking with others in the field, or by reading more about science and other investigative activities.

These results are consistent with the SII Basic Interest Scales, in which her interests in teaching, mathematics, and data management may stem from her background as a math teacher. Her interests in religious activities and science may suggest areas for further pursuit. The Occupational Scales point to a few specific occupations that Leslie may want to consider if she should choose a new career; these may offer her opportunities to pursue further learning as well as seeming to be a good fit with her interests. These occupations are in the investigative area (chemist, pharmacist, biologist) and the conventional area (actuary, accountant, bookkeeper).

Leslie's Personal Style Scales also point to areas for more learning opportunities. Her scores on the Work Style, Leadership Style, and Learning Environment Scales are each in the midrange. This may indicate that with more opportunities to learn, Leslie may become more or less interested in working with people, more willing to take on positions of leadership, or more interested in placing herself in a traditional academic learning environment.

The Skills Confidence Inventory (SCI) may be used in conjunction with the SII to explore areas in which learning history may play a role. For example, Leslie's interest and confidence levels are slightly different in the social and investigative themes, which could be the result of Leslie's learning histories and experiences. Areas in which Leslie is low in both interests and confidence (realistic and enterprising themes) may also be explored.

Leslie's beliefs about career decision making may provide several areas for further learning. The counselor may use *Exploring Your Beliefs* (Levin, Krumboltz, & Krumboltz, 1995) to integrate the results from her CBI, SII, and Myers-Briggs Type Indicator (MBTI). Her low score on Scale 8 of the CBI (peer equality) indicates that she believes that she needs to excel over others. She may be perceived by co-workers as competing with them for recognition and may not be perceived as a team player. This combined with her predominant thinking type on the MBTI indicates that she may be making decisions at work objectively rather than considering personal values, perhaps logically expecting recognition for good work. This could be problematic for her but only if her belief that she needs to excel over others is a barrier to working cooperatively with co-workers. Her score of 49 on the Work Style Scale of the SII, however, indicates that she prefers to work alone *and* with people. The counselor may want to discuss this: "Let's look at the advantages of cooperation and competition in your current teaching job. How have you known when you have excelled over others?"

Several scales in Part 3 of the CBI (factors that influence my decision) were low for Leslie. Scale 12 (approval of others) was the lowest of these scales, but she also had low scores on Scales 10 (control) and 11 (responsibility). Together these indicate that Leslie believes that others strongly influence her career decisions. Leslie's score on Scale 12 was her lowest CBI score, indicating that approval by others is important to her. This is consistent with her career history. The counselor works with Leslie to identify whom she is trying to please and why: "Let's look at which specific decisions and behaviors will be approved or disapproved." One way the counselor may do this, identified in *Exploring Your Beliefs* (Levin et al., 1995), is to ask Leslie to identify an occupation on the SII of which her husband may disapprove, then find another of which he would approve. For example, she may think he would disapprove of her becoming a physicist because she would need to seek further education and that he would approve of her becoming a bookkeeper because she could do that with little further training.

The counselor may then ask Leslie, "Do you want to base a decision on your husband's disapproval of further education?" Leslie may indicate that she needs his financial support for her education. She may further express concern that the difference between their educational levels would bother her husband. But after reflection, she may think that these issues are not factors that should determine her decisions. This is consistent with her MBTI type of ISTJ, particularly the thinking type, where decisions are made logically and practically. The counselor then may help Leslie identify some ways that she can talk to her husband about his disapproval of further education and her concern about their educational differences. These reflections are consistent with Leslie's score on Scale 6, that a college education is necessary for a good job.

Scales 10 and 11 (control and responsibility, respectively) indicate that Leslie feels that her career decisions are influenced and controlled by others and also that she thinks that an expert can make a better decision than she can. If Leslie has already talked about her need for her husband's approval, the counselor may use Scale 10 to talk about his influence on her decisions, as well as her family-of-origin's influence. The counselor may explore the ways that Leslie perceives influence is exerted and the effect of that influence on her. For example, she may feel that her family influences her by direct negative comments about her inability to make decisions and that she believes that she cannot make decisions on her own. The counselor may further explore her beliefs about the potential of the assessment tools and of counseling, helping Leslie to understand that, ultimately, she has to make her own decision. Another important area for exploration is in what ways Leslie feels that she needs approval from the counselor and how to balance her own views with those of the "expert" counselor.

At this point, the counselor may include some discussion with Leslie about the ways that others have influenced some of her personal decisions and how her decision-making style may be similar across the domains of her life. Leslie is struggling with her desire to have a child, her anger at her husband's lack of communication about various issues, and her general depression following the miscarriages. Leslie also appears to be unhappy with the division of labor in her home, yet she accepts her husband's decision about the way it is apportioned. She may be influenced by her perception of his Hispanic background, going along with the overt messages her mother-in-law has given her about an appropriate role for a wife. She also appears to have accepted her family's and her husband's expectations that she would stay out of the labor force while her child or children are small. The counselor may explore these issues with Leslie: "Let's examine your assumptions about others' perceptions and how they influence your decisions. We want to make sure that these are decisions that are yours rather than decisions you are going along with to win others' approval."

The counselor explores two additional CBI scales with Leslie. They discuss Scale 18 (relocation) and may determine that Leslie's reluctance to relocate is related to the importance of her personal relationships with her husband and her family. They also discuss Scale 3 (acceptance of uncertainty), which indicates that Leslie believes that she should have made a decision by now and is uncomfortable with the uncertainty of the future. Her judging type on the MBTI also indicates that she prefers to reach closure, preferring not to leave options open. The counselor helps her explore, however, the benefits of remaining uncertain versus making a quick decision before she has all the information she needs.

*Interventions*

Krumboltz (1996) discusses (a) developmental and preventive interventions and (b) targeted and remedial interventions. The former consists of activities aimed toward groups of individuals in structured or programmatic ways, such as career education activities, job clubs, and the more recent school-to-work transition movement. The latter category consists of activities more typically conducted as part of career counseling, such as cognitive interventions (goal clarification, cognitive restructuring, countering troublesome beliefs, and cognitive rehearsal) and behavioral interventions.

Mitchell, Levin, and Krumboltz (in press) extend social learning theory by pointing out how unplanned events affect career development. They advocate that career counselors should help clients to expect that unplanned events will inevitably affect their careers and that such effects are normal. They suggest that counselors teach their clients how to take an active role in creating beneficial events. They also point out that indecision need not necessarily be a problem. They contend that indecision is desirable in enabling a flexible response to constantly changing circumstances. Too much planning may result in clients missing new opportunities.

*Cognitive Interventions.* An important issue to consider early in career counseling is *goal clarification.* Leslie's reasons for entering counseling are fairly clear cut. She would like to sort out some options she is currently considering—that is, quitting her present job, staying in her career, or considering a career change. She also is trying to incorporate her plans and hopes for a family into her career decision-making process. Although these are clearly stated concerns, it would be helpful for Leslie and the counselor to further explore the parameters of these counseling goals so as to clarify them. Moreover, she does have expectations that the counselor will provide information, particularly about which option is "best" for her. This, clearly, is a counseling goal that needs further elaboration and clarification.

*Cognitive restructuring,* or "reframing," is focused on developing a different perspective. Cognitive restructuring is a particularly valuable tool in working with Leslie, to help her explore the feelings and beliefs that underlie her dissatisfaction with her job and her consideration of perhaps major changes in her career and life. For example, her frustration with her current situation could be viewed as a sign that she is ready for new challenges and moving on to other things in her life. In addition, exploration of the aspects of her job dissatisfaction might reveal areas in which cognitive restructuring would be useful. Part of her job dissatisfaction clearly stems from expectations that she has for herself, for which she then denigrates herself: "Why do I let myself get so emotionally drained by the difficult students?" Cognitive restructuring allows her to view her investment as a positive characteristic, although the way in which it affects her personally is not beneficial and might be modified through behavioral interventions (discussed later).

Another area in which cognitive restructuring is beneficial relates to Leslie's expectations about her current decision-making process. Although Leslie verbalizes a willingness to explore a variety of career options, she also feels some anxiety about being in the middle of a career decision. This anxiety would appear to be rooted in her previous experience with the teasing she received from her family about her indecision during college. The counselor encourages Leslie to give herself permission to suspend decision making for a period of time, which the counselor might even specify (e.g., "because this process takes some time, you should not plan to have a firm decision made until at least April"). The counselor may also use direct positive verbal reinforcement, such as "You're making good progress on this decision."

Another cognitive technique is *countering a troublesome belief*. This technique is indicated when there are long-standing messages that clients hold about themselves or the world of work. Leslie has incorporated many beliefs about herself as a teacher but also about herself as a woman in the workforce. Leslie has nagging doubts about herself as a teacher: She appears outwardly confident about her competencies as a teacher, yet she finds herself worrying each night about whether she has done enough preparation for the following day and secretly harbors the idea that other teachers must be doing something better than she does in the classroom. The counselor helps her express and explore these beliefs and points out the evidence that contradicts these worries.

Leslie also has beliefs about herself as a "career woman" that could benefit from intervention. She has received mixed messages from her family about the role of achievement in her life, and these internalized beliefs seem to enter into her confusion about career issues. For example, she holds conflicting beliefs about whether she should be invested in her career, reflected in her seeming ambivalence about pursuing further education and what role her career will have when she has children.

*Cognitive rehearsal* is used to help Leslie combat some of the negative messages she has incorporated. For example, her daily worries about her skills as a teacher are counteracted with positive self-statements generated with the help of the counselor. Leslie has no difficulty in identifying her strengths as a teacher but does not fully believe that they are true, particularly when she is feeling stressed and vulnerable. Leslie and the counselor may prepare a list of positive self-statements, which she can either rehearse on a scheduled basis or use as she is feeling herself becoming negative.

*Behavioral Interventions.* Behavioral interventions are techniques that incorporate experiential components. *Role-playing* is a method of trying out new behaviors in the counseling session. As Krumboltz

(1996) notes, trying a new behavior may result in a change in beliefs, as a client observes himself or herself in a new light. Leslie's dissatisfaction with her new principal is exacerbated by frustration with her own behavior related to him; that is, she accepts what he says during their interactions, then becomes angry later that he doesn't understand her position. Through role play, the counselor helps her develop and practice some assertiveness skills so that she feels more prepared for future interactions with the principal. Role-playing in session allows the counselor to give Leslie immediate feedback about the effectiveness of her behavior. If her dissatisfaction with teaching is due mainly to her inability to cope with an ineffective principal, the counselor's teaching of good coping skills may enable her to enjoy teaching again.

Krumboltz (1996) recommends *desensitization* as a way to combat phobias related to career issues. Despite the fact that "career decisions are crucial to human happiness" (p. 70), people often arrive at career counseling exhibiting "zeteophobia," or a fear of the career decision-making process. Leslie's fears about career decision making appear to be twofold: As just discussed, she is concerned about being undecided, but she also is concerned about making the "wrong" decision. These two fears need to be clearly identified and separated from one another so that they can be addressed in counseling. The former fear may force a premature decision, whereas the latter fear may prevent an appropriate decision. The counselor uses desensitization techniques to confront the fear about approaching the decision.

*Using paradoxical intention to discover disconfirming evidence* asks clients to adopt or exaggerate a behavior so that they may experience the feared outcome of the behavior. Paradoxical intention may be effective in addressing Leslie's worries about preparation for class: The counselor might ask her to experiment with putting a time limit on her evening class preparation one night and to prepare until she feels completely ready another night. Paradoxical intention should be applied cautiously, however: The counselor needs to feel confident in his or her understanding of the client's concerns before assigning a paradoxical intention as an intervention.

Finally, the counselor *investigates assumptions to discover disconfirming evidence*. In Leslie's case, her inclination to avoid her husband's disapproval by not pursuing occupations requiring further education may be based on faulty assumptions about his reaction. The counselor's previous interventions that encouraged Leslie to discuss this issue with her husband may result in a more accurate (and positive) view of her husband's beliefs and concerns.

## DISCUSSION QUESTIONS REGARDING LESLIE FROM KRUMBOLTZ'S THEORETICAL PERSPECTIVE

1. What specific hypotheses would you develop about Leslie from Krumboltz's social learning theory? How does using social learning theory help you understand Leslie? How might it help Leslie understand herself?

2. What other specific interventions might be used to address the concerns that Leslie brings to counseling?

3. From what types of learning experiences might Leslie benefit?

4. What additional self-observation generalizations does Leslie have about her interests and values?

5. What worldview generalizations does Leslie hold?

6. What are Leslie's key beliefs about the career of teaching? What are her key beliefs about graduate school and about women entering technical careers?

7. What are Leslie's key beliefs about her role as a mother and worker and as the wife of a Hispanic man? Should a counselor challenge the validity of those beliefs and, if so, how?

## ADDITIONAL CASES

### Case 1: Dorece

Dorece is a 21-year-old African American woman who is a student at a major urban university on the East Coast. She was referred to career counseling by her academic adviser because she had not yet declared a major despite accumulating enough credits to be considered a junior. Dorece presents herself as quite self-assured yet seems unnerved by the prospect of making a decision. She comes to counseling each week with a different idea of what she might choose, which she states with considerable enthusiasm. However, she does not complete the tasks assigned by her counselor, such as investigating the requirements of the major or what the job might entail, nor does her enthusiasm carry into the following week.

Dorece is the youngest child of four and grew up in an upper-middle-class home in suburban Washington D.C. Her father is an advertising manager for a radio station, and her mother is a government attorney. Dorece attended an exclusive all-girls' private high school, where she excelled in all her courses and graduated with a 3.8 grade point average. She enjoyed choir, French club, and the sailing club. Her older siblings have successfully completed graduate or professional degrees and are working in the Washington, D.C., area.

When she entered college, Dorece was encouraged by her parents to not choose a major too hastily but, rather, to explore various opportunities before she settled on the "right choice." She initially enrolled in standard freshman year courses and did well in all of them. She particularly enjoyed her English classes and found that she appreciated the challenge of creative writing. Despite this, however, she did not declare English as a major because her father expressed concerned about what she could "do" with a degree in English. After rejecting English as a major, she experienced similar concerns with other majors and soon found herself ruling out most of the possibilities. She has considered becoming a broadcast journalist, because many have told her that she her good looks and presentation style would serve her well in that field. She has considered nursing, because she enjoys caring for others and has considered teaching for the same reason. Her sisters, however, were horrified when she mentioned these possibilities, claiming that she would disgrace the family if she entered such a gender-stereotypic occupation. She continued to search for the "right choice" for a major.

Dorece is in a very serious relationship with an African American man who is attending graduate school at the same university. He is completing his doctorate in political science and has some aspirations to a political career; if that is not possible, he would like an academic career. He and Dorece have discussed her lack of decision making; he thinks she should become an English major. He also has expressed concern that it may be detrimental to his future political career if she were to enter broadcast journalism.

## Questions for Discussion

1. How have Dorece's learning experiences affected her career decision making?
2. Under what career beliefs is Dorece operating?

3. What interventions might be effective in addressing her current career status?
4. What role are others playing in Dorece's career decisions?
5. What would you do as a counselor from the perspective of social learning theory to help Dorece make a career decision?

### Case 2: Steve

Steve is a Caucasian man, aged 39, and a divorced father of an 8-year-old son. He is employed as a writer for a greeting card company. He seeks career counseling because he is not satisfied as a greeting card writer but is not sure he wants to continue his original goal of becoming a college professor. Steve majored in English as an undergraduate and pursued a doctorate in American Literature. However, he dropped out of his graduate program in the middle of his third year and has not returned to finish his degree.

Steve met his ex-wife, Mariela, while he was an undergraduate. She had already finished her degree and was working as a secretary. She worked while he finished his undergraduate degree and continued supporting him while he was in his first year of graduate school. In his second year, however, she quit working when she became pregnant with their son. He took out loans to support them but realized in the third year of his graduate program that he needed to leave school and work while she stayed home with their child. Their plan was that she would return to work when their son was 3 years old, at which point Steve would return to finish his degree and pursue a career as a college professor.

Their marriage, however, failed, and Steve's financial obligations for child support and alimony are significant enough that he feels he cannot quit his job to return to school to finish his degree. He is also questioning his original plans to get a doctorate and become a professor. He is the oldest son of eight children born to lower-working-class parents; his mother stayed home with the children, and his father worked in a factory. His father often worked two jobs to make ends meet. Steve is the first child in his entire extended family to attend college, much less graduate and enter graduate school. His parents are disappointed that his marriage failed but have been very supportive of his decision to quit school to support his family.

When he took the job as a greeting card writer, he anticipated that he would be with the company only temporarily. However, he has now worked there for over 5 years and has worked his way to increased levels of responsibility. There are some aspects of the greeting card business that he enjoys or at least some parts of business decisions that he enjoys. He does not like having to create trite greeting card phrases but does enjoy the marketing meetings that he attends.

## Questions for Discussion

1. How have Steve's learning experiences affected his career decision making?
2. Under what career beliefs is Steve operating?
3. What interventions might be effective in dealing with his decision making?
4. How has Steve's family influenced his decision making?
5. How might you help Steve with his career concerns?

### Case 3: Lori

Lori is referred for career counseling by a good friend who is a social worker and is concerned about Lori's lack of energy and possible depression. Lori is a 45-year-old Caucasian woman. She is married to John, who is running his family's farm in southeastern Iowa. Lori met John when they were both in college, where John was studying agricultural economics and Lori was studying home economics. They both finished their bachelor's degrees and moved to John's hometown, a small farming community. When they were first married, they lived in town while John's parents lived on the farm. John worked with his father, incorporating more modern agricultural practices into the farm operation, and gradually took over the farm business from his father. John's mother was a very traditional farm wife, raising chickens, and helping her husband on the farm when necessary, but primarily taking care of her seven children.

Lori and John have two children, both daughters. They moved to the farm when John's father had a stroke, and they needed to take care of him and John's mother, who also was in poor health. Lori had worked as a home economist for the local extension office after she and John married, but at the encouragement of her husband and mother-in-law, she quit her job when her first daughter was born. She had enjoyed working, especially the teaching aspects of her work, as well as meeting lots of new people.

Lori's daughters are now in high school, and the older one just received her driver's license. Her daughters have been spending more time away from home than in the past, with activities in town and at the consolidated school several miles away. The oldest daughter's newly acquired driver's license means that Lori is not asked to drive the girls to and from their activities as often as she had previously done. Her father-in-law died the previous month, and Lori and John are struggling with decisions about caring for her mother-in-law, who requires daily assistance from Lori due to deteriorating health.

Lori feels quite isolated on the farm. She would like to return to work but does not know what she wants to do or even what options are open to her. Lori and John are not able to relocate, because John is committed to maintaining the family farm for their daughters. She had enjoyed her work as a home economist, but because women are now less often at home, Lori doesn't know if that job even exists anymore.

## Questions for Discussion

1. How have Lori's learning experiences affected her career decision making, and how have her life circumstances affected her learning experiences?
2. Under what career beliefs is Lori operating?
3. What interventions might be effective in dealing with her decision making?
4. How would you incorporate the personal issues that Lori is facing into career counseling?
5. How would you incorporate Lori's possible depression into career counseling from a social learning perspective?

# SEVEN

# *Social Cognitive Career Theory*

The theoretical approaches we have examined thus far have been well-established theories that have shaped vocational psychology for several decades. However, the theory we will discuss in this chapter is relatively new, with the first introduction of the concepts in 1981 (Hackett & Betz, 1981) and a complete description of the theory published only in 1994 (Lent, Brown, & Hackett, 1994). We include this emerging theory because of its utility and because of the impact this theory has already had on the field. It differs from the other theories in its focus on the personal constructions that people place on events related to career decision making.

Social cognitive theory (Bandura, 1977, 1986, 1997) has been recently applied in vocational psychology to help explain how individuals' career interests develop, how they make career choices, and how they determine their level of performance. Bandura hypothesizes that individuals' conception of their confidence to perform tasks (self-efficacy) mediates between what they know and how they act and that people's beliefs in their ability to accomplish things helps to determine the actions they will take. Self-efficacy comes from individuals' previous performance accomplishments, vicariously by observing others, from verbal persuasion, and from physiological states and arousal.

Bandura also postulates that self-efficacy is distinct from outcome expectancies, or the expectations that one has of the result of behavior. Bandura (1986) notes that self-efficacy and "outcome expectancies judgments are differentiated because individuals can believe that a particular course of action will produce certain outcomes, but they do not act on that outcome belief because they question whether they can actually execute the necessary activities" (p. 392). The constructs of self-efficacy and outcome expectancies are an individual's perceptions of reality; as such, those perceptions may or may not be realistic perceptions. It is important to note that in decision making, individuals' perceptions of reality are hypothesized to be greater determinants of their behavior than objective reality.

Hackett and Betz (1981) were the first to apply Bandura's social cognitive theory with its emphasis on the role of self-efficacy to career choices. They focused on self-efficacy theory to explain women's traditional career choices, suggesting that low self-efficacy may explain the restricted range of women's career options. Their work led to investigations of the role that self-efficacy may play in a variety of career-related behaviors, although it is only recently that the constructs of self-efficacy and outcome expectancies have been incorporated into a theoretical framework related to career decisions. Lent et al. (1994) have proposed a social cognitive framework that explains and predicts career behavior. Specifically, their three-part model links interests, choices, and performance based on Bandura's (1986) social cognitive model.

Basic to all three of the segments of the model, Lent et al. (1994, 1996) propose that performance accomplishments, verbal persuasion, vicarious learning, and physiological states and arousal forge an individual's self-efficacy expectations. For example, a young woman who does well in French class, is persuaded by others that she could be mistaken for a native French speaker, observes others speaking French, and is mildly anxious about performing well would be expected to have high self-efficacy beliefs for speaking French. It is important to note that Bandura's conceptualization of self-efficacy is situation specific. In the preceding example, the young woman may have high self-efficacy for speaking French but lower self-efficacy beliefs for speaking German or Russian.

Lent et al. (1994) also propose that demographic and individual difference variables (such as sex, race and ethnicity, and socioeconomic

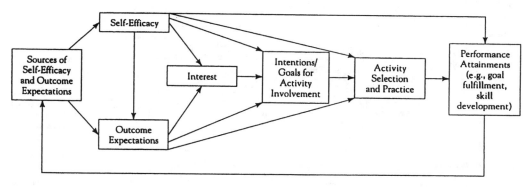

**Figure 7.1.** Predicting Interest Development in Social Cognitive Career Theory
SOURCE: Lent, Brown, and Hackett (1994). Used with permission.

status) interact with background and contextual variables to influence learning experiences that play a role in forming self-efficacy beliefs. Those self-efficacy expectations, in turn, are related to outcome expectations that individuals have about the outcomes of behavior. In the earlier example of the young French-speaking woman, a high socioeconomic status may have provided her with opportunities to learn French and may lead to her outcome expectations of speaking French, such as opportunities to travel or live in France.

In the *interest* segment of Lent et al.'s model (see Figure 7.1), outcome expectancies and self-efficacy beliefs both predict interests. Interests (together with self-efficacy beliefs and outcome expectancies) predict goals, which in turn lead to behaviors related to choosing and practicing activities, which then lead to performance attainments. For example, a young man may have developed an interest in playing the drums based on his self-efficacy beliefs that he is competent as a drum player. He also expects positive outcomes from playing the drums, such as social interaction with friends or enjoying the music, as well as verbal reinforcement from his family. He then is predicted to intend to continue to play the drums and perhaps to form a goal to join a band. This leads to his increased choice to practice the drums and eventually to his skill development in drum playing.

Lent et al. (1994, 1996) also propose that background and contextual variables help to explain why an individual does not pursue an area in which he or she has strong interest. Background and contextual variables may serve as perceived barriers to entry or to poor outcome expectations. For example, a young man with high interests in helping others and in medical fields may not go into nursing because of his

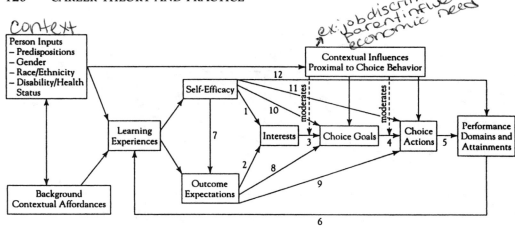

**Figure 7.2.** Predicting Vocational Choice in Social Cognitive Career Theory
SOURCE: Lent, Brown, and Hackett (1994). Used with permission.

perception that nursing is not an appropriate occupation for a man. He may further perceive weak support from others to enter that occupation, support that may have helped him to overcome that barrier. Barriers may be objective or subjective; what is important is an individual's perception of the barrier (Swanson, Daniels, & Tokar, 1996).

The *choice* segment of the model (see Figure 7.2) proposes that person inputs (e.g., gender, race, disability, personality, and predispositions) and background context together influence learning experiences, which influence self-efficacy beliefs and outcome expectancies. As already described, these influence interests, which influence choice goals; goals influence actions, and actions influence performance attainments. For example, a young girl from an affluent background is taken to science museums, encouraged to read and learn about science and famous scientists, and given opportunities to take science classes and to attend summer science camp. These learning experiences, afforded by her socioeconomic status, influence the development of her beliefs in her ability to do well in science. Her performance in science and her knowledge that doing well in science will lead to positive outcomes, such as good grades, parental approval, and time spent with friends, and to the development of her interest in science. She believes she can do well in science in college, she learns that science is a field that is well compensated and one that is not typical for women, and she develops an intention to enter a science major in

③

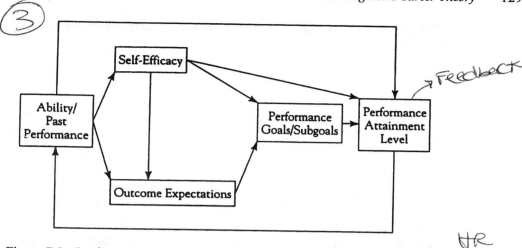

→ Feedback

HR

**Figure 7.3.** Predicting Task Performance in Social Cognitive Career Theory
SOURCE: Lent, Brown, and Hackett (1994). Used with permission.

college. Lent et al. (1996) note that the process of making a career choice involves choosing a goal (e.g., becoming a scientist), taking action to implement that goal (completing courses in a biology major), and the subsequent consequences of those actions (successful graduation in biology).

The *performance* part of the model (see Figure 7.3) predicts the level of performance as well as the persistence an individual has in pursuing goals. This segment proposes that past performance accomplishments influence self-efficacy and outcome expectancies, which in turn influence performance goals; these lead to performance attainment level. In other words, past performance influences self-efficacy beliefs along with the expectations individuals have about the outcomes of their future behavior. These expectations affect the goals that people set for themselves. These goals will then affect the level of performance they may attain. Thus, a woman who did well in basketball while in high school has confidence in her ability to play and decides to try out for the basketball team in college. After making the team, she sets challenging goals for her offensive and defensive performance (e.g., averaging at least 12 points a game), based on her past successes and current self-efficacy and outcome beliefs. Lent et al. (1996) differentiate their choice and interest models from the performance model. The former involve the content of career choices, such as the field or specific occupation in which one would like to work, whereas the performance model predicts the level of performance toward which one aspires within one's chosen field.

Bandura (1997) comments that "in making career decisions, people must come to grips with uncertainties about their capabilities, the stability of their interests, . . . the prospects of alternative occupations, . . . and the type of identity they seek to construct for themselves" (p. 422). Individuals' perceptions of their own efficacy in mastering various skills and tasks play an important role in predicting their choices as well as in their perseverance to accomplish their goals. Social cognitive theory thus is readily applicable to development of interventions targeted at increasing individuals' self-efficacy in a variety of areas. Other areas for intervention include fostering positive and realistic outcome expectations, setting specific goals, increasing coping self-efficacy, and developing strong performance skills. Interventions may be targeted at expanding vocational interests, increasing decision-making skills and exploratory behavior, helping clients explore various careers, and increasing consideration of nontraditional careers.

## APPLYING SOCIAL COGNITIVE CAREER THEORY TO THE CASE OF LESLIE

### Conceptualizing Leslie's Career History

In conceptualizing Leslie's career history, counselors using a social cognitive model (Lent et al., 1996) focus on the learning experiences Leslie has had. They would examine how those learning experiences may relate to the self-efficacy beliefs and outcome expectations Leslie had as an adolescent and how those may have influenced her interests and, in turn, how those affected performance and choices as she grew older.

Leslie's family had the resources to expose her to a variety of opportunities when she was a child. Her mother was very involved in the arts in their community, and thus Leslie visited the art museum with her mother, took art and music classes, and attended symphony concerts with her family. Leslie also had significant learning experiences while in school; her active roles as a math tutor and as a leader in the French club and her successful participation in her school's science fair were opportunities for her to learn about herself and to gain confidence in her skills. Leslie did well academically, as well as socially, in high school. Others perceived her as a leader, although she did not view herself as a leader, because she did not seek out leadership positions.

Leslie's learning experiences were related to her eventual occupational choice. In other words, the activities in which Leslie was engaged as a child and adolescent, such as becoming a tutor, helped in preparation for a career as a teacher. However, there were barriers to her translation of her learning experiences into a major occupational direction. She knew she was going to attend college, consistent with her parents' expectations, but she did not declare a major until well into her sophomore year in college. She took general courses in the community college she attended after high school and then was "undecided" for several semesters after she transferred to a larger university.

In the performance model proposed by Lent et al. (1994), the level of goals toward which Leslie aspired were influenced by her self-efficacy beliefs and the outcomes she expected would result from pursuing her goals. Leslie did very well academically in high school yet chose to attend a community college rather than the university. Leslie set lower goals for herself than were consistent with her level of performance. This may have been due to faulty self-efficacy beliefs about her ability to do well academically; this is evidenced in her uncertainty about being successful in college. Such lowered self-efficacy beliefs may have been due to a lack of role models or verbal encouragement to seek an academically challenging curriculum. Leslie also may not have had a good knowledge of the outcomes associated with attending a community college versus the university, although she did expect that her parents would approve of her decision to go on for some postsecondary education. Once she was enrolled in the community college, however, she was frustrated by the lack of challenge. This may have led to increased self-efficacy beliefs about her ability to do well academically and to her decision to transfer to the university.

Even after she enrolled in the university, Leslie still struggled with making a career decision. She did well in many of her classes, although she did not do well in mechanical drawing, which led her to conclude that she would not do well in engineering. Her overall self-efficacy beliefs in her ability to do well academically were relatively high; however, her self-efficacy beliefs in her ability to do well in the specific areas related to engineering were low. She also appeared to have low self-efficacy beliefs related to advanced training, or she might have had low self-efficacy beliefs in her ability to juggle the multiple roles required of balancing career and family obligations. These beliefs led her to foreclose career options that required postgraduate training.

Leslie did not want to consider options that were nontraditional for a woman. This was influenced by the outcomes she expected of a nontraditional career, such as continuing to be among the few women in a career setting or difficulty in combining her career with raising a family. Leslie also received little encouragement to consider nontraditional careers; in fact, she was at times actively discouraged by her professors.

Leslie's learning experiences led her to know that she was proficient in math and that she was interested in teaching and in helping others. She had developed self-efficacy beliefs in her ability to teach when she was a math tutor in high school. Leslie's decision to major in secondary math education was influenced by her self-efficacy beliefs in her math and teaching abilities and her lower self-efficacy beliefs about advanced training, because teaching did not require a graduate degree. Her student teaching experience gave her a sense of accomplishment and verbal encouragement, which led to increased self-efficacy beliefs in her teaching ability, which led to greater interest in being a teacher and then to her subsequent implementation of that choice. Her choice also was influenced by the outcomes she expected of a teaching career: She would have a career that she could combine with raising a family as well as a career in which she would not be singled out as one of the few women. In addition, Leslie expected that the choice of teaching would meet with her family's approval. Leslie's decision, then, was strongly influenced by her pattern of self-efficacy and outcome beliefs, which perhaps led to her setting a lower performance goal than she was capable of (Lent et al., 1996). However, her decision to be a math teacher was a choice consonant with her self-efficacy beliefs and with her outcome expectations.

Leslie's early career years were a time of increasing her self-efficacy beliefs in her teaching ability. Lent et al. (1996) note that the social cognitive model "asserts that people form an enduring interest in an activity when they view themselves as competent at it and when they anticipate that performing it will produce valued outcomes" (p. 383). Leslie viewed herself as a good, perhaps even as a very good, teacher. She also began to anticipate that being a teacher would have outcomes that she enjoyed and appreciated. The outcomes included approval from her family, approval from her students and peers, and feeling competent as a teacher. Leslie also enjoyed the challenge of teaching a variety of math classes and being able to be autonomous and creative in her own classroom.

Lent et al.'s (1996) performance model suggests that Leslie's performance accomplishments as a teacher and positive outcome expectations of a teaching career would lead her to set higher accomplishment goals. However, Leslie made a lateral move to a teaching position in a larger city to be closer to her family. This change of environment brought with it some unwelcome changes in the rewards of her work and, subsequently, in her outcome expectations. She did not pursue a graduate degree, even though she took several continuing education classes, thus suggesting that she may have low outcome expectancies about the student role or the rewards that an advanced degree might bring her. She also might have anticipated barriers to pursuing a graduate degree, either from her family or from her husband.

## Conceptualizing Leslie's Present Situation

Leslie has been a teacher for over 13 years, suggesting that she has high self-efficacy beliefs in her ability to teach, that she expects positive outcomes from the occupation, and that she has formed a long-lasting interest in the occupation. However, Leslie reports considerable dissatisfaction with her job. Some of her concerns may be related to changes in outcomes she has come to expect from the job; others may be related to her own changing self-efficacy beliefs regarding certain aspects of her current teaching role. Or conversely, she may have developed interests in another field in which she has higher self-efficacy beliefs and higher outcome expectancies.

Leslie states that she is a good teacher, suggesting high teaching efficacy overall. She enjoys the outcomes associated with direct interactions with her students. However, she also notes frustration in not reaching some students, and this may be threatening her self-efficacy beliefs about her teaching ability. She has also had some difficult interactions with parents, which have led her to question her teaching efficacy, at least within the context of her current school and teaching assignment.

Some of the outcomes associated with being a teacher, such as approval from parents and students, autonomy in her classroom, and ability to challenge herself through teaching advanced classes, have recently diminished for Leslie. She reports frustration with the principal's new accountability measures. She may perceive this as feedback on her teaching, interpreting that the principal does not trust her ability to teach, which in turn could lead to lower teaching efficacy. She also is distrustful of participating in reporting on her teaching goals and activities. She may fear, for example, that she will be evaluated negatively or that she will lose the ability to set her own goals and activities in the class. Other outcomes that Leslie has expected of teaching have also changed. Approval from students and parents is not as frequent as it once was for Leslie. She has had fewer opportunities to teach challenging courses, even though she has been in this high school for 10 years.

One of the outcomes that Leslie expected from her teaching was the ability to combine teaching with raising a family. However, she is experiencing difficulty having children, which may lead her to question the premise on which that expectancy was based. She also reports some dissatisfaction with the division of labor in her marriage, suggesting that she might be questioning the way in which she had intended to combine work and family.

Leslie reports that she is willing to consider graduate school at this point, indicating that her efficacy beliefs in her academic skills have become more congruent with her documented skills in doing well academically, that her expectations of the outcomes of attending graduate school have changed, or both. Leslie is considering a wide range of occupational areas, although she continues to have weak self-efficacy beliefs in her ability to make a career decision. Her family has given her little encouragement in her career exploration; her brother has actively discouraged her from changing careers, and her mother and sister feel that she should quit work to concentrate on having a family. It is not known whether Leslie has had any role models of individuals who have changed careers in midlife. It would appear that Leslie is less inclined than earlier in her life to foreclose options that are nontraditional for women; she indicated, for example, that she would consider engineering as a career. Leslie may perceive the relatively traditional division of labor in her marriage as a barrier to choices, however, particularly because she reports that her husband and family expect her to stay home if and when she does have children.

### Directions and Implications for Career Counseling

Career counseling within the framework of the social cognitive career model focuses on helping clients identify faulty efficacy beliefs and unrealistic outcome expectations that have led them to make poor career decisions. Brown and Lent (1996) suggest three basic tenets inherent in career counseling from a social cognitive framework. The first is to identify those options that clients have foreclosed because they have unrealistic or faulty self-efficacy beliefs or outcome expectancies. The second is to identify and evaluate barriers to various career choices that may have led clients to prematurely eliminate a career possibility from consideration. The third tenet is to help clients modify and counteract faulty efficacy beliefs and faulty occupational information. These are not necessarily done in a linear order. For example, it may be necessary to work with clients to identify options that they have eliminated from consideration. It may be important then to help clients modify efficacy beliefs or to correct their occupational information so that they may consider a career that seems to be a particularly appropriate choice, and then move to help them identify and eliminate barriers to implementing that choice.

### Goals of Counseling

The overarching goal of the social cognitive career model is to help clients make a career choice that "correspond[s] well with important aspects of their work personality" (Lent et al., 1996, p. 402). In other words, the goal of career counseling within this framework is to help clients find a career that matches their interests, values, and skills. An important part of this process is to help clients explore possibilities that are a good match but that were discarded from consideration due to poor self-efficacy perceptions or inaccurate outcome expectations.

*Identifying Foreclosed Options.* Career counseling begins with helping clients clarify their goals for career counseling. The career counselor works with Leslie to help her identify whether she was seeking counseling to help her choose an entirely new career path or whether she wanted to make some changes to be more satisfied in her current position. It appears that Leslie is not very certain of her own goal for counseling. Initially, then, the counselor works to help her clarify her goals. The counselor asks her the question, "When will you know counseling has been successful?" Clarifying the counseling goals helps Leslie and the counselor focus the assessments and interventions toward that goal and helps them both evaluate the process and result of counseling.

Once Leslie and the counselor have clarified the goals for counseling, the counselor focuses on exploring those paths that Leslie has dropped from consideration and to expand the possibilities that Leslie could consider. The counselor also encourages Leslie to explore options to become more satisfied with her current career. The counselor might say, "Leslie, I noticed that you were considering the occupations of engineering, psychology, and medicine. Let's examine why you decided those weren't for you. We can also spend some time looking at ways to make teaching a more viable career option for you."

Brown and Lent (1996) identify three approaches to identifying specific foreclosed options. One is to focus on the results from an interest inventory, using both high-scoring interests and those interest scales on which clients scored lower. In the latter, the counselor incorporates an analysis on the basis of those areas of less interest. This approach may also include an analysis of the relationship between areas of interest and level of confidence in that area, such as that provided by the Skills Confidence Inventory (SCI).

Leslie's results on the Strong Interest Inventory (SII) indicate high interest in the General Occupational Themes in social, conventional, and investigative areas and on the Basic Interest Scales for mathematics, data management, teaching, religious activities, and science. Leslie had much less interest in the General Occupational Themes in enterprising and artistic areas and indicated low interest in the Basic Interest Scales associated with the artistic General Occupational Theme, such as music/dramatics, art, culinary arts, and writing. She also indicated little interest in medical service, law/politics, merchandising, and agriculture. The counselor explores these areas to examine the basis for a low level of interest in the areas. For example, as noted earlier, Leslie had a variety of opportunities to be exposed to careers related to the arts through her mother's work in community arts organizations. The basis for her lack of interest in the arts area may be due to a realistic appraisal of her skills in the area. However, Leslie also may have decided early in her adolescence that she did not want to pursue careers in the arts areas for reasons unrelated to her skills. For example, she may have decided that she did not want to pursue a path followed by her mother, she may have negative outcome expectations associated with entering the arts field, or she may have erroneously decided that she did not have the skills to pursue a career in the arts. The counselor spends some time exploring this as a possible avenue for further consideration: "Leslie, the Strong Interest Inventory results indicate that, compared with a large group of women, you aren't very interested in the areas represented in the artistic General Occupational Theme. Can you think back to a time when you may have been interested in this area? Perhaps there are some occupations that you would like to explore for further consideration?"

The counselor also discusses the scales on which Leslie scored high but that she has not pursued in her career, specifically the areas indicated by the Basic Interest Scales for science, mathematics, and data management, as well as those related to the Basic Interest Scale for social service. Occupations for which Leslie scored high included mathematician, computer programmer/systems analyst, actuary, biologist, physicist, and pharmacist. She also scored high on the Occupational Scale for mathematics teacher, indicating that she is a good match for her own career. The latter may indicate that career counseling should focus on helping her to find a different occupational environment rather than a different career. However, the counselor may also encourage her to explore the occupations on which she scored similar to women in that occupation: "Leslie, your pattern of likes and dislikes was similar to women who are speech pathologists and special education teachers; these two are in the social General Occupational Theme area. Tell me what you think of these occupations."

Leslie's Learning Environment Scale score on the SII indicates that she is interested in practical, hands-on learning, as opposed to more traditional academic modes of education. This may be a further clue to her reluctance to pursue a graduate degree. Her decision to not seek advanced training may have been related to her negative outcome expectations related to the type of learning required in graduate school rather than to her low self-efficacy beliefs related to graduate training.

Examination of the comparison between Leslie's interests and skills confidence on the SCI lends some support for the counselor to encourage Leslie to explore options in both the investigative and social General Occupational Theme areas. Interventions for areas in which a client has lower interest than confidence would target outcome expectancies. Self-efficacy beliefs would be the target of interventions in areas in which confidence is lower than interest. Leslie's results indicate that Leslie has more confidence in her skills than interest in the investigative area and more interests than skill confidence in the social area. The lower interest in the investigative theme may be due to her lower outcome expectations in this area. The counselor explores this with Leslie: "I notice that the Strong and SCI results indicate that you have more confidence in your ability to do the tasks related to the investigative area than you have interests in the area. This may be related to the outcomes you would expect from tasks and occupations in this area. Tell me what you would expect if you were to pursue the occupation of chemist or dentist." The counselor then helps Leslie to determine if this is related to her negative outcome expectations related to further education and helps her to reevaluate those outcome expectations or determine if other investigative occupations are more consonant with her educational goals.

The difference in Leslie's confidence and interest in the social area may be due to lack of learning opportunities available to Leslie in the areas tapped by the Social Skills Confidence Scale, such as directly working to help people with their problems, or counseling an unhappy couple. The counselor works with Leslie to assess areas that she wants to consider, particularly focusing on those areas that might be fruitful for further investigation but that Leslie is not considering due to poor self-efficacy beliefs or low outcome expectations. If, for example, Leslie indicates that she might be interested in being a social worker but does not feel she could actually help people, social work would be an area the counselor would target for further exploration.

A second approach for identifying foreclosed options is to analyze discrepancies between occupations identified on an interest inventory and those identified on an aptitude inventory or those identified on a needs inventory, such as the Minnesota Importance Questionnaire (MIQ). The assumption behind the latter analysis is that occupations predicted to be satisfying based on needs would also be predicted to be satisfying based on interests unless faulty efficacy or outcome perceptions had prevented the development of interest in that area. Identifying those discrepant occupations may help the client to expand the possible range of occupations she or he is considering. This should be used only as a guide, however, because the occupations on each inventory do not overlap entirely; that is, not all occupations on the MIQ are found on the SII and vice versa. It is important to note that social cognitive career theory views needs and values as outcome expectations and would consider the MIQ as providing information related to the outcome expectations (i.e., rewards) that a client may have about an occupation.

Occupations on which Leslie had high scores in both the SII and MIQ included secondary teacher, speech pathologist, engineer, and programmer. Occupations in which Leslie was predicted to be satisfied based on her needs results but in which she did not indicate an interest included architect, interior decorator, librarian, technical writer, minister, nurse, occupational therapist, recreation leader, social worker, realtor, psychologist, and police officer. These provide additional areas for the counselor to explore with Leslie: "Leslie, I note that several occupations may provide the rewards you would expect from an occupation, but you did not indicate you were interested in that occupation. In particular, I wonder what you think of those occupations in the social area, such as nurse and occupational therapist, as well as in the artistic area, such as librarian and architect." Two occupations may deserve further discussion. Leslie's interests in religious activities suggest that the occupation of minister may be an occupation worthy of in-depth consideration, particularly if her lack of efficacy beliefs regarding helping others has caused her to preclude it as an option. The other occupation to discuss is technical writing, because she entered counseling having listed that as an option. She may have low efficacy beliefs in her writing ability that have led to low interests in this area; these merit further investigation to determine the accuracy of those efficacy beliefs.

A third approach to identifying foreclosed options is to use a card sort (Dewey, 1974; Dolliver, 1969). In this strategy, the counselor gives Leslie a set of cards with an occupation listed on each card and asks her to sort them into three piles. The first pile consists of occupations she might choose, the second pile is occupations she would not choose, and the last pile consists of occupations "in question." The counselor then focuses on the occupations in the "in question" and "would not choose" piles. Leslie is asked to further sort these occupations into occupations she might choose if she felt she had the skills to do the job well, those she might choose if she felt it would result in positive outcomes, and occupations she would not ever choose. The counselor then focuses on occupations targeted either for further skill development, if in fact Leslie did not have the skills to accomplish the job, or for modification of efficacy beliefs, if her perceptions of her skills are inaccurate. The latter may be the case if Leslie feels she could not enter engineering because she does not have the skills to take the advanced math courses that such training would require. The counselor then focuses on the "might choose if result in positive outcomes" pile. The counselor asks Leslie: "Tell me what you would expect from the occupations in this pile. How accurate do you think your perceptions of the outcomes might be?" The counselor also encourages Leslie to obtain more information if her knowledge of outcomes expected of various occupations is incomplete or inaccurate. For example, if Leslie still believed that she would not be able to combine work as an engineer with a family, the counselor refers her for informational interviewing to women engineers who are combining both.

*Reevaluate and Modify Efficacy Beliefs.* A second tenet of the social cognitive career model is that counselors need to help their clients modify faulty self-efficacy beliefs that prevent them from considering viable career options. Lent et al. (1996) suggest that counselors working with clients who have evidence of skills but who have weak self-efficacy develop strategies that promote efficacy. These strategies may be designed specifically to encourage performance accomplishments, to rethink previous performance accomplishments, or "to interpret their past and present successes in a manner that promotes, rather than discounts, perceived competence" (p. 406).

Brown and Lent (1996) identify several strategies to help clients modify their efficacy beliefs, including helping clients create opportunities to experience successful performance accomplishments. One strategy is to give Leslie additional opportunities to form efficacy beliefs about her ability to do graduate work—for example, encouraging her to talk to current graduate students or to examine syllabi for graduate courses. The counselor also needs to help her to correctly attribute her performance as related to her abilities when she performs well, as opposed to attributing it to some other external source, such as ease of the test, or to mere effort on her part. It is important that Leslie gain a more accurate view of her abilities to raise her efficacy beliefs.

In addition, the counselor works with Leslie to help her further reanalyze previous experiences that led her to conclude she would not do well in school. For example, the counselor encourages Leslie to identify the faulty efficacy beliefs she had as an adolescent that led her to choose entering a community college instead of a university or that led her to close off a number of options that required graduate training. The counselor helps Leslie analyze which of those efficacy beliefs are still operating and identify methods to change those beliefs. The counselor could, for example, encourage Leslie to gather more information about how she compares with others. Her beliefs in her ability to perform well in graduate school may have been due to inaccurate perceptions of the performance level required of graduate students. Gathering more accurate information about graduate school expectations, as well as gaining a more accurate picture of herself, may help Leslie modify her efficacy beliefs.

*Identify Barriers.* The third tenet in career counseling from a social cognitive model is that counselors need to work with clients to help them identify barriers to implementing career options. Once barriers are identified, counselors need to help clients to evaluate whether the perceptions of barriers are based on a realistic appraisal of the environment and to help clients evaluate how likely they are to encounter those barriers.

The Career Beliefs Inventory (CBI) provides some information related to the barriers Leslie is encountering in making a career decision. Leslie's greatest barriers appear to be related to her focus on others, such as how well she does compared with others and others' approval and involvement in her decisions, as well as what appears to be her lack of willingness to take risks. The counselor works to help Leslie identify strategies to overcome the identified barriers. One strategy identified by Brown and Lent (1996) is to ask clients to complete a decisional balance sheet (Janis & Mann, 1977) for each career alternative under consideration. Clients are asked to indicate positive and negative consequences related to each alternative; they identify consequences anticipated for themselves and for others, in both the short and long term.

Leslie's counselor asks her to complete a decisional balance sheet for staying in her current occupation and for each alternative career she was considering. Leslie may, for example, identify her husband's and mother's traditional views of women's role in child rearing as a barrier to pursuing a career as an engineer or her own discomfort with being in a nontraditional field as a barrier. She may identify her lack of confidence in helping others as a barrier to entering the ministry, also perhaps voicing a fear that her family would not support such a choice. She may also identify her anger at the principal and lack of challenge as barriers to continuing in her current position.

Leslie's counselor then helps her to identify how realistic each of those barriers may be: "Leslie, you indicated that your family may not approve of your pursuing a degree in engineering. What information have they given you that has led you to this conclusion? What might happen if you discussed the possibilities of further education with your husband or if you talked about engineering as a possible option with your family?" Her fears of their reaction may, in fact, be well grounded, or they may be inaccurate. If her fears are realistic barriers to her pursuing these options, the counselor would encourage her to identify possible ways to manage or prevent those barriers. For example, the counselor may encourage her to talk further with her husband to enlist his help in a more role-sharing model of child rearing. Leslie may, however, also decide that the consequence of losing familial support is too great, and that may help her decide to stay in her current position as a teacher.

If Leslie decides to remain a math teacher, identification of the barriers associated with that position might help her to determine specific actions to make her more satisfied in that occupation. For example, she may decide that the barriers include her principal, and that she has little power to change his specific actions. This may lead her to seek a position as a math teacher in another school, knowing that she would be happier in a smaller school system in which she could teach a greater variety of classes.

## DISCUSSION QUESTIONS REGARDING LESLIE FROM A SOCIAL COGNITIVE FRAMEWORK

1. What specific hypotheses would you develop about Leslie from social cognitive career theory? How does using social cognitive theory help you understand Leslie? How might it help Leslie understand herself?

2. Leslie appears to be struggling to make some midlife career changes. How would you address the issues that Leslie is dealing with regarding her career from a social cognitive career model perspective? How would you address the issues that she is dealing with in her marriage?

3. How may Leslie's efficacy beliefs be influenced by the messages she has received from her husband and family about the role of work in her life?

4. How might you incorporate information from the additional inventories that Leslie completed?

5. What interventions or techniques from social cognitive theory might you use with Leslie?

6. What role did Leslie's gender socialization play in her career decisions as an adolescent? What role is her gender socialization playing in her career decisions as an adult?

7. What additional barriers may Leslie encounter if she decides to stay in her current profession of teaching? What barriers may she encounter if she chooses to become a social worker? Engineer? Minister? Technical writer?

## ADDITIONAL CASES

### Case 1: Jerry

Jerry is a 32-year-old gay Caucasian man seeking career counseling because he was diagnosed as HIV-positive several years ago. When he was first diagnosed, he expected his health to deteriorate rapidly, and initially, he thought he was given only 4 years to live, so he decided to continue working as a hairstylist. However, his regimen of treatments has enabled him to be well enough to work, and he is in a position of realizing that he never really liked his work as a stylist. He continued to do that work because it paid the bills. Now he is seeking career counseling because he is ready to make a different career choice.

Jerry is a licensed hairstylist working in a suite of hair salons; he shares his leased space with another stylist, Latasha. Jerry initially became a hairstylist because he enjoyed the creativity of working with different styles and liked helping people look better; he also was "sick of school" and did not want an occupation that entailed a college degree. Jerry had been struggling with his sexual identity through high school and did not do well in his high school classes, precluding options for postsecondary training. He had taken drafting in high school, and he enjoyed that, as well as a shop class he took as a senior. Jerry was also on the basketball team during his first two years in high school but dropped out during his junior year. He came out to his parents during his senior year in high school; they were initially unhappy but were eventually supportive of his decision. His decision to become a stylist was also influenced by his perception that it was an occupation in which others would be supportive of a gay man.

His counselor began to clarify Jerry's goals and found that Jerry also had some interpersonal conflicts in his current work environment with Latasha. Jerry complained that Latasha was stealing his items and was forming alliances with others in the suite against him. Jerry was reluctant to directly confront her, however, suggesting that if he ignored the problems they would go away. However, Latasha informed him that she was breaking their agreement and moving to a salon by herself, leaving Jerry solely responsible for the rent on their shared suite. Again, Jerry was reluctant to confront the issue, choosing not to take legal action against her. His career decisions then included whether he should quit being a hairstylist altogether, declare bankruptcy, and move back to his parents' home while he considered what to do; expand his services to make more money to cover the rent in the salon; or seek and train another partner.

Jerry indicated that he really "got sick of hearing people talk all day" and did not enjoy the interpersonal conflicts that others seemed to create. He was frustrated at having to be inside a lot, when he would rather be outside. He did enjoy being able to work with his hands and still enjoyed some of the creative aspects of his job. He appreciated some of the flexibility of his work, as well, because it enabled him to schedule around days when he was not feeling well.

Jerry's SII scores indicated that his highest interests were in the realistic and social General Occupational Themes, with high Basic Interest Scales scores for social service, culinary arts, mechanical activities, athletics, teaching, and mathematics. He was most similar to men who were police officers, auto mechanics, athletic trainers, occupational therapists, and small business owners. Jerry's MIQ profile indicated that it was very important for him to get along well with his co-workers, do things for other people, and do something that makes use of his abilities. His scores on the General Aptitude Test Battery indicated that he was at least one standard deviation above the mean in all tested areas and had particularly high level of ability in verbal reasoning, numerical reasoning, and general learning ability.

## Questions for Discussion

1. How might have Jerry's self-efficacy beliefs or outcome expectations foreclosed options? What are specific examples of options he may have foreclosed?
2. What barriers is Jerry facing in his career alternatives?
3. What are Jerry's likely outcome expectations about his various career alternatives?
4. How would you incorporate the information presented by Jerry's career history and his assessment results?
5. How might Jerry's learning opportunities have been partly shaped by his sexual orientation?
6. How might you modify Jerry's self-efficacy beliefs?
7. How may Jerry's interpersonal conflicts affect his career decisions? What role might have self-efficacy beliefs and/or outcome expectancies played in his interpersonal conflicts?

### Case 2: Kamisha

Kamisha is a 21-year-old African American woman in her third year of college. She is seeking counseling because she is undecided about her college major. She attends a private liberal arts college and has done very well in all of her courses. She originally declared a major in chemistry, changed to English during her second year, and finally changed to psychology. However, although she is getting an A in the class, she does not like the psychology course she is currently taking and has begun to have doubts about her entry into the field. She knows she will need to continue on to graduate school if she wishes to be a psychologist. She is confident she would do well if she would choose to pursue this avenue; she is concerned, however, that it may not be the right choice for her.

Kamisha is the daughter of two successful corporate lawyers; she is the older of two sisters. Her parents, although busy with their careers while she was growing up, were able to provide her with numerous educational opportunities. She attended a prestigious private high school, traveled abroad extensively with her family, and spent her junior year in high school studying in France. Kamisha also attended various summer camps, as well as participating in several classes provided by the local university specifically targeting African American girls. She particularly enjoyed her classes in science, English, math, and social studies. The latter included courses in political science, sociology, and psychology.

Kamisha's parents have high expectations for their daughters. They believe that they both should not only finish college but should seek some additional postgraduate training, such as a law degree or a doctorate. They provided them both with many opportunities, and they also feel that their daughters "owe it to their race" to do well. Kamisha's parents have also worked hard to shield their daughters from overt discrimination, sending them to private educational institutions known for their racially egalitarian policies and practices. Kamisha's sister is currently on an athletic scholarship at another private university, where she is excelling as a soccer player and doing well in her premedical studies.

Although Kamisha has done well in all her courses and is interested in most of the material she has studied, she is genuinely confused about which avenue to pursue. She has changed her major so often because she has been pressured by the college to declare a major but has not felt that she is able to determine which one is best for her. Her interest inventory results indicate that she is interested in artistic, investigative, and social areas and that she is similar to women who are psychologists, college professors, mathematicians, biologists, chemists, and English teachers.

## Questions for Discussion

1. How may Kamisha have foreclosed her career options? What are specific examples of options she has foreclosed, if any?
2. What barriers is Kamisha encountering, if any?
3. What might be Kamisha's outcome expectations about her college major decision?
4. How may a counselor incorporate Kamisha's assessment results into counseling?
5. What additional information may the counselor seek?
6. How have Kamisha's learning opportunities been shaped by her socioeconomic status and by her cultural background?
7. What social cognitive strategies would you employ to help Kamisha make a career choice?

### Case 3: Jim

Jim is a 27-year-old Caucasian male who suffered a spinal cord injury in the neck area four years earlier, which has severely limited his mobility. How his injury occurred is unknown to Jim. He related that he was attending a party in honor of his completion of the Reserve Officer's Training Corp (ROTC), and the last thing he remembers is opening the bathroom door and closing it behind him. The next thing he knew he was lying on the bathroom floor and could not move. He underwent 6 months of hospitalization and therapy. Jim returned to finish his baccalaureate degree, is currently enrolled in a graduate program, and is seeking counseling because he has begun to have doubts about whether he is taking the right career path.

During his high school years, Jim was involved in volunteer work at two schools for children with physical and cognitive disabilities. He enjoyed working with the kids individually and in groups. One of the things he liked most was seeing the progression the children made over time. He also enjoyed sports and being active. The aspects of sports he enjoyed the most were the teamwork, motivation, and sense of achievement he received after successfully accomplishing a goal. He wanted to incorporate both of these factors in choosing a career and chose to pursue physical education with an adaptive emphasis to include children with special needs.

Jim was very active in college, becoming involved in many campus activities, such as student government, intramural sports, and ROTC. He also continued to volunteer working with children. After 4 years in college, he was a year and a half from finishing his degree, a well-respected student leader on campus, and near completion of the ROTC program when the accident occurred.

Following the accident, Jim knew he could no longer pursue physical education and decided to major in recreation therapy because it involved actively participating with a client or groups and also might include sporting activities. He completed his degree 3 ½ years later and decided to enroll in graduate school. He hoped to one day pursue a doctorate, so he decided to first enroll in a master's program; he also hoped to move away from home and establish his independence.

Jim found a few things that were difficult in going to a school out of state. Two roadblocks were wheelchair-accessible housing accommodations and insurance and medical benefits. After researching the possibility of a move, he found that it would be more difficult than it was worth, and feeling pressured by the time constraints of the deadlines for applications, he applied to a local graduate program in rehabilitation counseling. He chose rehabilitation counseling as a good complement to his bachelor's degree in recreation therapy. He was admitted and began to take classes.

Although his conflict had been solved, Jim felt rushed by the decision and was not 100% sure this was the right direction for him. He took one class in the summer session to ease himself into attending classes again, get familiar with the campus, and establish himself in the program. This class was a basic counseling introductory class that exposed him to a few different aspects of counseling he had not considered. He now wants to determine whether to leave rehabilitation counseling and enter a more general counseling curriculum for his master's work or finish his master's degree and seek a doctorate in counseling or counseling psychology.

## Questions for Discussion

1. How may Jim have foreclosed his career options? What are specific examples of options he has foreclosed, if any?
2. What barriers is Jim encountering, if any?
3. What might be Jim's outcome expectations about his decisions about graduate training?
4. How would you incorporate Jim's disability into your approach to counseling?
5. What additional information would you seek?
6. How have Jim's learning opportunities been shaped by his disability and by his cultural background?
7. What social cognitive strategies would you employ to help Jim make a career choice?

# EIGHT

## Gender–Aware and Feminist Approaches

In contrast to the theories discussed in the previous five chapters, gender-aware and feminist approaches are not theories of career development; rather, they are approaches to career counseling; this distinction was discussed in Chapter 1. Attention is usually given to women's career psychology in discussions of theories of career development; however, feminist career counseling rarely is included. Moreover, the virtual explosion of empirical literature regarding women's career development has not been matched by theoretical development.

Much of the literature cited in this chapter is drawn from earlier writings about feminist therapy in general. In addition, several authors have recently translated these feminist therapy concepts to career counseling, and we will draw heavily on these writings to describe feminist career counseling and its applications to Leslie and other clients. Our goal, then, is to synthesize previous literature regarding gender context in career development and in therapy so that readers may view how gender-aware and feminist principles can be applied in career counseling.

Gysbers, Heppner, and Johnston (1998) describe three counseling orientations that take gender into account. First, *nonsexist counseling* (Marecek & Kravetz, 1977) is based on the idea that there should be equity in the treatment of men and women within counseling, and clients should be treated as individuals, not as "women" or "men." Second, *gender-aware counseling* (Good, Gilbert, & Scher, 1990) recognizes that gender is integral to counseling and that client concerns are best viewed within a larger societal context. Counselors are encouraged to actively address gender injustices and to work together with the client in a collaborative relationship. Finally, *feminist counseling* (Brooks & Forrest, 1994; Sturdivant, 1980) represents an adaptation of feminist tenets to the practice of counseling.

Gender-aware and feminist counseling approaches share many similar philosophical assumptions, primarily their common emphasis on the centrality of gender in working with clients. Nonsexist counseling, on the other hand, differs in that it advocates a "gender-blind" perspective of clients, which presents some disadvantages in comparison with the two previous approaches.

Hare-Mustin and Marecek (1988) discuss two perspectives on studying the social construction of gender, one that emphasizes the differences between men and women and one that minimizes those differences. They characterize the former perspective as prone to "alpha bias," or the tendency to exaggerate differences, whereas the latter perspective is prone to "beta bias," or the tendency to ignore differences. Alpha bias is the predominant view in American society and underpins most psychological theories about gender, including some feminist theories such as Gilligan's (1982). These theories propose fundamental gender differences as constellations of opposing traits or characteristics (such as feminine vs. masculine, instrumental vs. expressive). Beta bias, on the other hand, has received less attention but also exists in many theories of psychological development. Beta bias is evident in theories and practices that attempt to treat men and women equally yet may inadvertently perpetuate the inequality they hope to redress.

One consequence of alpha bias is that observed sex differences may be overinterpreted as essential "male" or "female" qualities, when they may be due to differences in the social hierarchy. For example, demonstrated sex differences in vocational interests, such as women's interest in social activities, may not be due to women's inherent relational nature but because social-type careers include lower-prestige occupations that are more accessible to women. Moreover, by emphasizing between-group variability, alpha bias leads to minimization of within-group variability. Thus, theories concerning gender tend to overlook differences among women that may be related to race and ethnicity, age, disability status, social class, marital status, parental status, sexual orientation, and so on.

Consequences of beta bias are more subtle in nature and, on the surface, may seem trivial. After all, what's wrong with arguing for little difference between men and women and therefore treating them similarly? However, ignoring special needs of women may also underestimate differential allocation of resources and power and ultimately disadvantage women: "In a society in which one group holds most of the power, seemingly neutral actions usually benefit members of that group" (Hare-Mustin & Marecek, 1988, p. 460).

### Gender-Aware Counseling

Gender-aware therapy (GAT; Good et al., 1990) was developed by integrating feminist therapy with emerging knowledge about gender. The impetus for developing GAT was (a) the perception that feminist therapy was not applicable to male clients and (b) the growing evidence that gender-role socialization also has deleterious effects on men's development and mental health. It is important to distinguish among terms used in this body of literature. *Sex* refers to one's biological status as male or female, whereas *gender* refers to the way in which one perceives and expresses being male or female. *Gender roles* and *gender-role socialization* thus refer to the behaviors and roles that society expects of individuals, based on their biological sex.

Gender-aware approaches highlight the pervasive influence of early gender-role socialization on expectations about work and careers, for both men and women. For men, gender-role socialization in childhood and adolescence encourages boys to restrict their emotional expressiveness and to strive for achievement and competition. Men's expectations of the work world often include assuming a provider role, upward career progression, and acquisition of material possessions that reflect their success. Gender-role socialization for women includes messages that place limits on career aspirations and achievements, as will be discussed in more detail later in this chapter.

Gender-aware counseling acknowledges that male and female role expectations also enter into the counseling process. For example, counseling itself may be "antithetical to the male role" (Mintz & O'Neil, 1990, p. 382), which may influence how the client interacts with the counselor, such as engaging in competitive behavior. Women clients may assume a passive role in the counseling process and may rely on the expertness offered by test results and interpretations. Another focus of gender-aware counseling is the gender-role socialization of the counselor and how it interacts with the gender-role socialization of the client (Mintz & O'Neil, 1990).

### Feminist Counseling

As presented by Brooks and Forrest (1994), the basic underlying belief of feminism is the social, political, and economic equality between women and men. They describe four tenets of feminist therapy, which they then apply to career counseling. First, *sociocultural conditions* are viewed as the primary source of women's problems: "Social structures have molded and limited women's experiences and opportunities" (Brooks & Forrest, 1994, p. 111). An implication of this tenet is that the symptoms that women exhibit actually represent adaptive solutions to societal expectations rather than psychopathology or intrapsychic problems. For example, a "dependent" style of career decision making might be viewed as the natural consequence of the role that young women were expected to fulfill in their families and in society at large.

Second, the *personal is political:* Because all women in American society are oppressed, political understanding and solutions are necessary to address the problems that individual women experience. A goal of feminist therapy is to assist the client in differentiating what has been imposed on her by society and what is truly internal, or "to differentiate between external, relatively uncontrollable sociocultural conditions (such as prejudice in the job market) and internal feelings and reactions to these conditions (which are changeable)" (Sturdivant, 1980, p. 79).

A classic example of this tenet is the politics of housework. The manner in which home responsibilities are divided is viewed as not just a personal decision between a woman and her partner but also as a larger political issue because of the gendered nature in which work and home worlds are constructed. The arena of work is the domain of men; the arena of home is the domain of women. Women may be expected to do more housework because their time in the work world is viewed as less valuable to the family (in terms of their level of compensation) and as less important to their self-concept. In a reciprocal fashion, they may have less time to invest in the work world because of their home and child care responsibilities. Thus, an interplay exists between the personal realm and the political realm and, in this case, between the personal realm and the career realm. Personal decisions in the home about the division of labor have political ramifications; political and organizational decisions in the work world have personal ramifications.

The third tenet of feminist therapies is that the relationship between counselor and client is *egalitarian.* The feminist counselor acknowledges her expertise but works to develop a relationship based on equal worth and that is collaborative rather than hierarchical. Power is inherent in the client-counselor relationship, and the feminist counselor needs to be aware of the sources of her power and the ways in which power may be abused. Moreover, the counselor needs to work to diminish any power differentials that are harmful or exploitative and that reinforce client passivity and dependence (Gannon, 1982). Power-sharing techniques are recommended to reduce the power differential, such as self-disclosure by the therapist and encouraging the client to consider herself the expert on her own experiences.

Finally, the fourth tenet is related to the *goals of feminist therapy,* which may be viewed as diametrically opposed to the goals of traditional therapy. Namely, feminist therapies reject social conformity and adjustment to unhealthy social conditions, in favor of personal self-definition and self-determination. One fundamental belief is that women must achieve both psychological and economic independence.

As noted earlier, both gender-aware therapy and feminist therapy may be applied to career counseling; in fact, they are particularly relevant given the "gendered context" of career choice and development (see Cook, 1993; Gysbers et al., 1998). This terminology reflects the fact that gender-role socialization permeates all aspects of individuals' development and is therefore crucial in understanding how they perceive their available opportunities as well as their limits. Moreover, recognizing the gendered context of a client's career development entails making those influences an explicit part of the discussion within career counseling so that the client can be empowered to make choices based on a more informed consideration of the intersection of his or her gender-role socialization and the gendered nature of the work environment.

How do these three approaches—nonsexist counseling, gender-aware therapy, and feminist therapy—relate to career counseling? What are the advantages and disadvantages of a counselor attending to gender issues? Counselors are likely to struggle with the role of gender in career counseling. When should we pay attention to gender differences, and when should we downplay or ignore them? An obvious example is how clients choose to integrate parenting with their careers, and the issues become complex. Clearly, pregnancy and child-bearing are unique to women, with implications for career planning and workplace accommodations. Parenting, however, is increasingly shared by mothers and fathers, also with clear yet overlooked implications for the workplace and career planning. Counselors may routinely ask female clients about their plans for children yet neglect to ask the same questions of male clients.

## Gender and Assessment

Gender also is relevant to the use of assessment in counseling. Worrell and Remer (1992) discuss four major sources of sex bias in testing: (a) sex-biased items, (b) inappropriate norm groups, (c) sex-biased interpretation, and (d) sex-biased constructs. Because of the focused attention given to gender issues in career development research, most of these sources have decreased substantially in the last 20 years. However, counselors should continue to be concerned about the ways in which sex bias may enter into standardized assessment, particularly related to how the counselor interprets the results.

It is imperative that counselors understand the way in which a specific inventory is developed and normed so that they can interpret the results accurately for female and male clients. For example, sex differences in vocational interests have been well documented. However, consensus has not been reached about how to treat these differences, so inventories vary in their approaches.

Brown (1990) offers a set of guidelines for explicitly incorporating gender into assessment, which were adapted for career counseling by Brooks and her colleagues (Brooks & Forrest, 1994; Brown & Brooks, 1991; Forrest & Brooks, 1993). Two guidelines are pertinent prior to assessment. First, counselors need to be familiar with theory and research regarding the role of gender in career development and the differential factors or processes influencing men's and women's career choices. Many resources exist for acquiring this type of information (see Betz, in press; Betz & Fitzgerald, 1987; Fitzgerald & Weitzman, 1992; Walsh & Osipow, 1994). Second, counselors need to examine their own biases, conscious and unconscious, about women and career development. These biases have the potential to affect counselors' work with their clients.

The remaining guidelines pertain to inclusion of gender in the assessment process (Brown, 1990). First, counselors gather information about clients' views of themselves in various roles over the life span, including messages from their families of origin and the current or future expectations they perceive for work and family roles. What types of roles do clients anticipate, and how do gender-role expectations relate to these roles? Second, counselors elicit information about the meaning that clients attach to gender relative to their careers. For example, how does a client think about her decision to be an engineer in the context of its being a nontraditional choice for women? Third, counselors explicitly assess the degree to which clients comply with gender-role prescriptions and the positive and negative consequences of their degree of compliance or noncompliance. Brooks and Forrest (1994) suggest three patterns of how gender roles may influence female clients' perceived career options: (a) Overly stereotyped clients may respond passively to career problems and may express interest only in traditionally female occupations; (b) those attempting to conform more to stereotypes may struggle with the ways in which they do not "fit" with expectations; and (c) those attempting to conform less to stereotypes may exhibit more nontraditional behaviors and explore gender-nontraditional occupational choices.

The fourth guideline (Brooks & Forrest, 1994; Brown, 1990) is that counselors need to monitor their reactions during counseling, particularly to clients' noncompliance with gender-role expectations. Fifth, counselors can develop specific hypotheses about the influence of gender-role expectations within the counseling process. Finally, counselors need to evaluate diagnoses and conceptualizations of clients for gender-stereotypic assumptions. These guidelines all serve a single purpose: to integrate a consideration of gender into all that a counselor does with a client, both covertly in the counselor's own reactions and internal processes and overtly in discussions in counseling sessions.

## GENDER AND THEORIES OF CAREER DEVELOPMENT

Theorists generally agree that women's careers may not be adequately explained by traditional theories of career development, at least in their original versions. However, there continues to be some disagreement about whether it is better to modify existing theories, create new theories to specifically address women's career issues, or create theories that explain both men's and women's careers more adequately. Some of this debate parallels the earlier discussion of alpha and beta bias (Hare-Mustin & Marecek, 1988). More specifically, the primary debate is whether separate theories are necessary or desirable. To some, separate theories overemphasize our differences (alpha bias), whereas to others, separate theories are necessary to understand special needs. For example, women continue to perform a larger proportion of child-rearing responsibilities, and therefore, this needs to be addressed in theories of career development. Harmon (1997) discusses "neglected theoretical categories" that occur when theories are geared toward women. As Harmon (1997) notes, counselors "fail to operate from the broadest possible stance in opening topics for discussion with their clients" (p. 465) such as neglecting to assess a man's self-efficacy for combining multiple roles.

## APPLYING GENDER-AWARE AND FEMINIST APPROACHES TO THE CASE OF LESLIE

### Conceptualizing Leslie's Career History

Leslie's career history contains evidence of early gender-role socialization and corresponding limits placed on her options due to gender expectations. Moreover, she seemed to be struggling throughout her life with balancing nontraditional interests with traditional gender-role expectations. She received mixed messages about careers considered appropriate for women to consider. She did receive support and encouragement for her nontraditional interests, and she was not actively discouraged from pursuing those interests. However, the support was not offered universally by the important people in her life, and often, she felt that other people, particularly her family, were "humoring" her aspirations and choices. For example, her mother indicated that the specific major or career direction that Leslie chose was not crucial, because she probably would marry and have a family rather than be active in the workforce.

Leslie experienced some negative events during college related to her sex, such as being put on the spot by professors as the only woman in her advanced math classes and being discouraged from pursuing engineering because it was difficult to combine with her interest in having a family. Although none of these individual events were overly traumatic, they had the cumulative effect of diverting her from pursuing a math degree.

Moreover, there seem to be times when Leslie was aware of or struggled with the constraints she felt as a woman, although the degree to which these were conscious struggles is unclear. For example, her decision to pursue math education represented a compromise between traditional and nontraditional career paths, yet at the time she could not articulate what she might be giving up in such a compromise.

Leslie did benefit from the influence of role models early in her life, most notably a female math teacher in seventh grade. This teacher served as Leslie's most important role model and source of support. Leslie generally found school to be a supportive environment, beginning in grade school and through high school. However, her success in school and recognition for academic achievement was consistently tempered by clear gender-role expectations about the relatively lesser role of work in her life, compared with marital and family roles.

Gysbers et al. (1998) suggest two factors within the gendered context of adolescence that have particular relevance in understanding Leslie's history. First, boys and girls often receive differential treatment in the classroom, which may occur more often according to gender-role expectations. For example, girls are less assertive about contributing to classroom discussions or offering answers to questions posed by teachers. These differential behaviors may be even more apparent in classes such as math and science. Leslie experienced some teasing by her classmates during middle school and high school and at times chose not to speak in class to avoid being teased.

Second, the college years may be characterized by the "culture of romance" (Holland & Eisenhart, 1990), in which women's career aspirations decrease as they spend more energy in relationship-enhancing activities and make career decisions to accommodate their partners' plans. This pattern was true for Leslie, who transferred from a community college to the university that her boyfriend attended. Luckily for her, however, it turned out to be a good decision because the university provided her with more challenging classes and greater educational opportunities.

### Conceptualizing Leslie's Present Situation

Several aspects of Leslie's current situation may be illuminated by a consideration of their gendered contexts, most notably (a) the circumstances in her specific work environment and (b) her perceptions about her current and future work and family roles.

Leslie's work environment provides opportunities for both growth and development, as well as ways in which her behavior is constricted, based on her role as a female employee. Although Leslie has not experienced any blatant examples of sex discrimination, she has occasionally wondered if her male colleagues have received better teaching assignments. The principal has championed the importance of male role models for the adolescent boys in their school, particularly for those who are having problems at home, and Leslie has overheard other female teachers complaining about feeling undervalued by the principal. She has not yet joined in those discussions but has begun to think more seriously about the validity of their concerns. Moreover, some female teachers have voiced their suspicions that male teachers may be receiving higher merit raises, because of the principal's statements about their relatively greater value.

Another factor related to gender at work is that Leslie is the only woman in the math department at her school. Her immediate work environment, then, tends to consist of more traditional "masculine" than "feminine" attributes, even in minor details such as what the math teachers discuss about their weekend activities. Leslie also has less experience than most of her colleagues, which interacts with her being the only woman in how she is perceived by others and how she perceives her treatment by others.

Acknowledging the gendered context of Leslie's current situation allows several different perspectives to emerge. For example, part of her frustration with her principal may be due to gender-role expectations that enter into their professional and interpersonal interactions. During her intake, Leslie described the principal's style as "oppressive." One hypothesis is that he treats his teaching staff, most of whom are female, in a sexist manner.

Teachers within Leslie's school volunteer for or are assigned duties that follow sex-typical expectations. For example, female teachers are expected to chaperone dances, and male teachers are expected to supervise athletic events. Furthermore, there are clear messages about female teachers who have or are planning to have children, whereas male teachers' decisions about children are discussed only in the context of salary needs. Leslie has not discussed her desire to have children, and she has kept her difficulties with pregnancy to herself.

Yet during a discussion of teaching assignments and an upcoming retirement in her department, the principal asked Leslie about whether she was planning to ask for maternity leave in the next few years. Leslie was uncomfortable discussing her plans and personal life with her principal.

Taking a gendered-context perspective also has implications for a second issue in Leslie's life: taking on the role of parent. Choosing to have children brings many changes in one's life, including major questions about life roles as well as the "minor" decisions that need to be made on a daily basis. All of these changes are influenced by gender-role expectations and vice versa. Here, too, Leslie seems to have received many mixed messages about societal and familial expectations. Her mother and sister believe that her current career crisis is a good reason to quit her job and have children. Her husband expects that Leslie would stay at home until their children are in school and also expects that she will not move ahead with any career decisions at this time because of her desire to have children.

Leslie struggles with articulating her expectations about combining work and family, particularly because her beliefs and hopes are somewhat at odds with her husband's and with her mother's and sister's beliefs. She very much wants to have a child, and she also wants to maintain her involvement in the work role. She continues to view teaching as an ideal occupation to combine with family roles, which made it an attractive feature for her initial choice of teaching as a career. Moreover, she has had numerous co-workers as role models, women who have had children and returned to their teaching positions.

When Leslie's mother and sister express their opinions that she quit her job, Leslie finds it easiest just to ignore them. She has tried to explain how she would like to combine work and family roles, but she doesn't feel that they understand why she would want to continue working. Joe's expectations, on the other hand, are more important for Leslie to address, and they have had some arguments about the roles that each of them would assume as parents and as workers. Leslie hopes that Joe will cooperate fully in child rearing once they have a child, although she also expects that she will take primary responsibility for a child. She is more concerned, however, about his expectation that she stay at home until the child enters school, because she has no intention of doing so. She worries that she would "go stir crazy" if she were not working outside of the home.

## Directions and Implications
## for Career Counseling

Feminist therapy has been described as more of a philosophical stance than a school of therapy. As such, the tenets of feminist therapy clearly have important implications for the goals of counseling. Perhaps most important, the issue of gender becomes an explicit focus of career counseling and may even permeate every aspect of counseling, including definition of the presenting problem, building a working alliance, choosing and interpreting assessments, designing and implementing interventions, and terminating the counseling relationship.

The four tenets of feminist therapy, described earlier, have been applied to the practice of career counseling (Brooks & Forrest, 1994) and, more specifically, to career assessment (Forrest & Brooks, 1993). In addition, several authors have suggested specific techniques for addressing gender within counseling, which will be applied to Leslie.

### Sociocultural Conditions as
### a Primary Source of Women's Problems

This first tenet addresses how problems are conceptualized by the counselor and the client. Feminist counselors emphasize sociocultural explanations and de-emphasize intrapsychic explanations in considering a client's problems. Common career problems that women experience, such as work-family conflict, underuse of abilities, limited opportunities, and work adjustment problems, are viewed as resulting from the patriarchal society in which they live (Forrest & Brooks, 1993).

The feminist counselor would begin working with Leslie with an eye toward assessing how societal expectations have shaped her career experiences thus far. One way to do so is to interpret traditional types of assessment (interests, values, skills, personality, work history). A second method is to specifically search for ways in which gender-role issues have affected the client (Forrest & Brooks, 1993; Swanson & Woitke, 1997).

Leslie's Strong Interest Inventory (SII) profile contains scores reflecting same-sex norms, opposite-sex norms, and combined-sex norms—sometimes for the same scales—and the counselor needs to know how to properly interpret these scores. Leslie is likely to ask the counselor why there are two scores for each Occupational Scale and why some of her male-normed scales are higher than the corresponding female-normed scales.

Another perspective on Leslie's SII profile is that her interests are common for women—namely, the primary code of social in Holland's (1997) theory, as well as her conventional-type interests. Her investigative type is less typical for women. The counselor is likely to explore the gender-role origins of Leslie's interests and discuss societal expectations for women regarding "social" behavior. Throughout her life, Leslie clearly has been aware that her interest in math was atypical for her sex. She has not, however, really thought about the "gendered context" of her career decisions. One focus of counseling might be analyzing how Leslie has experienced her decisions regarding her nontraditional interests. What benefits has she received from "being different"? What negative experiences has she had because of being different?

Gysbers et al. (1998) suggest a set of questions to guide an assessment of the gendered context of a client's environment. These questions provide examples of how a counselor might explicitly integrate gender into an assessment of a client's career-related history:

- What messages did you receive as a child about the career options you might pursue?

- In school, did you feel support, discouragement, or a neutral reaction to the development of your interests? Who supported the development of your interests and skills? Who discouraged you about a potential interest area?

- Were you actively encouraged to pursue interests because they were appropriate to your role as a woman (man)? Were you encouraged to pursue interests that were nontraditional for you as a woman (man)?

- What occupational dreams did you discard at some point in your life? Why did you discard them?

Gysbers et al. (1998) also suggest questions to assess the gendered context of a work environment. These questions would be particularly useful for a client dealing with issues related to work adjustment:

- In general, how does your work environment feel to you? What words would you use to describe your work atmosphere?

- What messages have you received about your career opportunities within your work environment? Do they seem limited because you are a woman (man)?

- Are your skills and interests being actively promoted and developed within the organization?
- Have you experienced either subtle or blatant instances of harassment or discouragement in your work environment?
- Have there been times when you felt treated differently because of your sex?

The counselor also may use a gender-role analysis (Brown, 1986, 1990; Brown & Brooks, 1991). As described by Forrest and Brooks (1993), gender-role analysis begins with the counselor's assuming a sociological perspective to gather information about the client's family of origin and her beliefs about societal gender-role expectations. The counselor then takes a phenomenological perspective to examine the ways in which the client has created meaning for herself within her background. What did it mean for Leslie to be female in her family while she was growing up? What does it mean for her now with her husband and within her family of origin? What lessons did she learn about gender-role expectations? From Leslie's experience, what happens when women deviate from gender-role expectations? What does gender mean to her when she thinks about her career thus far? When she thinks about her future career and family roles?

The counselor needs to be aware of external barriers to career development that Leslie has encountered in her academic or work environments (Swanson, Daniels, & Tokar, 1996; Swanson & Woitke, 1997; Worrell & Remer, 1992). Moreover, the counselor needs to be attentive to ways in which these barriers have been internalized into low self-efficacy or self-esteem. Identifying internal barriers as originally emanating from external sources is a unique perspective of feminist therapy.

Another technique that the counselor could use to assess Leslie's gender role prescriptions is to use a sentence completion exercise, either in-session or as homework. Forrest and Brooks (1993) suggest the following:

Since I am a woman,
    I am required to be _____
    I am allowed to be _____
    I am forbidden to be _____

If I were a man, I would be
    required to be _____
    allowed to be _____
    forbidden to be _____

*The Personal Is Political*

Application of this tenet in career counseling suggests that a client must be aware of the political and economic realities of society to fully understand her own personal problems. Furthermore, this tenet implies that individual action alone will not resolve the problems that a woman brings to career counseling (Forrest & Brooks, 1993).

Career counseling with Leslie thus would incorporate the "personal is political" tenet by analyzing her concerns within the context of the larger group of women in general and focusing on the sociopolitical commonalities between Leslie's situation and that of other women. Furthermore, this tenet may be applied by focusing on the power dynamics in her work environment and relationships. The counselor could use a power analysis (Forrest & Brooks, 1993; Worrell & Remer, 1992) to help Leslie identify the types of power that she can and does use in various situations. The goals of a power analysis would be to increase Leslie's understanding about the nature of power, particularly in how power is connected to gender and how she might expand her use of power.

*Egalitarian Counseling Relationship*

This tenet encourages development of a collaborative, nonhierarchical relationship between counselor and client, in which both participants have equal worth regardless of whatever differential expertise or power they bring to their interactions. The counselor can use a number of power-sharing techniques with Leslie. First, the counselor assumes, and encourages Leslie to acknowledge, that she is the expert on herself. This is particularly important to emphasize in the context of using and interpreting standardized assessment results, during which computer-generated profiles are often inappropriately reified. Second, the counselor and Leslie work together in developing hypotheses about her career issues and avoid using jargon in doing so. The egalitarian approach also applies to decisions about assessment, and Leslie would have been involved in choosing specific instruments.

In the context of developing a good working alliance, Leslie and the counselor will begin to discuss their beliefs about gender-role issues. It is important to assess Leslie's level of awareness or acceptance of feminist ideas, because this will affect how she views the gendered context of her career issues and whether she may be in a different place than the counselor in terms of her readiness to discuss gender-role expectations and experiences.

### Essentials for Women's Mental Health: Self-Definition and Self-Determination

This tenet is the one most closely related to counseling goals, in that it redefines appropriate goals for women. One explicit goal of feminist therapy that is particularly relevant in career counseling is for individuals to be financially independent; as Fitzgerald (1986) notes, "It is not in anyone's best interest to be totally economically dependent on the good will and good health of another person" (p. 129). Pursuit of this goal with Leslie would entail discussion of how gender-role expectations have limited her choices and how the low wages associated with traditionally female occupations, such as teaching, keep women from achieving independence. Moreover, the counselor could help Leslie view the gendered aspects of her work environment and discuss how she might overcome external and internal barriers (Forrest & Brooks, 1993).

In addition, feminist therapists are enjoined to not overlook critical issues affecting women's lives. With Leslie, the counselor would discuss a wide range of issues, beginning with possible instances of discrimination or sexual harassment in her work environment. A second set of issues concerns the degree to which Leslie's career decisions are governed by economic or financial dependence and how she and Joe will negotiate their respective career or job changes. Moreover, Leslie expressed dissatisfaction with how she and Joe divide household responsibilities and concerns about how they might approach child-rearing responsibilities.

Leslie's capacity for self-definition and self-determination can be assessed by listening carefully to how she talks about her career decisions to date and by her thinking about future career decisions (Forrest & Brooks, 1993). Does she frame her career history in terms of how it has conformed to the desires or influences of other people? Are her interests and goals clearly defined, separately from those of people such as her family and husband?

A nonsexist card sort (Brown & Brooks, 1991; Dewey, 1974) also may be used to determine Leslie's perceptions of gender-appropriate options. The cards consist of equal numbers of traditionally male and traditionally female occupations, and Leslie would sort them into three piles: those she would consider, those she would not consider, and those about which she is unsure. The counselor then separates the first two piles of cards into the traditionally female and male occupations and asks Leslie to describe advantages and disadvantages.

The gender-socialized limits that Leslie perceives may also be assessed via the "discarded dreams" technique (Sargent, 1977, cited in Forrest & Brooks, 1993). Leslie would list her career dreams that have been encouraged or discouraged by important people in her life. As she discussed these dreams, the counselor would listen for negative messages that continue to influence her decisions.

---

## DISCUSSION QUESTIONS REGARDING LESLIE FROM A GENDER-AWARE OR FEMINIST FRAMEWORK

1. What specific hypotheses would you develop about Leslie from gender-aware or feminist approaches or both? How does using these approaches help you understand Leslie? How might it help Leslie understand herself?
2. In what other ways has gender influenced Leslie's career development throughout her life—as a child, an adolescent, and an adult?
3. How might you work with Leslie from a nonsexist perspective? From a gender-aware perspective? From a feminist perspective?
4. What types of gender role expectations did Leslie learn from her family of origin? From the educational system? From her work experience? From her husband and his family?
5. How might Leslie's assessment results be influenced by gender? How might the counselor address these influences?
6. Conceptualize Leslie's relationship with her husband from a gendered perspective. In what ways might each of their roles be constrained due to gender-role expectations?
7. How has "the personal is political" been manifested in Leslie's life?

---

### ADDITIONAL CASES

#### Case 1: Ellen

Ellen is a 50-year-old Caucasian woman who entered counseling at a women's center in her community. Her husband, Tim, recently filed for divorce after 27 years of marriage, and Ellen is feeling bewildered. They have three children—two sons aged 21 and 19, who are both in college, and a daughter aged 16.

Ellen and Tim met and married while in college—Ellen as a sophomore and Tim as a senior. Ellen quit school to take a secretarial job to support them while Tim went to graduate school in anthropology. He finished his Ph.D. in 5 years and obtained a faculty position at a prestigious state university. Their oldest child was born during the first year of Tim's new job, and Ellen did not look for work outside of the home. When the youngest child went to elementary school, Ellen contemplated getting a job, but Tim's career was so demanding that she felt it was more important for her to focus her attention on the children and household responsibilities.

Ellen knew that Tim had seemed dissatisfied in the last few years, but his decision to ask for a divorce came as a shock to her. He told her that he wanted to leave the marriage because he was disappointed in how "traditional" their relationship was and that he wished she could be more like the professional women he dealt with daily at the university. Ellen reports feeling "betrayed," because he never expressed these concerns at any time earlier in their 27 years together. She feels that they had an unspoken arrangement, in which she would take most of the responsibility for raising their children, entertaining his colleagues, and generally doing whatever was necessary to support Tim's career advancement. Yet now she feels that he is changing the rules and criticizing her for what she felt he wanted her to do.

In addition to her emotional distress about Tim's announcement, Ellen is also thinking about many practical details resulting from the divorce. Tim seems amenable to a fair financial settlement and is committed to college education for all three children. However, he has told Ellen that he doesn't intend to provide her with any financial support after their youngest daughter leaves home, and Ellen is feeling quite concerned about her future. Ellen will no longer be able to anticipate financial security at retirement, and so, at age 50, she would like to plan how she will use the next 15 years to prepare for her own retirement. Because she hasn't been in the workforce for 20 years, however, Ellen feels very unsure of what she could do to support herself. Ellen is thus entering counseling with a variety of pressing issues.

## Questions for Discussion

1. How would you conceptualize Ellen's current situation from a gender-aware or feminist perspective?
2. How might it help Ellen to view her situation from a gender-aware or feminist perspective? How would examining gender-role expectations assist her?
3. How might you work with Ellen regarding career planning? How could she identify work-related skills?
4. In what ways would you foster an egalitarian therapeutic relationship with Ellen?
5. What specific interventions or techniques would you like to use with Ellen?

### Case 2: Diana and Bill

Diana and Bill are a dual-career couple in their mid-40s. Diana is a systems analyst within the communications industry; Bill is an actuary, most recently with an insurance company. They moved to a new state 10 months ago so that Diana could accept a major promotion within her company. They have two children in high school.

Bill sought counseling because he is having difficulty finding a new job. In the first few months, he tried to find a position similar to the one he'd just left but expanded his search when he was unable to find such a job. Before moving, Bill had been successful at his job but was beginning to experience some burnout. The vice president in his division was grooming him to take over a supervisory position, yet Bill had been feeling ambivalent about the promotion. He felt pressured by Diana to take the position, because it was accompanied by a hefty raise and more status within the organization.

Diana reentered the workforce 5 years ago after a 10-year hiatus for child rearing, and she has been very successful at her job. The position for which they recently moved represented a major move up the corporate ladder for Diana. Bill has been supportive of Diana's career and also felt relieved that he was no longer the primary breadwinner. On the other hand, he is somewhat uncomfortable with her success, because of their shifting roles: He was becoming less committed to his job and career as Diana was becoming more committed to hers. He became angry when his former co-workers made comments that Bill was quitting his job so he could be supported by his wife, and the vice president that wanted to promote him wrote him a weak letter of reference, questioning his drive and ability to achieve.

## Questions for Discussion

1. In what way have gender-role expectations influenced Bill? How are they affecting Bill and Diana?
2. How might you help Bill deal with the changes that have occurred because of his inability to find a job?
3. What does the occupational role mean to Bill? How does it fit with his image of himself as a man?
4. How might you help Diana deal with the changes that have occurred because of Bill's unemployment?
5. What does the occupational role mean to Diana? How does it fit with her image of herself as a woman?

## Case 3: Tony

Tony is a 19-year-old African American sophomore who came to the university counseling center because he is undecided about a major. He has considered physical education or restaurant management, although he does not know much about either of these majors or occupational fields. He states that he wants to make a lot of money, and also wants a job where he is his own boss. What he'd really like to do is own and manage a nightclub, and he has thought about many of the details, such as the name and format of the club, the kind of manager he would be, and so on.

Tony is a first-generation college student, and he feels pressure from his parents to complete his bachelor's degree. College was not entirely what he expected, however, and he wishes he could quit and find a job in a nightclub. He wonders if getting a degree will help him anyway. Tony is engaged to a woman who is a junior majoring in marketing, and she is encouraging him to stay in school. They plan to get married after she graduates next year.

During counseling, you ask him about how he envisions his job or career fitting with the rest of his roles in life and use a guided imagery exercise to help Tony think about his lifestyle and his daily activities. When you ask him how working in a nightclub will fit with other aspects of his life, he talks about how it won't affect other aspects of his life because his friends will probably "hang out" with him at the nightclub. You then specifically ask about whether he wants to have children; Tony responds by saying that "Why does that matter? It will be my wife's job to take care of any kids."

## Questions for Discussion

1. How would you deal with your feelings and reactions to Tony's statements?
2. How would you encourage an egalitarian relationship with him?
3. What techniques might you use to help Tony explore the various roles in his life? How might you convince Tony of the value of doing so?
4. What gender-role expectations might Tony be experiencing from his parents, particularly as an African American man?
5. What factors might be occurring between Tony and his fiancée? How might their careers and their relationship be conceptualized from a gender-aware or feminist perspective?

# NINE

# *Culturally Appropriate Career Counseling*

In Chapter 8, we departed from the format of the rest of the chapters by examining gender-focused approaches to career counseling. We follow that model in this chapter, as well, although here we are focusing on approaches that explicitly emphasize race and ethnic background as part of career counseling.

The United States has a long history of attempting to come to terms with the changing demographic makeup of its population. The last decade of the 20th century is no exception. The changing racial and ethnic makeup of educational systems and workplaces has been perceived as both a problem and a tremendous opportunity for the United States. As a problem, the changing demography is forcing employers, educators, and members of the helping professions to rethink their practices and policies. But the changes are also bringing a new energy and vitality to many environments as multiple perspectives and diverse viewpoints help to create more powerful and effective solutions to complex issues.

These changes are also affecting the counseling profession. Counselors are faced with a growing urgency to develop competencies to be both culturally sensitive and culturally responsive. They are questioning whether current policies and practices are effective for diverse populations, and old notions of uniformity are being eliminated in favor of designing programs to meet the individual needs of various cultural groups. Leaders within the profession are demanding that counselors provide culturally appropriate services (Bingham & Ward, 1994; Fouad & Bingham, 1995; Leong & Brown, 1995; Sue & Sue, 1990; Ward & Bingham, 1993), and clients from diverse racial and ethnic groups are demanding that they receive those services (Brown, Minor, & Jepsen, 1991). Brown et al. (1991) found that racial and ethnic clients report a need specifically for career services, yet Sue and Sue (1990) and Ponterotto and Casas (1991) report that racial and ethnic minority clients are not seeking or staying in traditional counseling services. Career counseling must take place within a cultural context, helping clients set goals that are appropriate from their worldview (rather than the counselor's worldview) and using culturally appropriate techniques to best serve all clients. For their part, career counselors are willing to provide appropriate services but are often at a loss to learn *how* to be more culturally responsive to their clients.

Unlike theories discussed in Chapters 3 through 7, no one theoretical framework has been developed to explain the career behavior of racial and ethnic minorities. Rather, several individuals have called for culturally appropriate career counseling, and some have also described models for appropriate intervention. In this chapter, we will give a brief overview of the issues salient to culturally appropriate career counseling and will provide a review of three models. One model, the culturally appropriate career counseling model (CACCM; Fouad & Bingham, 1995) will be discussed in greater depth and then will be applied to the case of Leslie. Readers wishing additional information are referred to Leong (1995) for further discussions on career counseling for specific racial and ethnic groups.

All clients operate within a cultural context. Clients are shaped in part by factors such as their gender, racial identity and background, sexual orientation, socioeconomic status, or disability, all of which help to form their environments and their responses to it. A central tenet of all approaches to cross-cultural career counseling is that the most effective career counseling explicitly incorporates those contextual factors. Effective career counselors will not treat all clients the same, assuming that their cultural experiences are uniform, but will approach each client as belonging to one or more cultures. For example, a client may be an Asian American married to a white woman, working in a company headed by an African American and living in an ethnically diverse middle-class neighborhood. He may feel that he belongs to several cultures; some may be more salient to him than others. His counselor needs to be aware of his multiple cultures and how they interact. His goals will reflect his cultural contexts, indicating which are most salient to him.

Culturally responsive career counseling is good for *all* clients. All clients come to counseling with unique biological, social, and developmental experiences that are products of the cultures to which they belong. However, it is also critical to note that belonging to a culture does not automatically mean that a client will display one characteristic or another. Rather, there is great heterogeneity within groups. Counselors need to be flexible enough to incorporate the cultural variables salient to the client. This requires that the counselor has developed multicultural competencies and is prepared for culturally appropriate counseling (Sue et al., 1998).

Culturally appropriate counseling requires that the counselor have knowledge and skills to work with specific cultural groups. For example, a counselor working with Hmong clients in the Midwest needs to know the history of the Hmong immigration to the United States, the development of their written language, and their cultural norms and values. But although there are culturally specific issues that counselors need to know, there are also several overlying variables that counselors need to be aware of that may affect many minority group clients. These include the influences of racism, social class, discrimination, acculturation, and immigration status on career behavior as well as the involvement of family in career decision making.

Racial discrimination and social class have strongly affected the career behavior of racial and ethnic minorities in the United States but have not been taken into account in most traditional career counseling (Fitzgerald & Betz, 1994; Leung, 1995). External issues such as discrimination and poverty have a disproportionate effect on racial and ethnic groups, limiting the options that individuals may consider and restricting their access to a wide variety of opportunities (Fitzgerald & Betz, 1994). There is an overrepresentation of racial and ethnic group individuals in the lower socioeconomic levels. The strong relationships between socioeconomic status and educational attainment and occupational level have led to a continuous cycle of poor and poorly educated minority individuals (Arbona, 1996). Discrimination has also played a role in keeping individuals trapped in this cycle.

To be most effective, career counselors need to understand the role that discrimination has played in the choices their clients make and help their clients realize how discrimination may have limited their perceptions of opportunities as well as barring them from opportunities. Counselors need to understand the relationship between social class and educational level and how those together may affect the real choices available to clients. Poverty, poor academic training, and the psychological factors related to feeling powerless and unable to plan for the future are realities for many clients. As Fitzgerald and Betz (1994) note, the very notion of helping clients find an optimal occupational area is unrealistic for many poor clients. For them, a job that pays for rent and food for their families is of much greater importance than self-realization.

Acculturation and immigration status are also important variables to assess in cross-cultural career counseling. Acculturation refers to the ongoing process by which individuals come into contact with a new culture and how they change and adapt to that culture in behavior, emotion, and thought. It is not a simple linear process, nor is it a process through which individuals automatically lose their original culture. Some individuals may be able to operate quite well in two cultures, in essence becoming bicultural. It is important to ascertain clients' level of acculturation, because this may affect their consideration of various career choices. It may also affect the process they find most useful in career counseling. For example, counseling may be most effective for an Asian American client with strong traditional values if it includes her family.

This previous example illustrates the fourth overarching variable—that is, for many racial and ethnic groups, the weight placed on individual values is less important than the weight placed on collective values. Traditionally, career counseling has focused on the individual, with an emphasis on independent decision making, but this may not be as appropriate for some individuals from traditional ethnic cultures. Rather, they may feel strongly that family approval is the most important variable in choosing a career. Family approval may, in fact, be much more important than their own interests and needs. Although effective career counseling has always considered variables such as family obligations, it has been done within the context of also examining interests, abilities, values, and personality. We are suggesting that culturally responsive career counseling acknowledges that cultures vary in the weight placed on all those variables and that in many cultures the standard individualistic approach to career decision making may be inappropriate.

## CAREER INTERVENTION MODELS

Three models have recently been developed to help counselors conceptualize ways to incorporate culture into career counseling. These models complement one another, each expanding areas that the others do not cover. The most comprehensive model is Leong and Hartung's (1997) integrative-sequential conceptual framework for career counseling. The second model by Leung (1995) focuses exclusively on career interventions, explicating the outcomes of those interventions. Finally, Fouad and Bingham's (1995) model delineates the career counseling process, identifying specific areas in which culture may play a role. Each model addresses a specific aspect of cross-cultural career counseling.

Leong and Hartung's (1997) model consists of five stages. The first stage is recognition by the client of vocational problems. In this stage, Leong and Hartung suggested that the client's cultural background affects the process by which a client recognizes a problem. For example, two individuals may work in an environment that does not make full use of their abilities, but only one views it as a problem, whereas the other is grateful to have work that pays a salary. Their cultural background will help shape when situations are viewed as problems.

Stage 2 focuses on help seeking and using career services. Leong and Hartung (1997) note that clients' attitudes toward mental health services will influence whether they seek help for problems. They suggest that it is important in this stage to assess barriers to seeking career counseling. They identify lack of bilingual staff, lack of culturally appropriate services, and cultural mistrust as possible factors that have led to underuse of career services by culturally diverse clients.

During Stage 3, career problems are evaluated. Leong and Hartung (1997) extend other models examined in this chapter by delineating that career problems can be evaluated only if a problem is recognized and if the client seeks professional help for career problems. Once a client comes for counseling, the counselor may use a five-dimension

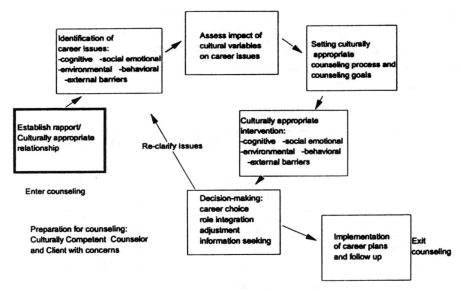

**Figure 9.1.** Culturally Appropriate Counseling Model
SOURCE: Fouad and Bingham (1995). Used with permission.

cultural formulation model as a guideline, which incorporates the cultural identity of the individual, a cultural explanation of the problem, an examination of cultural factors in the environment, influence of cultural variables that may affect the relationship between the client and counselor, and an overall cultural assessment and plan.

Once the client's career problems have been evaluated, the counselor moves to Stage 4, implementing career interventions. Leong and Hartung (1997) include assessment as a primary career intervention, advocating that the counselor and client collaborate to "help the client derive meaning from the assessment results" (p. 198). The fifth and final stage is the outcome of the intervention, in which the client returns to the community.

Although Leong and Hartung's (1997) is a comprehensive model of career services for minority clients, Leung (1995) focuses on one aspect, that of career interventions. His model has three levels—systemic, group, and one-to-one—and focuses on educational as well as career outcomes. Leung advocates that the model should incorporate educational outcomes, because education is critical to the career development of racial and ethnic minorities, to counteract the cyclical effect of poverty and discrimination. Systemic interventions for career

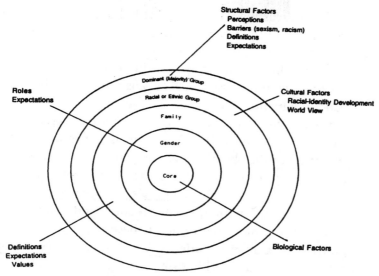

**Figure 9.2.** Spheres of Influence of Cultural Variables
SOURCE: Fouad and Bingham (1995). Used with permission.

outcomes may include helping school counselors develop special career-related programs that target racial and ethnic minorities; systemic educational outcomes may include developing multiculturally affirming schools. Group educational and career interventions include group career counseling. This is strongly advocated by Bowman (1993) as well. Leung (1995), however, suggests that group career counseling may be more effective if it is structured and if the groups consist of one racial and ethnic group so that similarity of values and beliefs may be explored. In one-to-one career and educational counseling, Leung advocates that "career issues of minority clients must be understood in terms of the cultural background and beliefs of the client" (p. 562).

Fouad and Bingham (1995) proposed the CACCM, which specifically assesses the impact of cultural variables in each step of career counseling (Figure 9.1). Note that this model is less comprehensive than the Leong and Hartung (1997) model, because it does not explicate the process by which clients arrive at the recognition that they need to seek counseling for help with career problems. The CACCM is an extension of models originally proposed by Ward and Bingham (1993; Bingham & Ward, 1994).

The model begins with establishing a culturally appropriate relationship in Step 1. In this critical first step, the counselor must work to establish a trusting relationship with the client to develop a working consensus. Culturally appropriate relationships, will, of necessity, differ with clients' cultural norms and expectations of counseling and of the counseling relationship. It is important for the counselor to be aware of general cultural expectations but also to be flexible and to suspend judgment.

In the second step, the counselor identifies career issues that the client brings to counseling. This step is conceptualized as a broad examination of the client's concerns that may be related to vocational issues; these are examined within the client's cultural context. Fouad and Bingham identify five categories of career issues: cognitive, social/emotional, behavioral, environmental, and external. Clients may, of course, bring more than one of these issues to career counseling. Cognitive issues may include faulty information processing or irrational beliefs about working or career decision making. Emotional issues may include anxiety at work, or a client may be managing anger related to racism that bars him or her from a work-related opportunity. Behavioral concerns may include being referred to career counseling because of a poor interpersonal style or work habits. Environmental issues are those related to the work environment, including working conditions, co-workers, or supervisors. Fouad and Bingham (1995) distinguish environmental concerns from external barriers, which include racial discrimination, oppression, and sexual harassment. External barriers are explicitly defined because racism and oppression influence career choices for many racial and ethnic group clients. These may operate implicitly, as part of restricting options that clients may consider, or explicitly, as they are eliminated from positions due to race or gender.

In the third step of the CACCM, the counselor works with the client to assess the impact of cultural variables on those career issues. Fouad and Bingham (1995) conceptualize a series of concentric circles forming a sphere to help identify the way that culture influences vocational behavior (see Figure 9.2).

The first, innermost, circle represents the core, which comprises the unique aspects of the individual. The next circle influencing the self most directly is gender. Gender influences the types of careers that individuals will consider and the way that they implement their career choices. The interaction of gender and culture also affects career choices in that some cultures have more clearly defined expectations of men and women, particularly in relation to gender-appropriate occupations.

The next circle influencing vocational behavior represents individuals' families. Familial expectations and familial norms and values play an important role in forming individuals' views of work and their own work-related decisions. As noted earlier, for some individuals, this will be a strong influence; for others, the influence of the family will not be as strong. The fourth and fifth circles are the outermost layers. The fourth layer is the individual's racial and ethnic group, including cultural factors such as cultural values, racial identity, and acculturation level. Finally, Fouad and Bingham (1995) conceptualize the dominant culture as the outermost layer of influence on individuals' career decision making. These spheres are intended to be dynamic rather than static. Thus, at a particular point in one individual's life, the family sphere may be predominant, with strong influence also from the dominant culture. Then, as individuals gain a greater sense of identification with a racial and ethnic culture, the fourth sphere may increase in influence, whereas the dominant culture sphere reduces in influence on their vocational choices.

Once the counselor and client have determined the career issues and the influence of culture on those career issues, Step 4 is setting culturally appropriate processes and goals. The counseling process must be culturally appropriate, and the goals of counseling must fit within the client's cultural framework. An example of an inappropriate process is the use of insight-oriented counseling for clients whose culture places little emphasis on individual introspection (e.g., traditional Asian cultures) or when counselors insist on solely addressing the individual rather than his or her family. Inappropriate goals for the client may include encouraging career choices based on dominant culture values, such as choosing occupations based on prestigious occupations or nontraditional careers for women.

Once the goals and processes have been determined, Step 5 is determining and implementing a culturally appropriate intervention. Bowman (1993) recommends that group interventions might be particularly effective with racial and ethnic clients. She also recommended the inclusion of the family in career counseling and encouraging clients to seek same-gender and same-ethnic group role models. Career interventions have included assessment, which has unique issues when applied across cultures. Fouad (1993) recommends that counselors be aware of the way that culture may influence traditional vocational assessment and suggests that counselors seek additional ways to help clients clarify and identify the variables important in their career decision making. In the final two steps in the CACCM, Step 6 is helping the client make a culturally appropriate decision, and Step 7 is implementing the client's plans and follow-up.

## MULTICULTURAL CAREER COUNSELING TENETS

Neville, Gysbers, Heppner, and Johnston (1998) outline five central tenets that are hallmarks of traditional career counseling and that must be guarded against as counselors work from a multicultural perspective. The first is the tenet of individualism and autonomy. As noted earlier, most traditional career counselors focus on the individual as the primary decision maker. In fact, the family unit is the decision maker for many clients, particularly those from cultural minority groups. The second tenet is that most career theories assume a certain level of affluence. In other words, they assume that clients can afford to spend time exploring their interests, values, and abilities and then seek additional training prior to implementing a career choice. However, as discussed earlier, many individuals do not have the economic luxury to do anything other than find a job that pays for necessities, and in fact, for many working poor, their salaries do not even cover basic needs. This is particularly the case for racial and ethnic minorities, who are disproportionately overrepresented in lower socioeconomic levels.

A third tenet of traditional career counseling is that opportunities are available to all individuals who work hard. In reality, the American dream of success based on hard work is the American nightmare for individuals who are restricted in their career choices due to racial and sexual discrimination, as well as discrimination based on sexual orientation or social class. A fourth tenet is that work is central in people's lives. But work may not be central for some individuals, because of the experiences of institutional racism or because their culture places higher value on other aspects of life. The final tenet is that of linearity in the career counseling process. Traditional career counseling, consisting of knowledge of self, knowledge of the world of work, and finding a match between the two, is the epitome of the white cultural focus on linear, rational, and objective thinking. But for some racial and ethnic group clients, a more intuitive approach may be more beneficial than a linear one.

# APPLYING A MULTICULTURAL PERSPECTIVE TO THE CASE OF LESLIE

## Conceptualizing Leslie's Career History

Leslie grew up as the middle child of a relatively affluent white middle-class family in a large metropolitan area in the midwestern United States. Her ethnicity is not specified, other than to note that she is Caucasian. She is, however, a product of one or more cultures that transmitted values and messages about being a Caucasian woman in the United States. Giordano and McGoldrick (1996) note that "all people are ethnic. . . . It is a fact of our identities, one over which we have no choice" (p. 428). European Americans often conceptualize themselves as not having a culture, as being "regular" Americans. However, their cultural backgrounds, whether their ancestors came from the Mediterranean, Eastern Europe, or Western Europe, have shaped the way they view the world, their relationship with nature, the way they define family, the way they define work, and their view of time. To fully understand Leslie's career history, it is critical to understand the cultural messages she received growing up as a white woman.

Katz (1985) discusses several aspects of the white culture. She notes that "whites share similar cultural dimensions that constitute a separate, unique culture" (p. 616). She explicitly identifies several components of white cultural values and beliefs. These include a focus on individualism, with its emphasis on autonomy and independence, competition, and a value placed on winning. There is a strong pragmatic orientation, with an emphasis on doing something about a situation or problem. Future planning is stressed, and progress and growth is valued. The scientific method is the favored mode, with preference given to rational and linear thinking and to decision making based on objective as opposed to subjective information. Status and power are based on position and title, and value is placed on economic possessions. The world is viewed as a place to master rather than as a place to tolerate or in which to coexist with nature. Family is primarily viewed as the nuclear family rather than as an extended family including many generations. The Protestant work ethic predominates: Hard work is good, and working hard brings success. Time is viewed as a saleable entity apportioned out according to set schedules; deviations from time schedules are not tolerated.

Leslie received messages from her family consistent with white cultural expectations. She was taught to work hard, as evidenced by her excellent academic work in high school. Her family expected her to plan for the future, in expecting her to go to college. However, they also clearly conveyed a value on individualism and autonomy in not giving her much direction or guidance in choosing a career or a major. Her father communicated a value placed on pragmatic gain in recommending that she enter a business field, although this did not coincide with her interests. Her family also may have transmitted several values in showing their impatience with her decision-making process. They may have indicated that she ought to be more rational and linear in her decision making, taking the information she had and simply making a decision. This is also consistent with a preference for doing something about a situation perceived as problematic. Leslie's family also appears to have conveyed messages about appropriate careers for their children that allowed them to gain positions of power and status.

Leslie also received messages of appropriate behavior as a white woman; some of these messages are in direct conflict with appropriate behavior as a white individual. White women are expected to be nurturing and to put others' needs before their own. They are expected to be caring and to be kind and helpful to others, particularly other white people. They also are perceived as being emotional, weak, illogical, and needing security from others. Thus, the culture tells white women to be independent *and* dependent, logical *and* emotional. White women are expected to be passive *and* to take control of a situation. They are to be nurturing *and* autonomous. Leslie seems to also have received these mixed messages. She was to be autonomous in making a career decision, but her mother communicated that she should not pursue that career at the same time she was taking care of a family. Her parents may have communicated that the occupation of teacher is a more appropriate occupation for a woman than going into a math or science career, because she would be taking care of others as a teacher. She may also have received messages that it is appropriate to rely on others to help make decisions rather than being emotionally independent. She may have received messages to avoid positions of leadership and power.

It is not clear what Leslie's perceptions of other races were while she was growing up. She grew up in a suburb of a large midwestern city; she may have grown up in a racially segregated environment. She had little contact with individuals of other races while she was growing up and had little opportunity to develop a consciousness of herself as a member of a racial or ethnic group or to develop a knowledge or understanding of other groups. On the other hand, Leslie may have grown up in a racially integrated neighborhood and may have had significant interpersonal relationships with children from many cultural groups. She may have developed a strong sense of herself as a member of a racial group and an appreciation of and understanding for other cultures. She may, in fact, have spent a great deal of time exploring her own cultural heritage(s) and may have gained an appreciation of the role of white privilege in the United States. Whichever the case, her early upbringing and the messages that her family, neighborhood, and school gave her about her own race and about other races helped to form her later racial perceptions and attitudes.

Leslie moved to her first job in a small town in the Midwest, which was most probably homogeneously white. Her frustrations with the job appeared to have little to do with the culture of the town but, rather, with the workload in her job and with the lack of a social support network. She had ended her relationship with her boyfriend, whose ethnicity is not given. She met her husband, Joe when she was nearly 30. He is second-generation Mexican American. Joe appears to have had some ambivalence about identifying with his Mexican American heritage. He wanted to conform to the dominant culture's behavioral expectations when he was an adolescent, refusing to speak Spanish or to attend church with his family, but his first marriage was to a Hispanic woman from his neighborhood. He appears to have become more involved in his community and to have developed a greater appreciation for the traditions and values of his heritage. After his first marriage dissolved, he appears to have retained his sense of identity as a Mexican American. Although he eventually married a white woman, Leslie, and no longer lives in his family's neighborhood, he still self-identifies as a Mexican American and has embraced many traditional values.

Joe and Leslie's marriage appears to be problematic for both sets of in-laws. Leslie's marriage to a member of another ethnic group may have been an issue for her parents. There are indications that they accept him as a member of the family, because Leslie and Joe spend a fair amount of time with her family. Leslie's family's initial concerns for her marriage to Joe may have been due less to his ethnicity than to her marriage to a divorced father of one son; they also may have reacted due to their own prejudices and lack of racial awareness. Social class may be another factor that influenced Leslie's family's reaction to Joe, because Joe's educational and occupational level are quite different from the rest of her family. Joe's mother has said she thinks Leslie is too American. This may have caused conflicts for Leslie with her mother-in-law; it may also cause conflict between Joe and Leslie if Joe feels torn between his family and his wife.

### Conceptualizing Leslie's Present Situation

Conceptualizing Leslie's current situation from a multicultural perspective includes examining Leslie's behaviors and values from the multiple cultural contexts in which she lives. She is a close member of her white family and continues to be influenced by their expectations and values. She is married to a Mexican-American man who has expectations for her behavior that may stem from his own cultural background and values. She works in a high school setting that may have a racially diverse faculty and students.

Leslie's family has conveyed to her that she should be pursuing a career that will give her position and economic benefits and have also suggested that she should start a family; the latter connotes that she cannot both work and raise a family. They again show some impatience with what they perceive as her slow decision making. Her father is still advocating a business career; her mother and sister are suggesting that she stop work to have children. Her brother communicates that she is perhaps making an emotional decision in examining her career choices; he has labeled her dissatisfaction as complaints about inconsequential aspects of her job.

Leslie's husband, Joe, also expects that she would stay home if they have children. She feels that although he is supportive of her changing careers, he is less supportive of her returning to school. Joe appears to be ambivalent about adopting the traditional Hispanic values that his family espoused. The role of women in the traditional Hispanic family is one of being subservient to her husband and of caring for and nurturing children, a role to which his mother conformed. A woman is expected to be passive and dependent on her husband. Caretaker of the family is her predominant purpose in life. On the other hand, Joe indicates that he knows that women should be able to be independent. Leslie may be violating some of his expectations in her interest in pursuing a career change. Although she and Joe want to have a family together, she may be reluctant to assume the role he wants her to play in that family. It is not clear whether Joe expects her to play a particular role with his son. Leslie and Joe's lack of communication may be due to differences in cultural values; she may be focusing on discussing all her concerns with him, thereby creating conflict, whereas he may be motivated by the Hispanic value of smoothing over conflicts and having harmonious relationships.

Finally, Leslie works in a high school that may or may not be racially diverse in the students she is serving and the faculty with whom she works. Whichever the case, race may be playing a role in Leslie's decisions. Her perceptions that parents are uninvolved in their children's education may have actually been a cultural difference in attitudes and behaviors. What she is interpreting as lack of involvement may be a cultural respect for authority and viewing the teacher as the expert. Similarly, her perceptions that students are having more difficulties at home may be due to her own racial assumptions about problems. In other words, Leslie may be interpreting her students' behavior from a cultural-deficit model and concluding that they are dealing with many problems at home.

## Directions and Implications for Career Counseling

### Goals of Counseling

The goal of counseling from a multicultural perspective is for counselors to deliver culturally appropriate interventions for clients, recognizing that clients come from a unique set of environments and contexts. Before this can happen, however, counselors must have knowledge of their own culture and the way their values and biases and behaviors are reflections of that culture. They must have knowledge of and understanding of other groups' worldviews and how individuals' worldviews affect their values and behaviors. In other words, counselors must be multiculturally competent. The goal of multiculturally competent career counseling is to help clients make the most culturally appropriate career decisions that fit within the context of their lives. Readers are referred to Sue et al. (1998) for further delineation and explanation of multicultural counseling competencies.

Some of the tenets discussed earlier may be important for the counselor to keep in mind when examining Leslie's career history. Leslie has consulted with her family and her husband; her husband, in particular, appears to play an influential role in Leslie's career decisions. The counselor should be aware that Leslie might choose to incorporate her husband in her decision making. Leslie also may have perceived that opportunities were not available to her because she is a woman. The counselor can help her explore some of those assumptions.

*Culturally Appropriate Career Counseling Model*

*Step 1: Establishing a Culturally Appropriate Relationship.* In the first step, the counselor sets the context for a working consensus (Bingham & Ward, 1994). This includes exhibiting empathy, warmth, and positive regard. The counselor and Leslie discuss Leslie's expectations for counseling, which are shaped by her cultural background. The counselor asks Leslie, "What do you expect of counseling and of me as your counselor?" Leslie most likely expects that the relationship would be a fairly egalitarian one and that the counselor has some information to share with her. She also expects that the assessment tools will help her clarify her interests and needs and will help point her in a particular direction.

*Step 2: Identification of Career Issues.* Leslie's counselor then helps Leslie identify her career issues. Leslie may include her dissatisfaction with her job, her desire to explore other career possibilities, and her desire to make a career decision of which her husband can be supportive as initial issues for counseling. The counselor helps Leslie explore additional environmental issues, such as the role that race and ethnicity may play in her current environment, external barriers such as possible sexism operating in the work environment, and how gender-role expectations may have influenced her prior decisions.

*Step 3: Assessing the Impact of Cultural Variables on Career Issues.* In the third step, the counselor helps Leslie explore how her behavior has been a product of her culture and whether these are behaviors she wants to continue or to change. For example, the counselor may state, "Leslie, you have been dissatisfied with not being able to teach advanced classes but have not said anything when those were assigned to others. You indicated that your mother taught you to play along and that women don't make a fuss. You could choose to be more assertive, which may change the assignments you get. Is this something you would like to change?" The counselor also explores how Joe's Hispanic background and values have contributed to the role he expects his wife to play. The counselor also helps Leslie examine how her culture and her husband's culture have interacted to help create the conflicts she has experienced in her marriage.

Using the spheres diagram (Figure 9.2), the counselor helps Leslie examine how her gender has influenced her own and other's expectations of her and the roles that she has been taught she should play. The counselor then helps her examine how her family has influenced her career decisions and the values that they have conveyed to her. The counselor asks Leslie to identify her cultural heritage and helps her understand how her culture has influenced her behavior. The counselor may say, "Leslie, you indicate that you are white. Tell me what ethnic group your family identifies most with. Let's look at how that culture may have influenced you." Finally, the counselor helps Leslie examine how the majority culture has affected her, both in giving her privileges as a white woman and in restricting her options due to sexism.

*Step 4: Setting Culturally Appropriate Processes and Goals.* Leslie's counselor works with her to establish the goals she wants to achieve in counseling. Leslie may choose to decide whether to leave teaching or not. In addition, she may also want to gain further clarity on how she has accepted messages from her family about being indecisive and overly emotional and how cultural values have influenced her marriage.

*Step 5: Implementing Culturally Appropriate Interventions.* In Step 5, the counselor incorporates the assessments that Leslie has taken, as well as implementing additional interventions that appear appropriate for the goals that Leslie has set for counseling. Her first goal is to make a decision about staying in the teaching profession or choosing another career.

The counselor first incorporates the results of the Strong Interest Inventory (SII) in counseling. Because Leslie may have restricted her options to stereotypically feminine occupations, the counselor helps Leslie examine her interest areas other than the traditionally female ones. In other words, the counselor helps Leslie examine interests in the investigative and conventional areas, examining the General Occupational Themes and Basic Interest Scales. Thus, the counselor asks her to discuss her interests in math and science, as well as in data management and processing. The counselor also asks Leslie to discuss the occupations in the investigative and conventional areas. Leslie may, however, prefer to accommodate her husband's wish that she not seek further schooling; this will limit her options to those careers that she could enter with a bachelor's degree in secondary math education. Interestingly, her Skills Confidence Inventory (SCI) indicates that she is quite confident about her skills in the nontraditional investigative areas; her counselor may want to explore this further with her.

Leslie's Minnesota Importance Questionnaire (MIQ) indicates that her highest values are consistent with her cultural expectations: achievement, ability utilization, moral values, and social service are her highest needs. The counselor helps Leslie examine which of those values are important for her to find rewarded in an occupation and how she interprets those needs. For example, the counselor may ask, "Your highest need is achievement. Tell me what that means for you, when you feel that you have accomplished something."

Hartung et al. (1998) suggest that many of the assessment tools that Leslie completed may be used within a cultural framework, advocating the use of a qualitative approach. For example, the counselor may examine the items in the Adult Career Concerns Inventory (ACCI) and the Career Beliefs Inventory (CBI) from a cultural perspective within the interview. Thus, the counselor may ask Leslie to discuss an item on the CBI, such as "Others are preventing me from doing the work I want to do," within the context of the cultural differences in her marriage.

Additional interventions that the counselor employs include the 42-item Career Checklist (Ward & Bingham, 1993). Leslie identifies the issues that influence her career decision making, such as familial obligations; understanding of her abilities, interests, and needs; confidence; knowledge of the world of work; personal or sociopolitical obstacles; decision-making confidence; view of the relationship between education and work; ability to dream; and belief that personal parameters affect career choice. The Career Checklist may help Leslie clarify barriers and obstacles to achieving her goals.

If Leslie's counseling goals include examining the role that culture plays in her decision making and in her marriage, the counselor may invite Joe to be part of career counseling. The counselor uses fantasy exercises to help Leslie identify how she would like to shape her career. The counselor asks Leslie to find role models who are women in nontraditional occupations to help her explore how that would fit in her life. Additional strategies include the use of genograms to help Leslie examine how her family has defined appropriate careers for men and women. Finally, the counselor asks Leslie to examine the role that culture may play in her decision to leave teaching. "How comfortable are you with teaching a racially diverse student group? Could your decision be related to the different races of your students or of other faculty? Could your decision to leave be due to sexist policies or behavior on the part of your principal?" If so, these may be a result of a lack of racial understanding or lack of knowledge of various racial and ethnic groups' cultural values and behavior, and the issues could be addressed in counseling.

*Step 6: Decision Making and Step 7: Implementation.* Following the interventions, Leslie's counselor helps her make a decision relative to her goals and then helps her formulate a plan to implement it. For example, Leslie may decide to confront Joe and her family about their expectations that she behave in sex-appropriate ways. Leslie's counselor helps her formulate specific steps to implement her decision—such as helping Leslie to work on assertiveness skills or role-playing a confrontation. Her counselor helps her to identify some specific goals she wants as a result of the confrontation—such as more equitable sharing of household tasks or support for a decision to go to graduate school.

---

## DISCUSSION QUESTIONS REGARDING LESLIE FROM A MULTICULTURAL PERSPECTIVE

1. What specific hypotheses would you develop about Leslie from culturally appropriate counseling approaches? How does using these approaches help you understand Leslie? How might it help Leslie understand herself?

2. What role may Leslie's worldview have played in her career development and choices?

3. How could you balance increasing awareness of race and ethnicity as possible influences in Leslie's decision making with an appreciation of her racial consciousness? Where might this be problematic?

4. How could you empower Leslie to make different types of decisions?

5. How may culture have interacted with Leslie's family of origin and her familial obligations to shape her behavior?

6. What role may sexism and racism have played in Leslie's decisions and in the outcomes of those decisions?

7. How might cultural issues influence the relationship between Leslie and Joe?

## ADDITIONAL CASES

### Case 1: Linda

Linda is an 18-year-old college freshman. Both of her parents are Korean and immigrated to the United States when Linda and her sisters were small children. Linda was 10 when they arrived in the United States; her sisters were 8, 5, and 2. She grew up in a primarily Korean community in Los Angeles, living with her parents, three sisters, and her paternal grandmother. Linda's parents both completed college degrees in Korea prior to the immigration. Linda's father was in business in Korea, and her mother was a teacher. However, when they came to the United States, neither was able to find work commensurate with their education and work experience. Her father worked for another Korean family in a grocery store, and her mother took in sewing and took care of the children. When Linda was 15, her parents were able to buy the grocery store. Since then, her mother has worked in the store with her father.

Linda's parents learned to speak English, although her grandmother refused to learn and speaks only Korean at home. Linda's parents speak Korean at home, as well, out of respect for her grandmother. Thus, Linda grew up speaking Korean and English. Her parents come in contact with individuals from many cultures in the grocery store, but their primary social network consists of the Korean American community; much of this community is focused on their involvement with the Korean Church. Linda and her sisters were expected to also be very involved with the Korean community, participating in activities in the church and forming friendships with other Korean children.

Linda attended an elementary school that was predominantly Korean and African American. Her parents placed a very high emphasis on education, making sure that she and her sisters worked hard at their studies each evening. She made some friends at school but was discouraged from participating in after-school activities because those might interfere with her studies. She also was discouraged from making friends outside her parents' social circle. Eventually, she did not want to bring friends home, because she was embarrassed at her grandmother's inability to communicate with anyone who could not speak Korean.

Linda did well in school and was chosen to attend a high school known for its science and math instruction and college-preparatory curriculum. Linda's parents were very pleased with their daughter's accomplishment and wanted to ensure that she would do well enough to enter a very good university; they increased their expectations of the time she spent studying. The high school was a racially diverse school, with many gifted students. Linda became friends with students from a wide geographic region and began to want to participate in more school and off-campus activities. Linda and her parents entered into many conflictual situations during her high school years: They expected her to be home, working on her school work, but she wanted to have the same freedoms as her new friends. She was particularly interested in participating in theater and received much verbal encouragement to pursue her interest in acting from her teachers and drama coach.

Her grandmother was highly critical of her mother during this time, blaming her mother for what she perceived as Linda's disobedience and disrespect. Her mother expected her father to support her against his mother, but he also felt that Linda was disrespectful and selfish in her desire to be "more American." This led to increased conflict between her parents, as well. They were very concerned that her sisters not learn "bad lessons" from Linda, wanting them to find their primary social relationships within their Korean community.

Linda finished high school with a 4.0 grade point average and won an academic scholarship to a prestigious university in the Los Angeles area. She was enrolled as a biology major and did well in her classes during the first semester. The second semester, however, her grades began to slip. Linda was suddenly unsure of her decision to pursue a biology major and began to reconsider her interests in acting. She sought out the help of a career counselor on campus to decide whether to change majors.

*Questions for Discussion*

1. What cultural values may Linda's family have conveyed to her throughout her upbringing?
2. What role may acculturation have played for Linda, her parents, and her grandmother? How may acculturation differences affect her sisters?
3. What may have led Linda to recognize that there was a problem?
4. What cultural variables would you want to incorporate in career counseling?
5. What may be some possible career interventions that you could use?
6. What cultural strengths would you emphasize in working with Linda?

### Case 2: Norman

Norman is an 18-year-old African American male who was referred to a counselor to help him adjust his attitude; he is about to graduate from high school and needs to find a job. Norman is the youngest son of three children. His father is a cook for a large catering company and his mother is a nurse; they have been divorced for 10 years. His oldest brother is in college, majoring in business, and his older sister is currently working as a receptionist and hopes to return to school to become a paralegal assistant. Norman has lived primarily with his mother, although she has asked him to live with his father twice during his high school years when she felt she was not able to "manage" him.

Norman is graduating from high school with a C average and has taken elective courses in manufacturing and in computers. Norman entered high school with a B average. However, he did not do well in his eighth-grade math and science classes, and his eighth-grade counselor encouraged him to take classes that would prepare him for a vocational technical school, such as applied math courses and business writing. His mother initially expressed some concern about this plan of study, hoping that Norman would enter a college-preparatory curriculum, but Norman did not want to go back and ask his counselor to change his schedule. In addition, his friends were signing up for the same courses, and he thought he'd be able to change once he was in high school. Unfortunately, the curriculum was less flexible than he thought, and he was unable to shift to a college-preparatory track.

The course that Norman enjoyed the most during his first year in high school was manufacturing. He enjoyed the material, he enjoyed working on the class projects, and he enjoyed the practical nature of the course. He was less enthusiastic about his other classes; he thought they were either irrelevant or boring. His mother became concerned during his sophomore year that he was not doing well in school. They began to have conflicts at home about his grades and about his friendships with several boys at school. This was the first instance in which he lived with his father, who helped him refocus on school, and his grades improved. He returned to live with his mother during the summer after his sophomore year, because her schedule permitted her to be home more than did his father's. He lived with his father once more during his senior year for a period of 2 months, returning to his mother's home when he and his father disagreed about the time spent with his friends.

Norman's freshman year manufacturing teacher encouraged him to continue in this track and to apply for an apprenticeship with a manufacturing company. Although he did not secure a formal apprenticeship, he did join a cooperative program during his junior year that enabled him to work part-time during the afternoon and take classes in the morning. He enjoyed the work, although he also felt bored at times with the relatively mundane work he felt he had to do. He was learning about cell manufacturing and quality improvement techniques in his manufacturing classes at school but was not seeing those policies implemented in the manufacturing company. He began to question his supervisors about the discrepancy between what he was doing and what he had learned in class. The supervisor complained to the teacher, and the teacher referred Norman to the school counselor. The teacher was primarily concerned that Norman learn to adjust his attitude, because questioning supervisors might lead Norman into problematic situations on the job.

The counselor found that Norman's vocational interests were primarily in the realistic and investigative areas. Norman also scored high on the Basic Interest Scales for mechanical activities, math, and science, as well as those for organizational management and law/public speaking. Norman was most similar to men who are engineers, farmers, research and development managers, computer programmers, auto mechanics, and small business owners.

### Questions for Discussion

1. What cultural values did his family transmit to Norman?
2. What role may racism have played in Norman's school and career history?
3. What role may Norman's parents and brother have played in Norman's decisions?
4. What cultural variables would you want to incorporate in career counseling?
5. What are some possible career interventions you could use?
6. What cultural strengths could you emphasize in working with Norman?
7. How would you work to "adjust Norman's attitude"? Is that an appropriate request on the part of the instructor?

### Case 3: Monica

Monica is a 27-year-old woman who is of Native American and African American descent. She is seeking career counseling because she has lost her government subsidy and she must enter the workforce. Monica is the mother of three children, ages 10, 8, and 6. The oldest child is the daughter of a white man; the younger two are children of a relationship Monica had with an African American man who also accepted her first child as his own. The latter relationship has ended. Although the children continue to see their father, his contribution to the household income must be supplemented to support Monica and her three children.

Monica's parents are both biracial. Her mother is half Cherokee and African American, and identifies primarily with her Cherokee heritage. She volunteers at a local museum devoted to Native American history and culture. Her father is half Sioux and half African American; his primary identification is with the African American community where he is a community police officer. Monica grew up in a middle-class, racially mixed neighborhood, the younger of two children. Her sister is 5 years older and employed as a day care worker, which enables her to also care for her own children. Her sister is married to an African American man who owns his own plumbing company.

Monica did not finish high school, because she dropped out when she was pregnant with her first child. Although her high school had day care available and her counselor encouraged her to complete her high school degree, Monica wanted to concentrate on her baby and on her boyfriend. However, shortly after the child was born, the baby's father left town and Monica has not seen him since. She went on public aid after he left. She was too depressed to find a job, and then began her relationship with Rick. Her government subsidy continued. Rick helped support her and her daughter and eventually their two additional children until their relationship ended. Monica's primary support system consists of her family and friends in her apartment building, most of whom are African American, although she feels no particular identification with either the Native American or African American community.

Monica learned last fall that her government subsidy was going to be eliminated this month. She did not know what to do, because she had no skills, no degree, and no job history. Her family encouraged her to seek career counseling some time ago, but she was embarrassed at her lack of skills and did nothing until she learned her last check would be next week.

## Questions for Discussion

1. What is the first thing you would focus on as the counselor?
2. What role may Monica's biracial status and her ethnic identity play in her decisions?
3. What cultural values may her family have transmitted to Monica?
4. What cultural variables would you want to incorporate in career counseling?
5. What are some possible career interventions you could use?
6. What cultural strengths could you emphasize in working with Monica?

# T E N

# *Summary and Integration*

We wrote this book to give students an understanding of how theories of career development could be applied in career counseling. Our intent in each chapter was to give a brief overview of the theory, apply it to a client, Leslie, and then discuss how a career counselor with that theoretical perspective would work with her. We used additional case studies at the end of each chapter to encourage readers to develop hypotheses about a wide variety of clients and to practice applying each theory to realistic cases. In the process, we ourselves were frequently reminded how focusing on one theoretical perspective very much influenced the course of counseling. It determined the questions we asked about Leslie, it determined the behavior that was examined and brought into counseling, and it determined the goals we imagined Leslie would set for herself. We realized that in our own career counseling neither of us uses a single theory. Although we were both trained initially in the theory of work adjustment at the University of Minnesota, our approaches stem from a combination of theoretical perspectives and interventions.

At this point, many readers may ask, How do these theories compare? What are the strengths and weaknesses of each? How well do they apply to clients with whom I work (or will work in the future)? Is there any empirical support for these theories? How can I combine the theories in my own work? These are the questions we hope to begin to answer in this chapter. We will first summarize and compare each of the major theoretical approaches we examined in the book. As we did in Chapter 1, we then ask readers to stop and think of how each perspective applies to their own lives. Theories were designed to represent reality and help us understand and predict behavior, and it is helpful to think of how each has contributed to a greater understanding of our own career history and decision making.

Consistent with the format of the rest of the book, we examine how each theory or approach contributes to our understanding of Leslie. We will explicate the contributions of each theory to career counseling with Leslie and examine what may be the unique contributions of each theory to conceptualizing the case. Then, just as we have used cases throughout the book to exemplify the application of theories and approaches, we will present two cases to illustrate the integration of theoretical perspectives. We ask readers to thoroughly consider how each theoretical perspective would approach the new cases.

In the first case, George, we will discuss our view of what a counselor from each perspective would do. We summarize by outlining what we would do as counselors and identify the theoretical approaches on which we are drawing. We hope, in doing so, that we are modeling the integrative perspective that we discussed in Chapter 1. In the second case, Tom, we present the case and follow-up stimulus questions and then leave it to readers to consider how each theoretical perspective would approach Tom.

We then turn our attention to the questions readers may have about support for these theories. As strong proponents of the scientist-practitioner model, we believe it is important to evaluate the research foundation underlying each theory. We briefly examine the empirical support available for the constructs delineated in each theory and the empirical support for the application of the theory to a broad range of populations, regardless of sex, racial and ethnic background, socio-economic level, disability, or sexual orientation. Because no theory has been empirically supported for every construct and every population, we will also identify some areas we would encourage researchers to examine in the future. Finally, we will finish by suggesting areas for further training and skill development.

## SUMMARY AND COMPARISON OF THE THEORIES

Recall from Chapter 1 that it is useful to think of theories as road maps. We use maps to plan a trip, considering alternate routes to a final destination and locating interesting sights to visit along the road. Maps prevent us from arriving at the wrong destination (or not arriving at all) and from taking circuitous routes when more direct ones are available. Likewise, theories offer us alternate views of reality, of explaining human behavior, and of conducting counseling to assist clients with their concerns. Each of the five theories discussed in this book has many areas in which it overlaps with other theories. For example, each attempts to predict optimal situations for clients, whether a good career choice or a satisfying work environment. Each uses a variety of ways to help clients learn more about themselves, and although each theory uses different language to describe it, each assumes that individuals interact with their environment in some way. However, a review of the major constructs reveals that each theory does more than use different labels for the same behavior; rather, each focuses on a unique perspective of vocational behavior.

We summarize the major constructs for each theory in Table 10.1, along with the outcomes that each theory predicts. This information will aid readers in keeping track of which construct is used by which theory and which theoretical perspective is most likely to be used in helping clients make career choices or adjustments. We will discuss the last two columns of Table 10.1 in later sections.

Holland's theory describes vocational personalities and work environments and how they fit together. Individuals differ in their vocational personalities and seek out the environments that fit with their personality types. Outcomes predicted by Holland's theory include vocational choice as well as vocational adjustment; both of these are predicted by congruence with the environment. The theory of work adjustment (TWA) also describes individual differences, although this theory highlights individuals' abilities and needs. The environmental focus is on ability requirements and rewards rather than on vocational personality. The TWA delineates processes postulated to occur as an individual tries to decrease job dissatisfaction. Similar to Holland's theory, outcomes predicted by the TWA also include vocational choice and adjustment, although the focus is much more on adjustment and behavior within a work setting.

The developmental theories of Super and Gottfredson describe the development of an individual's career over the life span. Super's theory puts more emphasis on later life stages, ranging from implementing a career choice to retirement, than does Gottfredson's, which places more emphasis on childhood and adolescence. Developmental models explain how choices are made and implemented more than the other theories discussed in this book. Both theories predict vocational choice

**TABLE 10.1** Comparison of Theories

| Theories | Constructs | Outcome | Understanding Leslie | Support |
|---|---|---|---|---|
| Holland | Personality types (RIASEC) | Congruence | Congruence between her personality type and her current work environment | Well researched |
| | Environmental types (RIASEC) | Satisfaction | | Empirically supported |
| | Congruence | | | Mostly supported for women and racial/ ethnic minorities |
| | Consistency | | | |
| | Differentiation | | | |
| | Identity | | | |
| Theory of work adjustment | Abilities | Satisfaction | Dissatisfaction due to discorrespondence between her needs and environmental rewards | Well researched |
| | Ability requirements | | | |
| | Needs | Tenure | | Well supported for some constructs, less support for personality style variables |
| | Rewards (need reinforcers) | Work adjustment | | |
| | Satisfaction | | | |
| | Satisfactoriness | | | |
| | Reactive adjustment | | | |
| | Active adjustment | | | Has not been fully empirically examined |
| | Person-environment correspondence | | | |
| | Flexibility | | | |
| | Perseverance | | | |
| Developmental Super | Life stages | Vocational choice | Recycling through exploration tasks | Well researched |
| | Developmental tasks | Life role adjustment | | |
| | Implementation of self-concept | | Balancing roles in her life | Well supported |
| | Vocational maturity | | | Later formulations of the theory more explanatory of women's and racial and ethnic groups' career development— more research needed here |
| | Life roles | | | |
| | Salience | | | |
| Gottfredson | Circumscription | | Circumscription of investigative aspirations | Little empirical support for Gottfredson |
| | Compromise | | | |
| | Vocational aspirations | | | |
| | Life stages | | | |
| Social learning theory | Genetic endowment | Vocational choice | Learning opportunities | Moderate support |
| | Environmental conditions | | Beliefs about herself and about career decision-making | No specific studies examining gender or race |
| | Associative and instrumental learning | | | |
| | Task approach skills | | | |
| Social cognitive career theory | Self-efficacy | Interests | Self-efficacy for math and teaching | Relatively new theory, some support |
| | Beliefs | Occupational choice | | |
| | Outcome expectations | Level of performance | Changing outcome expectations | Supportive for application across populations |
| | Choice model | | | |
| | Performance model | | | |
| | Identifying barriers | | | |
| | Foreclosure | | | |

and development; Super's outcomes also include implementation of the self-concept and delineation of work as one of many life roles.

The focal point of Krumboltz's social learning theory is learning experiences, both in the past and in the future. Similar to Holland's theory and the TWA, social learning theory postulates that individuals interact with their environments and that they learn from those interactions. The emphasis in social learning theory, however, is on the results of those interactions on individuals, who learn characteristic ways of approaching tasks and general observations about themselves and their world. Individuals' learning histories, their genetic endowments, and their task approach skills interact with environmental conditions to predict vocational choice.

Social cognitive career theory also focuses on how individuals learn from others, but this model emphasizes the personal construction that individuals place on what they have learned. This model also highlights how interests develop and how choices develop, with an emphasis on an individual's beliefs about his or her competence in the related abilities and the outcomes expected of pursuing that field. The social cognitive model and social learning theory are the most explicit in their consideration of environmental conditions and events.

As we noted in Chapter 1, the counselor's theoretical perspective helps to determine the way the client and his or her concerns are conceptualized, determines the most appropriate tools to use with the client, and the overall goals of counseling. Choosing which theory to incorporate into your own map of your client's career behavior will depend on your own experiences as well as on the client's presenting problem. Osipow's (1996) description of the focus of theoretical perspectives may be helpful as readers evaluate which of these theories they will use in their own counseling, for it will depend on what you want to emphasize. Osipow summarized the theories by noting that Holland identifies *what happens,* developmental theories describe *how it happens,* the TWA depicts *how it happens and the outcome,* and social learning theory changes *how it will happen.* He did not include social cognitive career theory in his discussion, but that model would describe *how an individual's perceptions of reality help to make it happen.*

### *Applying Theories to Your Own Career Development*

Before reading the subsequent section on applying theoretical perspectives, use the following questions to evaluate how each theory may contribute to a greater understanding of your own career history.

1. What insights have you gained about your own career history from each of the theories?

2. Is one theory more applicable to your own career decision making than others?

3. How might a combination of two or more theories be more applicable than just one? Which parts of the theories would be more applicable?

4. How can you use the major concepts from each theory to explain your career history?

5. What aspects of your career history and decision making are *not* explained by the theories?

6. What role has your culture and gender played in your own career decisions?

## INTEGRATING THEORETICAL PERSPECTIVES

We have summarized the major constructs of each theory and discussed how they may shape a counselor's perspective in conducting career counseling. The manner in which that can happen is what we have tried to illustrate throughout the book as we have applied each theory to Leslie's situation (presented in Chapter 2). We have conceptualized her career history and present situation from each perspective and conducted career counseling with her from each theoretical viewpoint. In this section, we connect these pieces to examine what we believe has been each theory's contribution to a fuller understanding of Leslie's history, her expectations, and her career goals. This is summarized in the fourth column of Table 10.1. We then apply each theoretical focus to a new case, George. Following our discussion of each theory's perspective on George, we share how we would integrate theoretical approaches in career counseling with George.

### Contributions of Different Theories to Understanding Leslie

The two theories of person-environment fit help us understand the sources of satisfaction and dissatisfaction that Leslie perceives in her current job and in her career. Holland's theory does so by suggesting that her type (social-conventional-investigative) is relatively congruent with her occupation as a math teacher (coded on the Strong Interest Inventory [SII] profile as CIR for women). Furthermore, many other types of high school teachers are primarily social types, so the individuals in her environment are likely to be social types. Her dissatisfaction, therefore, is probably not due to being in an occupation that is incongruent with her type. This understanding helps the counselor to look at other factors that might contribute to her dissatisfaction, such as people and policies in her specific job environment.

The TWA also offers a perspective on how Leslie corresponds to her environment, in terms of her satisfaction and her satisfactoriness. Here, her dissatisfaction is conceptualized as related to whether her values and needs are being met by the reward structure available in her work environment. We know that part of her dissatisfaction is likely due to her frustrated needs for autonomy, even as her other needs continue to be met on the job. An important feature that the TWA adds to our understanding is the explicit attention to determining that she has been a satisfactory employee. We have some information that she has performed well on the job, but the TWA helps us to focus more specifically on her job performance.

Both of these theories also suggest other alternatives should Leslie decide that she wants to change jobs or occupations. In the case of Holland's theory, Leslie's type of social, conventional, and investigative can be used as a guide for identifying other occupations with which she might be congruent. In the TWA, her identified values and needs, as well as her identified dissatisfactions with her current job, provide the avenue for exploring new occupational choices. Her needs to achieve and to use her talents, as well as her need to help others, are important to consider in occupational exploration.

Developmental theories provide a life span perspective in understanding Leslie. Her career concerns are not atypical for someone of her age and career stage as she is trying to determine the role of work in her life, particularly in relation to her other current (and desired) life roles. She has established herself as a teacher, yet she is still struggling with Super's developmental tasks of consolidating and advancing in her career, and she is questioning whether she wants to continue in this occupation or move into a new career. Considering the totality of Leslie's life space allows the counselor to incorporate an explicit discussion of her various life roles and their relation to one another. Leslie's other life roles undoubtedly interact with how she experiences her work role; for example, her dissatisfaction with her job may influence or be influenced by her desire to have children. Super's focus on career choice as an implementation of the self-concept thus helps us to understand Leslie's life in context.

Furthermore, Gottfredson's theory adds hypotheses about how Leslie may have circumscribed her occupational aspirations as a child and adolescent and then compromised her choices from those remaining acceptable alternatives. Leslie's compromises corresponded to those predicted by Gottfredson in that she chose an occupation that appeared to preserve her sex-typed aspirations (teaching), perhaps at the expense of her interests (engineering, math, and science).

Social learning theory contributes an examination of Leslie's learning history. Her career directions are understandable in terms of her learning experiences, task approach skills, and self-observation generalizations. In other words, Leslie was rewarded for her abilities in math, she recognized that she was good at math and so continued to pursue math activities, and she was confident of her math ability as well as her ability to teach math to others. Using a learning approach also emphasizes the future in that Leslie can construct new learning opportunities for herself to improve her satisfaction in her current job or to head in a new career direction. Krumboltz's social learning theory also offers an avenue for discussing Leslie's beliefs about herself and about career decision making.

Social cognitive career theory also uses learning experiences in understanding Leslie, with a particular focus on her self-efficacy for specific activities and the expected outcomes she anticipates from performing these activities. Leslie has considerable self-efficacy about mathematics and about teaching, and she also values the outcomes provided by doing well in math and teaching. Social cognitive career theory also suggests that her job dissatisfaction might be due to changing self-efficacy or outcome expectations, particularly as related to her desire to have children.

The models of culturally appropriate counseling and gender-aware and feminist approaches remind us to consider the multiple contextual factors that exert influence in Leslie's life. Her educational and career experiences have been shaped by societal expectations for her as a white, middle-class, heterosexual woman, regardless of her level of awareness of these expectations. Exploring these contextual factors will help Leslie realize the influence that they have had on her choices and help her make future decisions with a clearer sense of who she is and who she wants to be. Moreover, the counselor's own contextual experiences might influence his or her interaction with Leslie in counseling.

## THE CASE OF GEORGE

We will use the case of George, to demonstrate the way in which different theoretical perspectives inform how career counseling might proceed with another client. Assume that the following information was gathered during an intake interview with George; as you read, think about each of the theoretical approaches described in this book.

George is a 54-year-old Caucasian male of German and English descent. He is seeking counseling because he is becoming increasingly dissatisfied with his career as a financial planner. George lives in a semirural area in the Northeast. He is married with two college-aged children, and his wife is a special education teacher.

George has a bachelor's degree in industrial engineering. He had been accepted at several major universities after high school graduation but chose the one he attended because of its reputation for engineering and because it was his father's alma mater (who also received a degree in industrial engineering). George knew at that time that math and science were his "strong suits," and he also had interest and skills in working with people. However, he states now that he "never felt engineering was the right fit" but that industrial engineering was the best fit of the possible specialties within engineering.

After college graduation, he sought a position in engineering sales; after interviewing with several firms, he was hired by a company that manufactured french fryers to sell to fast food restaurants. George reported that he enjoyed this job and was very good at it. After five years, however, he tired of the constant travel, and he did not like some of the company's policies nor some of the customers that he had to deal with routinely. He quit the job with no plans for what he might do next and despite the company's efforts to retain him.

While on a vacation shortly after he quit his job, George bought a large quantity of Oriental rugs and returned home to open a retail store in a historic district of his small town that was undergoing redevelopment. The business flourished for several years, until an economic recession dried up the market. A friend asked for his assistance in setting up a food business in another town, and when George visited him to help, he decided to close his own business and join with his friend. This business grew rapidly, and George and his friend split into two independent operations so that George was managing a restaurant on his own.

George thoroughly enjoyed managing the restaurant. He handled all catering sales, hired and trained personnel, and managed the orders and accounts. The restaurant was very successful for several years until a highway was rerouted, which caused the traffic into the restaurant to drop off precipitously. George then found himself somewhat stranded, and he worried that he would need to move elsewhere to find a sales job with a corporation. However, one of his customers at the restaurant had been recruiting him to join his life insurance office as a financial planner, and George decided to give it a try.

George felt out of place with the other agents and planners at first but quickly "learned the ropes." He felt that it was the first time in his life that he was doing something to help other people. He has been working in life insurance and financial planning for 11 years; as he stated, "I took the job because I had to, and I've continued because I'm good at it." However, lately he's been feeling like "it's not fun anymore." He enjoys meeting with clients, but he finds it harder to make the phone calls necessary to set up the meetings and to solicit new sales prospects. He also finds himself more consciously aware that he benefits from each sale and of whether that awareness affects how he works with clients. He's worried that he is not doing as good a job for his clients.

When asked what he would do if he could change careers, he answered without hesitation: "teach." He has had some experience teaching basic insurance courses to new agents, which he enjoyed. He is interested in teaching math but is unsure about the practicality of doing so at his age.

Seven years ago, George took the SII and Myers-Briggs Type Indicator (MBTI) as part of a continuing education workshop sponsored by his office. His highest General Occupational Theme scores were social (very high), enterprising (high), and artistic (high), and his investigative score was moderately high. Other notable features of his SII profile are that he had high Basic Interest Scale scores in athletics, military activities, medical science, teaching, social service, religious activities, public speaking, law/politics, merchandising, and sales, and he had a very high score on the Risktaking/Adventure Scale. High Occupational Scale scores include police officer, dentist, optometrist, nurse, parks and recreation coordinator, community service organization director, school administrator, life insurance agent, purchasing agent, nursing home administrator, realtor, and credit manager. His MBTI type was ESFP (extroverted-sensing-feeling-perceiving).

### *Working With George*

Before we turn to a consideration of George from the various theoretical perspectives, consider the following questions:

1. What are your impressions of George?
2. What more would you like to know about him?
3. What hypotheses would you develop about George from the perspective of each approach, including gender-aware and culturally appropriate career counseling?
4. How will you gather information to test your hypotheses?
5. How does each of these theoretical approaches influence the next step in counseling? What direction would you take from the perspective of each, including gender-aware and culturally appropriate career counseling?

### *Considering George From Various Theoretical Perspectives*

We will begin with culturally appropriate approaches (Chapter 9) and work back to Holland's theory (Chapter 3). We consider George from each approach or theoretical perspective, highlighting the unique contributions of each perspective.

#### *Culturally Appropriate Approaches*

George is a white middle-class heterosexual male, possibly belonging to the upper middle class. He is of German and English descent. It is not indicated what ethnic group his wife belongs to, nor is his religious background noted. One more aspect of his context is given in the case study; he is from the Northeast and lives in a small town.

The culturally appropriate approach would assume that as a heterosexual white male, George had a great deal of privilege in his life. His options appear not to have been restricted by racism or sexism. He was able twice to impulsively open a new business and was successful at it, apparently without a barrier due to his race or sex. He was affected when the highway was rerouted, but there is no indication that he construed that as anything other than a neutral environmental event. However, George may have felt restricted due to the cultural messages he may have received about appropriate behavior for men.

The culturally appropriate approach would examine what George's multiple cultural contexts have conveyed to him. George attended his father's alma mater, following his father's footsteps into a career that was not necessarily a good fit for him. Was this an expectation from his family to carry on a family tradition? If so, are there other similar expectations? What expectations did George have as a financial provider for his family? George's ethnic background was German and English; how were those different ethnic backgrounds integrated into his upbringing? How may they affect him now?

### Gender-Aware and Feminist Approaches

Several aspects of George's career history seem pertinent to a gender analysis. First, George clearly identified with his father early in his career: His decision of university and major were both influenced by his father's choices, and although engineering did not seem like a good fit at the time, he pursued it anyway. More information about George's father would be helpful, particularly related to how George perceived his father's expectations for him generally and for his career success specifically.

Second, there is a theme in George's career history of working hard at building businesses but also with an underlying interest in and concern for people. The latter interest seems to be increasing in strength, as evidenced by George's expressed desire to teach. The interest in people may be an area that he did not feel encouraged to express earlier in his life.

### Social Cognitive Career Theory

The social cognitive theoretical perspective would focus on George's self-efficacy beliefs and his outcome expectations. He has been in an occupation for several years that he feels he is good at but that he does not want to continue doing. George would appear to have high self-efficacy beliefs about his abilities as a financial planner, but the outcomes he is expecting from his occupation are not as positive as perhaps they once were. He does not like cold sales calls and would like to feel that he is of more help to people than he may be. He expects better outcomes from being a teacher.

George appears to have high self-efficacy beliefs related to change, including changing careers. He has changed careers several times and been successful at it. He has a large number of diverse interests, indicating a variety of areas that may be options for him to examine. A career counselor working from a social cognitive perspective would help George examine the option of becoming a teacher, identifying possible barriers he may have. The counselor would also examine whether George has prematurely foreclosed other options, many of which may be identified by the SII results.

### Social Learning Theory

George appears to be a very intelligent man, with a high level of mathematical ability and strong interpersonal skills. Environmental conditions that may have influenced his career decision making include strong familial expectations to follow his father into industrial engineering. He was influenced by company policies in his first job, including the expectation that he travel. Two more environmental events shaped his career history: He had to close the Oriental rug store because of an economic recession and his restaurant because of the rerouting of the highway that reduced his customer base.

George learned in his first job that he was good in sales but that he did not enjoy traveling. He learned that he enjoyed managing a restaurant, and as a financial planner, he has learned that he enjoys helping people, does not enjoy soliciting new business, and does not enjoy setting up meetings. His task approach skills appear to include the high level of performance he expected of himself, willingness to take risks and make changes, and a strong ethic of helping people.

A social learning theory counselor would identify George's self-observation skills (e.g., I am good at financial planning, I am good at but do not like cold sales calls). A counselor would also identify George's beliefs and expectations of his career decision making, determining possible barriers to George's occupational change. The career counselor would help George identify areas for growth and new learning, using the interest inventory to help him determine where those new experiences may occur.

### Developmental Theories

Developmental theories add explicit attention to how George's self-concept has evolved throughout his life. He seems to have long-standing interests both in entrepreneurial and social service activities, but perhaps the relative importance of these two areas has shifted with time. George's self-concept thus has remained stable throughout his life, with a clear sense of what he is good at doing and what is important to him.

In Super's formulation, George is in the age range corresponding to maintenance stage career tasks; however, he has made enough career shifts that he could be conceptualized as being in establishment. In fact, his current career dissatisfaction seems to be related to his transition into maintenance: He seems to be asking, "Should I do something new or continue with this until retirement?"

## The Theory of Work Adjustment

George has indicated that he is not satisfied in his occupation. The TWA would conceptualize George as a satisfactory employee, whose abilities have matched the job requirements for the past 11 years. However, George's needs have not been met by the job. He would appear to have high compensation and social service needs as well as achievement needs. It would also seem that his social service needs at times interfere with his compensation needs, and when they do, the social service needs are stronger. George's adjustment style would appear to have a relatively high level of flexibility but a low level of perseverance (he stayed in a job he did not like for 5 years, then quit with no other plans in place). He seems to have a high level of pace.

His counselor would begin by examining whether George can increase the correspondence with his environment either by changing his needs or by changing the environment. George may, for example, work to resolve the conflict between his social service needs and his compensation needs, perhaps finding ways to meet his social service needs by volunteering for a local youth group. Alternatively, he may work to change the environment, perhaps by taking on different aspects of financial planning within the organization, by encouraging his firm to offer more free seminars and workshops so that he can feel he is helping others.

If George decides that he would rather explore new occupations than make his current occupation a better fit, the counselor would give George additional assessments, particularly the Minnesota Importance Questionnaire (MIQ) to help identify occupations in which he would be predicted to fit. He would be assumed to have high abilities in a variety of areas, including math, reasoning, and interpersonal communication. Occupations that dovetail between the SII and the MIQ would be good options for more exploration.

*Holland's Theory*

A counselor working from the perspective of Holland's theory would examine George's aspirations from early in his life and the relation between George's personality type and the environments in which he has worked. Clearly, George has had entrepreneurial aspirations and has always excelled at occupations that require persuasive abilities and sales skills—enterprising-type occupations. According to the General Occupational Themes of the SII, George is an SEA type, and the work environments in which he has thrived have been predominantly enterprising and social in nature.

George's decisions to change jobs relatively frequently may not be viewed as an unstable pattern, because he remained in occupations with the same environmental type. In fact, he probably has moved into more congruent occupations, incorporating increasingly more of his social interests.

## Our Own Approach to Conceptualizing George

We blend a variety of approaches when we do career counseling based on our own experiences of career counseling approaches with diverse clients. We have tried to show how that may be done in this section. However, it is important to note that this is just an example and certainly not a prescription for working with all clients. There are many ways to blend and integrate various theoretical approaches that will vary both with the counselor and the concern brought by the client.

George may be seeking career counseling for help adjusting to his current occupation or for help choosing a new career. He has an idea of an area that he might like to explore—teaching—but is not certain that it is a viable option for him. George has a large number of strengths: He appears to have high abilities in a variety of areas, including general intellectual ability and strong interpersonal skills. He has been successful in a number of ventures, he has the skills and confidence to initiate and adapt to change, and he has interests in diverse areas.

We would use a combination of person-environment fit theories (Holland's and the TWA) as well as Super's developmental theory to begin to conceptualize hypotheses about George's current career concerns. We would use a combination of social cognitive theory and Super's developmental theory to conceptualize his career history.

His career history would appear to include increasing knowledge in high school about his abilities but perhaps not about his interests. For example, he notes that he knew he excelled in math and science and chose to enter an engineering curriculum, but he does not say why he chose engineering. He does not indicate whether this was based on an examination of his interests and abilities. Nonetheless, by the end of high school he had crystallized an occupation (engineering), and by the time he had graduated from college he had specified an occupation (industrial engineering). When he implemented that choice, however, he did not decide to pursue a traditional industrial engineering job; rather, he implemented his choice in engineering sales. It would seem that George was implementing a self-concept that combined engineering knowledge with greater use of interpersonal skills than a traditional engineering position would provide.

Developmental theory does not entirely explain some of George's decisions, however. Why did he choose industrial engineering, even though he felt engineering was not a good fit for him? Why did he continue in it, and how did he decide to go into engineering sales? Examining George's decisions from a social cognitive perspective may be useful in formulating hypotheses about his early choices. George reported that he knew he was good in math and science, thus indicating that he had high self-efficacy beliefs about his abilities in these areas. He attended his father's alma mater, in the same occupation as his father. It may be that George expected very positive outcomes from pursuing this avenue, such as strong approval from his father or other family members. What other occupations did George consider, and what were the barriers to pursuing those occupations?

Social cognitive theory may help to explain George's decisions when he quit his first job in engineering sales. He had high self-efficacy beliefs in his ability to find another job, and his outcome expectancies for leaving the position and finding a new job were more positive than the outcomes expected of staying. The TWA would explicate this further.

His correspondence with the first job was very poor; he may have tried to adjust himself or his environment, but despite being a satisfactory employee, his needs were not met and he chose to leave the environment. What may have been his adjustment style in that job? Has that been consistent in other jobs?

The TWA would suggest that George's subsequent jobs of owning an Oriental rug store and managing a restaurant were more correspondent occupations for him. Both of those jobs ended for reasons outside his control; there is no indication that he was dissatisfied in either position. In fact, he notes that he enjoyed them very much. It would appear that managing a restaurant met his compensation, social service, and achievement needs and that he was well able to do it, because the restaurant was quite successful. George is less correspondent with the occupation of financial planner. He complains that it is "no longer any fun," connoting that his needs are not being met. We would hypothesize that his social service needs, in particular, are not being met, as well, perhaps as his achievement needs.

George's current dilemma is what to do about his dissatisfaction with his job. Should he change jobs? The first approach we would take would be to talk with George about the context of this decision. What other factors are there that George needs to consider? He has two college-aged children; what responsibilities does he have for their education? How would a change in jobs or in life circumstances affect George's wife, and are there concomitant dual career concerns? Does he have aging parents for whom he is responsible? In other words, does this decision affect others? What about the context of his decision within the other roles George plays in his life? What role does he want work to have at this point? Are there other roles (e.g., leisurite, student, citizen) that may be just as salient for George, or that he would like to make more salient? What cultural messages does George have about the role of work in a man's life? Which of those messages would he like to include in the way he lives his life? He may, for example, decide that he likes to be the major breadwinner and provider in the family. On the other hand, he may choose to share this role with his wife if he returns to school.

We would incorporate the developmental perspective in examining George's life roles and the context of the decision. Another aspect of the developmental perspective we would include is encouraging George to talk about the development of his career as a financial planner. He has worked as a financial planner for 11 years; he may be moving out of the establishment stage into the maintenance stage and using this transition point to stop and examine his options.

One of the questions we would want to explore with George is whether it is the occupation of financial planner he is dissatisfied with or if he is feeling dissatisfaction with the specific job environment. This question is from the TWA approach. He is a satisfactory employee, but his needs and the rewards provided by the job do not correspond. Three options or combinations of options are possible. First, counseling may focus on either adjusting himself or his environment. Is it very important to him that his social service needs are met in the work environment, or can he meet those needs in other domains of his life? How amenable is the work environment to being adjusted? Is it possible to increase the social service activities he does as part of his job and reduce the activities he finds aversive? If this is not possible in this job, the second option is to determine if he would be more satisfied as a financial planner in another firm or agency.

The third option is that the activities he finds aversive are integral to the occupation of financial planner, and he will have to change his occupation to find a better fit. We would turn to Holland's theory to help George find a new occupational area. His General Occupational Theme code is SEA, with some moderate interest in investigative. This code illuminates the lack of fit for George as an engineer, an environment characterized as realistic and investigative. It also may illuminate why he has enjoyed a variety of enterprising types of occupations over the course of his career that capitalized on his experience in sales and his enterprising interests, such as owning a store and managing a restaurant. Financial manager is not an occupation included on the SII, nor is it included in the *Dictionary of Holland Occupational Codes* (Gottfredson & Holland, 1996). However, George is in an office that combines life insurance agents and financial planners, and life insurance agents have a Holland code of E on the SII. This would indicate that George has some interests that are congruent with his work environment but that he may be seeking an environment more congruent with his social interests. We would encourage George to begin to examine the occupations with a strong social component from the SII, such as nurse, parks and recreation leader, community service organization director, and special education teacher.

We would return to the questions raised earlier about context and life roles as George moves toward making a decision first about whether he would like to adjust to the occupation, move to another company, or choose a new career. Are these options that George would like to pursue, how do they fit in his life right now, and what would he need to do differently to fit them into his life in the future? How does this fit with the developmental stage he is in right now, and how he feels about the role of work in his life? How does he feel about taking on a role of student if he decides to go back to school for a teaching degree? How can George find out more information about the occupations he is considering?

## *Summary*

Each of the theoretical perspectives offers a different perspective about George's career history and his current career concerns. The theories also suggest different hypotheses and directions for counseling. As we just demonstrated, the theories are not necessarily incompatible or mutually exclusive, and there are benefits to using multiple approaches to conceptualize a single client. This is particularly true when the client has had considerable life and career experience. Now consider the case of Tom, who is a traditional college-aged student.

## THE CASE OF TOM

Tom is a 21-year-old Caucasian man of Irish descent, the younger of two brothers from a medium-sized town in the southern United States. He grew up in a lower-middle-class neighborhood; his mother works as a postal clerk and his father is an airplane mechanic. They live near many relatives, and much of the family's social life revolves around family celebrations and events.

Tom enjoyed high school. He was an average student. He enjoyed the material he learned in school, but his main goal in high school was to be with his friends. He was very social, and he participated in as many activities as he could while still playing football and basketball. He was an average athlete in high school, and he knew he could not compete athletically at the college level, but he had fun being a part of the team and playing when he could.

In contrast to Tom, his older brother, Jeff, was an outstanding student. He graduated from high school with a 4.0 grade point average, took several advanced placement courses, and received scholarships to many universities. He ended up attending a prestigious school about 70 miles away from his parents. Jeff is able to come home frequently and still participates in the family activities.

Tom and Jeff are 3½ years apart in age but are very close emotionally. Jeff was eager to give Tom advice about attending college and was very disappointed when Tom's grades were not high enough to enable him to attend the same university. Tom was unsure of whether to go to college or not. His parents, aunts, and uncles had not graduated from college, and he thought they were successful and happy. He is happy at home, enjoys his family, and enjoys his friends. Tom feels no particular need to leave his hometown or to move far away from his family. But his brother told him that increasingly more jobs require college degrees, and he would be severely hampered in the future if he did not go to college.

Tom enrolled in a college close to his hometown. He lived in a dorm with his cousin as his roommate. They went home frequently to be part of family gatherings. He had to declare a major when he enrolled, and he decided to major in police science. He thought it sounded good, and one of his friends was majoring in it. He had never really given much thought to choosing a major; his primary decision was whether to attend college or not. He had not had much career guidance in high school, so he really did not have a very clear idea of his interests or his alternatives.

Tom loved college life and became heavily involved in many of the social aspects of a residential college environment. He pledged a fraternity, made many friends, and decided to run for student government office. But he did not do well in his studies. His first year grades were slightly below a C average. He did even more poorly his second year. He had not realized that police science required such a strong math and science background; math was his weakest subject in high school. At the end of the first semester of his second year, Tom flunked out of college.

## Working With Tom

Use the following questions to consider how you are viewing Tom and how you might work with him in career counseling:

1. What are your impressions of Tom?
2. What more would you like to know about him?

3. What hypotheses would you develop about Tom from the perspective of each theory, including gender-focused and culturally appropriate approaches?

4. How will you gather information to test your hypotheses?

5. How does each of these theoretical approaches influence the next step in counseling? What direction would you take from the perspective of each, including gender-focused and culturally appropriate approaches?

## EVALUATION OF THE MAJOR THEORIES

One of the most important questions that readers should ask as they consider each of the theories presented in this book is, How well does it work? The next most important question should be, For whom does it work? These are critical questions and are answered by the research conducted on each theory by its author(s) and others in the field. The last column of Table 10.1 includes a brief evaluation of the level of empirical support for each theory. This is an overly simplistic summary evaluation, for we are not able to provide a comprehensive review of the empirical support for each theory. Readers are referred to Osipow and Fitzgerald (1996) and Brown and Brooks (1996) for extensive reviews of the empirical bases for these theories. However, this summary will provide some basis for evaluating the theories. We examined the literature related to each theory on the following criteria: how well the theoretical constructs have been operationalized, how much support those constructs have received, and how applicable each theory is across a wide variety of populations.

The theories in this book have all been developed by scholars dedicated to testing and revising their theories. Consequently, all have stimulated research in an attempt to support their constructs and the relationships among them. It is not surprising that the oldest theories (Holland's, the TWA, and Super's) are the most well researched and, consequently, and are the most well established of the theories.

Holland's theory has been operationalized in a number of instruments, among them the Strong Interest Inventory (Harmon, Hansen, Borgen, & Hammer, 1994) and the Self-Directed Search (Holland, Powell, & Fritzsche, 1994). With over 500 research studies conducted on it, Holland's theory has been the most extensively examined career theory (Osipow & Fitzgerald, 1996). One reason is how clearly and easily its constructs have been operationalized; Borgen (1991) notes that "its simplicity makes it eminently useful" (p. 274). For example, research has determined that the RIASEC types exist in both individuals and environments (Holland et al., 1994). Hypothesized relationships among constructs also have been supported. For example, congruence is related to satisfaction (Spokane, 1996), and the types appear to be related to each other as predicted by the theory (e.g., Day & Rounds, 1998; Fouad, Harmon, & Borgen, 1997).

The TWA also has received empirical support, although the constructs have not stimulated as much research as has Holland's theory. Several of the constructs are well operationalized, and one of the hallmarks of TWA is that the authors have developed tools to measure the constructs (e.g., Lofquist & Dawis, 1991). Support for the constructs is somewhat equivocal, although more support has been found for correspondence, satisfaction, and satisfactoriness than for the adjustment style and personality variables. Hackett, Lent, and Greenhaus (1991) and Osipow and Fitzgerald (1996) note that, unlike the extensive research on Holland's theory, empirical support for the TWA has come mostly from its authors and their students, with little independent verification.

Super's theory has been generally supported in over five decades of studies. As noted by Borgen (1991), "Super's comprehensive conceptual work has splendidly stood the test of time" (p. 278). Individuals' careers do develop as predicted by Super, and research supports the construct of self-concept implementation. Gottfredson's theory is the newer of the two developmental theories discussed here and is less well operationalized than Super's theory. It has received mixed empirical support, although Gottfredson (1996) notes that research has not tested many areas of the model.

Social learning theory has been described as the major new theoretical thrust of the 1970s (Hackett et al., 1991), and the same may be said of social cognitive career theory in the 1990s. Social learning theory is very well operationalized, although it has not stimulated much research, particularly in recent years. However, the research that has been conducted testing its constructs has been supportive. Hackett and Lent (1992) comment that much of the research supporting social learning theory has come from related models and that these have also supported the theory. Social cognitive theory, as the newest model in the book, has received the least amount of support. However, it is well operationalized and has already stimulated quite a bit of research since Hackett and Betz's (1981) introduction. Lent, Brown, and Hackett did not publish the full social cognitive career theory until 1994. Preliminary research summarized by Lent et al. (1996) is supportive of the model, although much more research is needed before conclusively stating that it is empirically supported.

All of the theories were developed with the intention of being applied across a wide variety of populations. However, all have been criticized (e.g., Fouad & Bingham, 1995; Hackett & Lent, 1992; Leong & Brown, 1995) for not incorporating gender and culture explicitly in the theory. All are equally open to criticism for not thoroughly examining how well the theory applies to various populations. In fact, most were originally developed based on research conducted on white, middle-class men. We simply do not know if the theories operate similarly for women and men, for individuals of different racial and ethnic groups, or for gay and lesbian individuals. If they do differ, we do not know specifically how, nor do we know how to incorporate that knowledge into more effective practice.

It is incumbent on researchers and practitioners alike to work together to create a joint research agenda that will more effectively inform practice. First, more research needs to be conducted on the theories themselves and whether the constructs in fact reflect reality. Second, we need to know if the theoretical relationship among constructs differs across populations. Third, we need to know what works for whom, and when; in other words, we need to know which particular interventions are effective with specific individuals at distinct times in their lives.

## TRAINING AND SKILL DEVELOPMENT

In Chapter 1, we described how to use career theories to guide your work with clients, primarily through generating and testing hypotheses about clients, and we hope that working with the cases in this text has convinced you of the value of doing so. Developing and implementing a theoretical approach to working with clients involves learning a set of skills, just like the process of learning any other counseling-related skills: It takes conscious attention and practice.

We recommend that you continue to hone your conceptualization skills by explicitly using them. Only with continued exercise does conceptualization become second nature. With every new client that you encounter, ask the following questions:

1. How and what am I thinking about this client?
2. What assumptions am I making about the client's career history? What assumptions am I making about the client's current career concerns?
3. Which theoretical approaches are most useful in thinking about this client, and what hypotheses do the approaches suggest?
4. What specific cultural and gender issues are relevant with this client?
5. How does my culture and gender influence how I am thinking about this client? Am I imposing my values on the client?

## PARTING WORDS

Finally, we want to return to the fundamental purpose of this book. We continue to be fascinated by the study of career development and by the career issues that clients bring to counseling. We sincerely hope that we have conveyed our excitement and enthusiasm in the pages of this book. We encourage you to allow yourself to be fascinated by career stories. Understanding the role that work plays in individuals' lives will serve to make you a better counselor and will help you assist the clients that come to you for counseling.

# References

Arbona, C. (1996). Career theory and practice in a multicultural context. In M. L. Savickas & W. B. Walsh (Eds.), *Handbook of career counseling theory and practice* (pp. 45-54). Palo Alto, CA: Davies-Black.

Bandura, A. (1977). Self-efficacy: Toward a unifying theory of behavioral change. *Psychological Review, 84,* 191-215.

Bandura, A. (1986). *Social foundations of thought and action.* Englewood Cliffs, NJ: Prentice Hall.

Bandura, A. (1997). *Self-efficacy: The exercise of control.* New York: Freeman.

Betz, N. E. (in press). Women's career development. In M. Paludi & F. Denmark (Eds.), *Handbook of the psychology of women.* Westport, CT: Greenwood.

Betz, N. E., Borgen, F. H., & Harmon, L. W. (1996). *Skills Confidence Inventory.* Palo Alto, CA: Consulting Psychologists Press.

Betz, N. E., & Corning, A. F. (1993). The inseparability of "career" and "personal" counseling. *Career Development Quarterly, 42,* 137-142.

Betz, N. E., & Fitzgerald, L. F. (1987). *The career psychology of women.* Orlando, FL: Academic Press.

Bingham, R. P., & Ward, C. M. (1994). Career counseling with ethnic minority women. In W. B. Walsh & S. Osipow (Eds.), *Career counseling with women* (pp. 165-195). Hillsdale, NJ: Lawrence Erlbaum.

Blustein, D. L., & Spengler, P. M. (1995). Personal adjustment: Career counseling and psychotherapy. In W. B. Walsh & S. H. Osipow (Eds.), *Handbook of vocational psychology* (2nd ed., pp. 295-320). Hillsdale, NJ: Lawrence Erlbaum.

Bordin, E. S. (1979). The generalizability of the psychoanalytic concept of working alliance. *Psychotherapy: Theory, Research, and Practice, 16,* 252-260.

Borgen, F. H. (1991). Megatrends and milestones in vocational behavior: A 20-year counseling psychology retrospective. *Journal of Vocational Behavior, 39,* 263-290.

Bowman, S. L. (1993). Career intervention strategies for ethnic minorities. *Career Development Quarterly, 41,* 14-25.

Bozarth, J. D., & Fisher, R. (1990). Person-centered career counseling. In W. B. Walsh & S. H. Osipow (Eds.), *Career counseling* (pp. 45-78). Mahwah, NJ: Lawrence Erlbaum.

Brooks, L., & Forrest, L. (1994). Feminism and career counseling. In W. B. Walsh & S. H. Osipow (Eds.), *Career counseling for women.* Hillsdale, NJ: Lawrence Erlbaum.

Brown, D., & Brooks, L. (1985). Career counseling as a mental health intervention. *Professional Psychology: Research and Practice, 16,* 860-867.

Brown, D., & Brooks, L. (1991). *Career counseling techniques.* Needham Heights, MA: Allyn & Bacon.

Brown, D., Brooks, L., & Associates (Eds.). (1996). *Career choice and development* (3rd ed.). San Francisco: Jossey-Bass.

Brown, D., Minor, C. W., & Jepsen, D. A. (1991). The opinions of minorities preparing for work: Report of the second NCDA National Survey. *Career Development Quarterly, 40,* 5-19.

Brown, L. S. (1986). Gender role analysis: A neglected component of psychological assessment. *Psychotherapy: Theory, Research, Practice, Training, 23,* 243-248.

Brown, L. S. (1990). Taking account of gender in the clinical assessment interview. *Professional Psychology: Research and Practice, 21,* 12-17.

Brown, S. D., & Lent, R. W. (1996). A social cognitive framework for career choice counseling. *Career Development Quarterly, 44,* 354-366.

Chartrand, J. M. (1991). The evolution of trait-and-factor career counseling: A person X environment fit approach. *Journal of Counseling and Development, 69,* 518-524.

Cook, E. P. (1993). The gendered context of life: Implications for women's and men's career-life plans. *Career Development Quarterly, 41,* 227-237.

Davidson, S. L., & Gilbert, L. A. (1993). Career counseling is a personal matter. *Career Development Quarterly, 42,* 149-155.

Dawis, R. V. (1994). The theory of work adjustment as convergent theory. In M. L. Savickas & R. W. Lent (Eds.), *Convergence in career development theories* (pp. 33-43). Palo Alto, CA: Consulting Psychologists Press.

Dawis, R. V. (1996). The theory of work adjustment and person-environment-correspondence counseling. In D. Brown, L. Brooks, & Associates (Eds.), *Career choice and development* (3rd ed., pp. 75-120). San Francisco: Jossey-Bass.

Dawis, R. V., & Lofquist, L. H. (1984). *A psychological theory of work adjustment.* Minneapolis: University of Minnesota Press.

Day, S. X., & Rounds, J. (1998). Universality of vocational interest structure among racial and ethnic minorities. *American Psychologist, 53,* 728-736.

Dewey, C. R. (1974). Exploring interests: A nonsexist method. *Personnel and Guidance Journal, 52,* 311-315.

Dolliver, R. H. (1969). An adaptation of the Tyler Vocational Card Sort. *Personnel and Guidance Journal, 45,* 916-920.

Duckworth, J. (1990). The counseling approach to the use of testing. *The Counseling Psychologist, 18,* 198-204.

Erikson, E. H. (1968). *Identity: Youth and crisis.* New York: Norton.

Fitzgerald, L. F. (1986). Career counseling women: Principles, procedures and problems. In Z. Leibowitz & D. Lea (Eds.), *Adult career development: Concepts, issues and practices.* Alexandria, VA: American Association of Counseling and Development.

Fitzgerald, L. F., & Betz, N. E. (1994). Career development in cultural context: The role of gender, race, class, and sexual orientation. In M. L. Savickas & R. W. Lent (Eds.), *Convergence in career development theories: Implications for science and practice* (pp. 103-117). Palo Alto, CA: Consulting Psychologists Press.

Fitzgerald, L. F., & Weitzman, L. M. (1992). Women's career development: Theory and practice from a feminist perspective. In H. D. Lea & Z. B. Leibowitz (Eds.), *Adult career development: Concepts, issues and practices* (2nd ed., pp. 124-160). Alexandria, VA: National Career Development Association.

Flamer, S. (1986). Clinical-career intervention with adults: Low visibility, high need? *Journal of Community Psychology, 14,* 224-227.

Forrest, L., & Brooks, L. (1993). Feminism and career assessment. *Journal of Career Assessment, 1,* 233-245.

Fouad, N. A. (1993). Cross-cultural vocational assessment. *Career Development Quarterly, 42,* 4-13.

Fouad, N. A., & Bingham, R. (1995). Career counseling with racial/ethnic minorities. In W. B. Walsh & S. H. Osipow (Eds.), *Handbook of vocational psychology* (2nd ed., pp. 331-366). Hillsdale, NJ: Lawrence Erlbaum.

Fouad, N. A., Harmon, L. W., & Borgen, F. H. (1997). Structure of interests of employed male and female members of U.S. racial-ethnic minority and nonminority groups. *Journal of Counseling Psychology, 44,* 339-345.

Gannon, L. (1982). The role of power in psychotherapy. *Women and Therapy, 1*(2), 3-11.

Gilligan, C. (1982). *In a different voice: Psychological theory and women's development.* Cambridge, MA: Harvard University Press.

Giordano, J., & McGoldrick, M. (1996). European families: An overview. In M. McGoldrick, J. Giordano, & J. K. Pearce (Eds.), *Ethnicity and family therapy* (pp. 427-441). New York: Guilford.

Gold, J. M., & Scanlon, C. R. (1993). Psychological distress and counseling duration of career and noncareer clients. *Career Development Quarterly, 42,* 186-191.

Good, G. E., Gilbert, L. A., & Scher, M. (1990). Gender aware therapy: A synthesis of feminist therapy and knowledge about gender. *Journal of Counseling and Development, 68,* 376-380.

Gottfredson, G. D., & Holland, J. L. (1996). *Dictionary of Holland occupational codes* (3rd ed.). Palo Alto, CA: Consulting Psychologists Press.

Gottfredson, L. S. (1996). Gottfredson's theory of circumscription and compromise. In D. Brown, L. Brooks, & Associates (Eds.), *Career choice and development* (3rd ed., pp. 179-232). San Francisco: Jossey-Bass.

Gysbers, N. C., Heppner, M. J., & Johnston, J. A. (1998). *Career counseling: Process, issues, and techniques.* Boston: Allyn & Bacon.

Hackett, G. (1993). Career counseling and psychotherapy: False dichotomies and recommended remedies. *Journal of Career Assessment, 1,* 105-117.

Hackett, G., & Lent, R. W. (1992). Theoretical advances and current inquiry in career psychology. In S. D. Brown & R. W. Lent (Eds.), *Handbook of counseling psychology* (pp. 419-451). New York: John Wiley.

Hackett, G., Lent, R. W., & Greenhaus, J. H. (1991). Advances in vocational theory and research: A 20-year retrospective. *Journal of Vocational Behavior, 38,* 3-38.

Hackett, N. E., & Betz, N. (1981). A self-efficacy approach to the career development of women. *Journal of Vocational Behavior, 18,* 326-339.

Hare-Mustin, R. T., & Marecek, J. (1988). The meaning of difference: Gender theory, postmodernism, and psychology. *American Psychologist, 43,* 455-464.

Harmon, L. W. (1997). Do gender differences necessitate separate career development theories and measures? *Journal of Career Assessment, 5,* 463-470.

Harmon, L. W., Hansen, J. C., Borgen, F. H., & Hammer, A. C. (1994). *Strong Interest Inventory: Applications and technical guide.* Palo Alto, CA: Consulting Psychologists Press.

Hartung, P. J., Vandiver, B. J., Leong, F. T. L., Pope, M., Niles, S. G., & Farrow, B. (1998). Appraising cultural identity in career development assessment and counseling. *Career Development Quarterly, 46,* 276-293.

Haverkamp, B. E., & Moore, D. (1993). The career-personal dichotomy: Perceptual reality, practical illusion, and workplace integration. *Career Development Quarterly, 42,* 154-160.

Heppner, P. P., Reeder, B. L., & Larsen, L. M. (1983). Cognitive variables associated with personal problem-solving appraisal: Implications for counseling. *Journal of Counseling Psychology, 30,* 537-545.

Herr, E. L. (1989). Career development and mental health. *Journal of Career Development, 16*(1), 5-18.

Herr, E. L. (1997). Super's life-span, life-space approach and its outlook for refinement. *Career Development Quarterly, 45,* 238-246.

Holland, D. C., & Eisenhart, M. A. (1990). *Educated in romance: Women, achievement, and college culture.* Chicago: University of Chicago Press.

Holland, J. L. (1994). *The occupations finder.* Odessa, FL: Psychological Assessment Resources.

Holland, J. L. (1996). Integrating career theory and practice: The current situation and some potential remedies. In M. L. Savickas & W. B. Walsh (Eds.), *Handbook of career counseling theory and practice.* Palo Alto, CA: Davies-Black.

Holland, J. L. (1997). *Making vocational choices: A theory of vocational personalities and work environments* (3rd ed.). Odessa, FL: Psychological Assessment Resources.

Holland, J. L., & Gottfredson, G. D. (1994). *CASI: Career Attitudes and Strategies Inventory: An inventory for understanding adult careers.* Odessa, FL: Psychological Assessment Resources.

Holland, J. L., Powell, A. B., & Fritzsche, B. A. (1994). *The Self-Directed Search professional user's guide.* Odessa, FL: Psychological Assessment Resources.

Janis, I., & Mann, L. (1977). *Decision-making: A psychological analysis of conflict, choice, and commitment.* New York: Free Press.

Kapes, J. T., Mastie, M. M., & Whitfield, E. A. (1994). *A counselor's guide to career assessment instruments.* Alexandria, VA: National Career Development Association.

Katz, J. H. (1985). The sociopolitical nature of counseling. *The Counseling Psychologist, 13,* 615-624.

Krumboltz, J. (1991). *Manual for the Career Beliefs Inventory.* Palo Alto, CA: Consulting Psychologists Press.

Krumboltz, J. D. (1993). Integrating career and personal counseling. *Career Development Quarterly, 42,* 143-148.

Krumboltz, J. D. (1994). Improving career development theory from a social learning perspective. In M. L. Savickas & R. W. Lent (Eds.), *Convergence in career development theories* (pp. 9-31). Palo Alto, CA: Consulting Psychologists Press.

Krumboltz, J. D. (1996). A learning theory of career counseling. In M. L. Savickas & W. B. Walsh (Eds.), *Handbook of career counseling theory and practice* (pp. 55-80). Palo Alto, CA: Davies-Black.

Krumboltz, J. D., & Jackson, M. A. (1993). Career assessment as a learning tool. *Journal of Career Assessment, 1,* 393-409.

Kummerow, J. M. (Ed.). (1991). *New directions in career planning and the workplace.* Palo Alto, CA: Consulting Psychologists Press.

Lent, R. W., Brown, S. D., & Hackett, G. (1994). Toward a unifying social cognitive theory of career and academic interest, choice, and performance. *Journal of Vocational Behavior, 45,* 79-122.

Lent, R. W., Brown, S. D., & Hackett, G. (1996). Career development from a social cognitive perspective. In D. Brown, L. Brooks, & Associates (Eds.), *Career choice and development* (3rd ed., pp. 373-422). San Francisco: Jossey-Bass.

Lent, R. W., & Savickas, M. L. (1994). Is convergence a viable agenda for career psychology? In M. L. Savickas & R. W. Lent (Eds.), *Convergence in career development theories* (pp. 259-271). Palo Alto, CA: Consulting Psychologists Press.

Leong, F. T. L. (Ed.). (1995). *Career development and vocational behavior of racial and ethnic minorities.* Mahwah, NJ: Lawrence Erlbaum.

Leong, F. T. L., & Brown, M. T. (1995). Theoretical issues in cross-cultural career development: Cultural validity and cultural specificity. In W. B. Walsh & S. H. Osipow (Eds.), *Handbook of vocational psychology* (2nd ed., pp. 143-180). Hillsdale, NJ: Lawrence Erlbaum.

Leong, F. T. L., & Hartung, P. J. (1997). Career assessment with culturally different clients: Proposing an integrative-sequential conceptual framework for cross-cultural career counseling research and practice. *Journal of Career Assessment, 5,* 183-201.

Leung, S. A. (1995). Career development and counseling: A multicultural perspective. In J. G. Ponterotto, J. M. Casas, L. A. Suzuki, & C. M. Alexander (Eds.), *Handbook of multicultural counseling* (pp. 549-566). Thousand Oaks, CA: Sage.

Levin, A. S., Krumboltz, J. D., & Krumboltz, B. L. (1995). *Exploring your career beliefs: A workbook for the Career Beliefs Inventory with techniques for integrating your Strong and MBTI results.* Palo Alto, CA: Consulting Psychologists Press.

Lofquist, L. H., & Dawis, R. V. (1991). *Essentials of person-environment-correspondence counseling.* Minneapolis: University of Minnesota Press.

Long, B. S., Kahn, S. E., & Schutz, R. W. (1992). A causal model of stress and coping: Women in management. *Journal of Counseling Psychology, 39,* 337-239.

Lucas, M. S. (1992). Problems expressed by career and non-career help seekers: A comparison. *Journal of Counseling and Development, 70,* 417-420.

Lucas, M. S. (1996). Building cohesiveness between practitioners and researchers: A practitioner-scientist model. In M. L. Savickas & W. B. Walsh (Eds.), *Handbook of career counseling theory and practice* (pp. 81-88). Palo Alto, CA: Davies-Black.

Marecek, J., & Kravetz, D. (1977). Women and mental health: A review of feminist change efforts. *Psychiatry, 40,* 323-329.

Meara, N. M., & Patton, M. J. (1994). Contributions of the working alliance in the practice of career counseling. *Career Development Quarterly, 43,* 161-177.

Mintz, L. B., & O'Neil, J. M. (1990). Gender roles, sex, and the process of psychotherapy: Many questions and few answers. *Journal of Counseling and Development, 68,* 381-387.

Mitchell, K. E., Levin, A. S., & Krumboltz, J. D. (in press). Planned happenstance: Constructing unexpected career opportunities. *Journal of Counseling and Development.*

Mitchell, L. K., & Krumboltz, J. D. (1990). Social learning approach to career decision making: Krumboltz's theory. In D. Brown, L. Brooks, & Associates (Eds.), *Career choice and development: Applying contemporary theories to practice* (2nd ed.). San Francisco: Jossey-Bass.

Mitchell, L. K., & Krumboltz, J. D. (1996). Krumboltz's learning theory of career choice and counseling. In D. Brown, L. Brooks, & Associates (Eds.), *Career choice and development* (3rd ed., pp. 233-280). San Francisco: Jossey-Bass.

Myers, I. B., & McCaulley, M. H. (1985). *Manual: A guide to the development and use of the Myers-Briggs Type Indicator.* Palo Alto, CA: Consulting Psychologists Press.

National Career Development Association. (1997). *Career counseling competencies.* Columbus, OH: Author.

Neville, H. A., Gysbers, N. C., Heppner, M. J., & Johnston, J. (1998). Empowering life choices: Career counseling in cultural contexts. In N. C. Gysbers, M. J. Heppner, & J. Johnston, *Career counseling: Process, issues, and techniques.* Boston: Allyn & Bacon.

Osborne, W. L., Brown, S., Niles, S., & Miner, C. U. (1997). *Career development, assessment, and counseling: Applications of the Donald E. Super C-DAC approach.* Alexandria, VA: American Counseling Association.

Osipow, S. H. (1996). Does career theory guide practice or does career practice guide theory? In M. L. Savickas & W. B. Walsh (Eds.), *Handbook of career counseling theory and practice* (pp. 403-409). Palo Alto, CA: Davies-Black.

Osipow, S. H., & Fitzgerald, L. (1996). *Theories of career development* (4th ed.). Needham Heights, MA: Allyn & Bacon.

Parsons, F. (1909/1989). *Choosing a vocation.* Garrett Park, MD: Garrett Park Press. (Original work published in 1909)

Phillips, S. D., Friedlander, M. L., Kost, P. P., Specterman, R. V., & Robbins, E. S. (1988). Personal versus vocational focus in career counseling: A retrospective outcome study. *Journal of Counseling and Development, 67,* 169-173.

Pinkerton, R. S., Etzel, E. F., Rockwell, J. K., Talley, J. E., & Moorman, J. C. (1990). Psychotherapy and career counseling: Toward an integration for use with college students. *College Health, 39*(3), 129-136.

Ponterotto, J. G., & Casas, J. M. (1991). *Handbook of racial/ethnic minority counseling research.* Springfield, IL: Charles C Thomas.

Rounds, J. B., Henley, G. A., Dawis, R. V., Lofquist, L. H., & Weiss, D. J. (1981). *Manual for the Minnesota Importance Questionnaire.* Minneapolis, MN: University of Minnesota.

Rounds, J. B., & Tracey, T. J. (1990). From trait-and-factor to person-environment fit counseling: Theory and process. In W. B. Walsh & S. H. Osipow (Eds.), *Career counseling: Contemporary topics in vocational psychology* (pp. 1-44). Hillsdale, NJ: Lawrence Erlbaum.

Savickas, M. L. (1994). Measuring career development: Current status and future directions. *Career Development Quarterly, 43,* 54-62.

Savickas, M. L. (1997). Career adaptability: An integrative construct for life-span, life-space theory. *Career Development Quarterly, 45,* 247-259.

Savickas, M. L., & Lent, R. W. (Eds.). (1994). *Convergence in career development theories.* Palo Alto, CA: Consulting Psychologists Press.

Savickas, M. L., & Walsh, W. B. (Eds.). (1996). *Handbook of career counseling theory and practice.* Palo Alto, CA: Davies-Black.

Seligman, L. (1994). *Developmental career counseling and assessment* (2nd ed.). Thousand Oaks, CA: Sage.

Sharf, R. S. (1997). *Applying career development theory to counseling* (2nd ed.). Pacific Grove, CA: Brooks/Cole.

Spokane, A. R. (1989). Are there psychological and mental health consequences of difficult career decisions? *Journal of Career Development, 16*(1), 19-23.

Spokane, A. R. (1991). *Career intervention.* Englewood Cliffs, NJ: Prentice Hall.

Spokane, A. R. (1996). Holland's theory. In D. Brown, L. Brooks, & Associates (Eds.), *Career choice and development* (3rd ed., pp. 33-74). San Francisco: Jossey-Bass.

Spokane, A. R., & Fretz, B. R. (1993). Forty cases: A framework for studying the effects of career counseling on career and personal adjustment. *Journal of Career Assessment, 1,* 118-129.

Sturdivant, S. (1980). *Therapy with women: A feminist philosophy of treatment.* New York: Springer.

Sue, D. W., Carter, R. T., Casas, J. M., Fouad, N. A., Ivey, A. E., Jensen, M., LaFromboise, T., Manese, J., Ponterotto, J. G., & Vasquez, E. N. (1998). *Multicultural counseling competencies: Individual, professional and organizational development.* Thousand Oaks, CA: Sage.

Sue, D. W., & Sue, D. (1990). *Counseling the culturally different: Theory and practice* (2nd ed.). New York: John Wiley.

Super, D. E. (1953). A theory of vocational development. *American Psychologist, 8,* 185-190.

Super, D. E. (1957). *The psychology of careers.* New York: Harper Collins.

Super, D. E. (1980). A life-span, life-space approach to career development. *Journal of Vocational Behavior, 13,* 282-298.

Super, D. E. (1983). Assessment in career counseling: Toward truly developmental counseling. *Personnel and Guidance Journal, 61,* 555-562.

Super, D. E., Osborne, W. L., Walsh, D. J., Brown, S. D., & Niles, S. G. (1992). Developmental career assessment and counseling: The C-DAC. *Journal of Counseling and Development, 71,* 74-80.

Super, D. E., Savickas, M. L., & Super, C. M. (1996). The life-span, life-space approach to careers. In D. Brown, L. Brooks, & Associates (Eds.), *Career choice and development* (3rd ed., pp. 121-178). San Francisco: Jossey-Bass.

Super, D. E., Thompson, A. S., & Lindeman, R. H. (1988). *Adult Career Concerns Inventory: Manual for research and exploratory use in counseling.* Palo Alto, CA: Consulting Psychologists Press.

Swanson, J. L. (1995). The process and outcome of career counseling. In W. B. Walsh & S. H. Osipow (Eds.), *Handbook of vocational psychology* (2nd ed., pp. 217-259). Hillsdale, NJ: Lawrence Erlbaum.

Swanson, J. L., & Chu, S. P. (in press). Applications of person-environment psychology to the career development and vocational behavior of adolescents and adults. In W. E. Martin, Jr. & J. L. Swartz (Eds.), *Person-environment psychology: Mental health strategies with adolescents and adults.* Mahwah, NJ: Lawrence Erlbaum.

Swanson, J. L., Daniels, K. K., & Tokar, D. M. (1996). Assessing perceptions of career-related barriers: The Career Barriers Inventory. *Journal of Career Assessment, 4,* 219-244.

Swanson, J. L., & Woitke, M. B. (1997). Theory into practice in career assessment: Assessing women's career barriers. *Journal of Career Assessment, 5,* 443-462.

Walborn, F. S. (1996). *Process variables: Four common elements of counseling and psychotherapy.* Pacific Grove, CA: Brooks/Cole.

Walsh, W. B., & Osipow, S. H. (Eds.). (1994). *Career counseling for women.* Hillsdale, NJ: Lawrence Erlbaum.

Walsh, W. B., Price, R. H., & Craik, K. H. (1992). Person-environment psychology: An introduction. In W. B. Walsh, K. H. Craik, & R. H. Price (Eds.), *Person-environment psychology: Models and perspectives* (pp. vii-xi). Mahwah, NJ: Lawrence Erlbaum.

Ward, C. M., & Bingham, R. P. (1993). Career assessment of ethnic minority women. *Journal of Career Assessment, 1,* 246-257.

Watkins, C. E., Jr., & Campbell, V. L. (1990). Testing and assessment in counseling psychology: Contemporary developments and issues. *The Counseling Psychologist, 18,* 189-197.

Watkins, C. E., Jr., & Savickas, M. L. (1990). Psychodynamic career counseling. In W. B. Walsh & S. H. Osipow (Eds.), *Career counseling* (pp. 79-116). Mahwah, NJ: Lawrence Erlbaum.

Williams, C. P., & Savickas, M. L. (1990). Developmental tasks of career maintenance. *Journal of Vocational Behavior, 36,* 166-175.

Worrell, J., & Remer, P. (1992). *Feminist perspectives in therapy: An empowerment model for women.* New York: John Wiley.

# Appendix A

# *Suggested Readings*

## TEXTBOOKS FOCUSING ON THEORIES OF CAREER DEVELOPMENT

Brown, D., Brooks, L., & Associates (Eds.). (1996). *Career choice and development* (3rd ed.). San Francisco: Jossey-Bass.

Osipow, S. H., & Fitzgerald, L. (1996). *Theories of career development* (4th ed.). Needham Heights, MA: Allyn & Bacon.

Savickas, M. L., & Lent, R. W. (1994). *Convergence in career development theories.* Palo Alto, CA: Consulting Psychologists Press.

Savickas, M. L., & Walsh, W. B. (1996). *Handbook of career counseling theory and practice.* Palo Alto, CA: Davies-Black.

Sharf, R. S. (1997). *Applying career development theory to counseling* (2nd ed.). Pacific Grove, CA: Brooks/Cole.

Walsh, W. B., & Osipow, S. H. (1990). *Career counseling: Contemporary topics in vocational psychology.* Hillsdale, NJ: Lawrence Erlbaum.

## ADDITIONAL READINGS FOR EACH THEORY

### *Holland's Theory (Chapter 3)*

Holland, J. L. (1997). *Making vocational choices: A theory of vocational personalities and work environments* (3rd ed.). Odessa, FL: Psychological Assessment Resources.

Spokane, A. R. (1996). Holland's theory. In D. Brown, L. Brooks, & Associates (Eds.), *Career choice and development* (3rd ed., pp. 33-74). San Francisco: Jossey-Bass.

## Theory of Work Adjustment (Chapter 4)

Dawis, R. V. (1996). The theory of work adjustment and person-environment-correspondence counseling. In D. Brown, L. Brooks, & Associates (Eds.), *Career choice and development* (3rd ed., pp. 75-120). San Francisco: Jossey-Bass.

Dawis, R. V., & Lofquist, L. H. (1984). *A psychological theory of work adjustment.* Minneapolis: University of Minnesota Press.

Lofquist, L. H., & Dawis, R. V. (1991). *Essentials of person-environment-correspondence counseling.* Minneapolis: University of Minnesota Press.

## Developmental Theories (Chapter 5)

Gottfredson, L. S. (1981). Circumscription and compromise: A developmental theory of occupational aspirations [Monograph]. *Journal of Counseling Psychology, 28,* 545-579.

Gottfredson, L. S. (1996). Gottfredson's theory of circumscription and compromise. In D. Brown, L. Brooks, & Associates (Eds.), *Career choice and development* (3rd ed., pp. 179-232). San Francisco: Jossey-Bass.

Super, D. E. (1994). A life-span, life-space perspective on convergence. In M. L. Savickas & R. W. Lent (Eds.), *Convergence in career development theories* (pp. 63-74). Palo Alto, CA: Consulting Psychologists Press.

Super, D. E., Savickas, M. L., & Super, C. M. (1996). The life-span, life-space approach to careers. In D. Brown, L. Brooks, & Associates (Eds.), *Career choice and development* (3rd ed., pp. 121-178). San Francisco: Jossey-Bass.

## Krumboltz's Social Learning Theory (Chapter 6)

Krumboltz, J. D. (1994). A learning theory of career counseling. In M. L. Savickas & W. B. Walsh (Eds.), *Handbook of career counseling theory and practice* (pp. 55-80). Palo Alto, CA: Consulting Psychologists Press.

Mitchell, L. K., & Krumboltz, J. D. (1996). Krumboltz's learning theory of career choice and counseling. In D. Brown, L. Brooks, & Associates (Eds.), *Career choice and development* (3rd ed., pp. 233-280). San Francisco: Jossey-Bass.

## Social Cognitive Career Theory (Chapter 7)

Lent, R. W., Brown, S. D., & Hackett, G. (1994). Toward a unifying social cognitive theory of career and academic interest, choice, and performance. *Journal of Vocational Behavior, 45,* 79-122.

Lent, R. W., Brown, S. B., & Hackett, G. (1996). Career development from a social cognitive perspective. In D. Brown, L. Brooks, & Associates (Eds.), *Career choice and development* (3rd ed., pp. 373-422). San Francisco: Jossey-Bass.

## Gender-Aware and Feminist Approaches (Chapter 8)

Betz, N. E., & Fitzgerald, L. F. (1987). *The career psychology of women*. Orlando, FL: Academic Press.

Brooks, L., & Forrest, L. (1994). Feminism and career counseling. In W. B. Walsh & S. H. Osipow (Eds.), *Career counseling for women*. Hillsdale, NJ: Lawrence Erlbaum.

Fitzgerald, L. F., & Weitzman, L. M. (1992). Women's career development: Theory and practice from a feminist perspective. In H. D. Lea & Z. B. Leibowitz (Eds.), *Adult career development: Concepts, issues and practices* (2nd ed., pp. 124-160). Alexandria, VA: National Career Development Association.

Forrest, L., & Brooks, L. (1993). Feminism and career assessment. *Journal of Career Assessment, 1*, 233-245.

Good, G. E., Gilbert, L. A., & Scher, M. (1990). Gender aware therapy: A synthesis of feminist therapy and knowledge about gender. *Journal of Counseling and Development, 68*, 376-380.

## Culturally Appropriate Career Counseling (Chapter 9)

Fouad, N. A. (1993). Cross-cultural vocational assessment. *Career Development Quarterly, 42*, 4-13.

Fouad, N. A., & Bingham, R. (1995). Career counseling with racial/ethnic minorities. In W. B. Walsh & S. H. Osipow (Eds.), *Handbook of vocational psychology* (2nd ed., pp. 331-366). Hillsdale, NJ: Lawrence Erlbaum.

Leong, F. T. L. (1995). *Career development and vocational behavior of racial and ethnic minorities*. Mahwah, NJ: Lawrence Erlbaum.

Leong, F. T. L., & Brown, M. T. (1995). Theoretical issues in cross-cultural career development: Cultural validity and cultural specificity. In W. B. Walsh & S. H. Osipow (Eds.), *Handbook of vocational psychology* (2nd ed., pp. 143-180). Hillsdale, NJ: Lawrence Erlbaum.

# Appendix B

## Leslie's Profiles

SKILLS CONFIDENCE EDITION

| Profile report for | LESLIE | 7601 |
| ID: | | |
| Age: | 0 | Date tested: 10/21/97 |
| Gender: | Female | Date scored: 7/30/98 |

Page 1 of 6

## SNAPSHOT: A SUMMARY OF RESULTS FOR

### LESLIE

### GENERAL OCCUPATIONAL THEMES

The General Occupational Themes describe interests in six very broad areas, including interest in work and leisure activities, kinds of people, and work settings. Your interests in each area are shown at the right in rank order. Note that each Theme has a code, represented by the first letter of the Theme name.

You can use your Theme code, printed below your results, to identify school subjects, part-time jobs, college majors, leisure activities, or careers that you might find interesting. See the back of this Profile for suggestions on how to use your Theme code.

| THEME CODE | THEME | VERY LITTLE INTEREST | LITTLE INTEREST | AVERAGE INTEREST | HIGH INTEREST | VERY HIGH INTEREST | TYPICAL INTERESTS |
|---|---|---|---|---|---|---|---|
| S | SOCIAL | ☐ | ☐ | ☐ | ☐ | ☑ | Helping, instructing |
| C | CONVENTIONAL | ☐ | ☐ | ☐ | ☑ | ☐ | Accounting, processing data |
| I | INVESTIGATIVE | ☐ | ☐ | ☐ | ☑ | ☐ | Researching, analyzing |
| R | REALISTIC | ☐ | ☐ | ☑ | ☐ | ☐ | Building, repairing |
| E | ENTERPRISING | ☐ | ☑ | ☐ | ☐ | ☐ | Selling, managing |
| A | ARTISTIC | ☑ | ☐ | ☐ | ☐ | ☐ | Creating or enjoying art |

Your Theme code is SCI—(see explanation at left).

You might explore occupations with codes that contain any combination of these letters.

### BASIC INTEREST SCALES

The Basic Interest Scales measure your interests in 25 specific areas or activities. Only those 5 areas in which you show the *most* interest are listed at the right in rank order. Your results on all 25 Basic Interest Scales are found on page 2.

To the left of each scale is a letter that shows which of the six General Occupational Themes this activity is most closely related to. These codes can help you to identify other activities that you may enjoy.

| THEME CODE | BASIC INTEREST | VERY LITTLE INTEREST | LITTLE INTEREST | AVERAGE INTEREST | HIGH INTEREST | VERY HIGH INTEREST | TYPICAL ACTIVITIES |
|---|---|---|---|---|---|---|---|
| I | MATHEMATICS | ☐ | ☐ | ☐ | ☐ | ☑ | Working with numbers or statistics |
| C | DATA MANAGEMENT | ☐ | ☐ | ☐ | ☐ | ☑ | Analyzing data for decision making |
| S | TEACHING | ☐ | ☐ | ☐ | ☐ | ☑ | Instructing young people |
| S | RELIGIOUS ACTIVITIES | ☐ | ☐ | ☐ | ☑ | ☐ | Participating in spiritual activities |
| I | SCIENCE | ☐ | ☐ | ☐ | ☑ | ☐ | Conducting scientific research |

### OCCUPATIONAL SCALES

The Occupational Scales measure how similar your interests are to the interests of people who are satisfied working in those occupations. Only the 10 scales on which your interests are *most* similar to those of these people are listed at the right in rank order. Your results on all 211 of the Occupational Scales are found on pages 3, 4, and 5.

The letters to the left of each scale identify the Theme or Themes that most closely describe the interests of people working in that occupation. You can use these letters to find additional, related occupations that you might find interesting. After reviewing your results on all six pages of this Profile, see the back of page 5 for tips on finding other occupations in the Theme or Themes that interest you the most.

| THEME CODE | OCCUPATION | VERY DISSIMILAR | DISSIMILAR | MID-RANGE | SIMILAR | VERY SIMILAR |
|---|---|---|---|---|---|---|
| CI | ACTUARY | ☐ | ☐ | ☐ | ☐ | ☑ |
| IR | COMPUTER PROGR./SYSTEMS ANALYST | ☐ | ☐ | ☐ | ☐ | ☑ |
| CIR | MATHEMATICS TEACHER | ☐ | ☐ | ☐ | ☐ | ☑ |
| IR | CHEMIST | ☐ | ☐ | ☐ | ☐ | ☑ |
| IRC | MATHEMATICIAN | ☐ | ☐ | ☐ | ☐ | ☑ |
| CE | ACCOUNTANT | ☐ | ☐ | ☐ | ☑ | ☐ |
| IRA | BIOLOGIST | ☐ | ☐ | ☐ | ☑ | ☐ |
| C | BOOKKEEPER | ☐ | ☐ | ☐ | ☑ | ☐ |
| ICR | PHARMACIST | ☐ | ☐ | ☐ | ☑ | ☐ |
| IRA | PHYSICIST | ☐ | ☐ | ☐ | ☑ | ☐ |

**PERSONAL STYLE SCALES** measure your levels of comfort regarding Work Style, Learning Environment, Leadership Style, and Risk Taking/Adventure. This information may help you make decisions about particular work environments, educational settings, and types of activities you would find satisfying. Your results on these four scales are on page 6.

8657

*CPP* CONSULTING PSYCHOLOGISTS PRESS, INC. • 3803 E. Bayshore Road, Palo Alto, CA 94303

**Figure 1.** Leslie's Strong Interest Inventory Profile

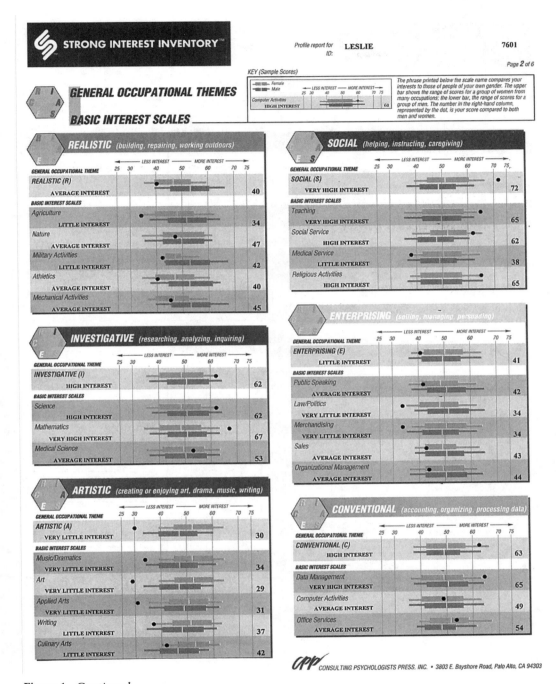

Figure 1. *Continued*

(continued)

## STRONG INTEREST INVENTORY™

Profile report for    **LESLIE**
ID:

7601

Page 3 of 6

KEY (Sample Scores)

| THEME CODES | YOUR SCORES | DISSIMILAR INTERESTS ——— SIMILAR INTERESTS |
| FEMALE MALE | FEMALE MALE | 15    20    30—MID-RANGE—40    50    55 |
| IES (SEC) Dietitian | 25 (SEC) | |
| * R Plumber | * 35 | |

( ) You can find your score compared to this gender under the Theme represented by the first letter of this code. For example, your score compared to male dietitians is shown under the S or Social Theme.

• The position of the dot shows how similar your interests are to those of individuals of your gender who say they are satisfied in their occupation.

* Not enough people of this gender who work in this occupation could be found to make a good comparison.

### OCCUPATIONAL SCALES

NOTES

## REALISTIC (building, repairing, working outdoors)

| THEME CODES FEMALE MALE | | YOUR SCORES FEMALE MALE | DISSIMILAR INTERESTS 15 20 30—MID-RANGE—40 50 SIMILAR INTERESTS 55 |
|---|---|---|---|
| RIS | (SIR) | Athletic Trainer | 5 (SIR) | |
| R | R | Auto Mechanic | 21 28 | |
| RIA | REA | Carpenter | 7 8 | |
| RIA | RIC | Electrician | 17 6 | |
| RCI | RI | Emergency Medical Technician | 19 20 | |
| RI | RI | Engineer | 40 41 | |
| (CSE) | RC | Farmer | (CSE) 36 | |
| RI | RI | Forester | 31 36 | |
| RC | RE | Gardener/Groundskeeper | 15 6 | |
| REI | REI | Horticultural Worker | 7 5 | |
| (CRE) | RCE | Military Enlisted Personnel | (CRE) 20 | |
| REI | REC | Military Officer | 12 18 | |
| * | R | Plumber | * 20 | |
| RE | R | Police Officer | 21 16 | |
| RIS | RI | Radiologic Technologist | 32 40 | |
| (CE) | RE | Small Business Owner | (CE) 11 | |
| RSI | RSE | Vocational Agriculture Teacher | 25 26 | |

## INVESTIGATIVE (researching, analyzing, inquiring)

| THEME CODES FEMALE MALE | | YOUR SCORES FEMALE MALE | DISSIMILAR INTERESTS 15 20 30—MID-RANGE—40 50 SIMILAR INTERESTS 55 |
|---|---|---|---|
| IS | IA | Audiologist | 43 31 | |
| IRA | IA | Biologist | 48 48 | |
| IR | IR | Chemist | 51 51 | |
| IR | IRA | Chiropractor | 26 20 | |
| IAR | IAS | College Professor | 36 48 | |
| IR | IAR | Computer Programmer/Systems Analyst | 55 53 | |
| IRA | IR | Dentist | 20 16 | |
| IES | (SEC) | Dietitian | 28 (SEC) | |
| IRA | IA | Geographer | 35 44 | |
| IRA | IRA | Geologist | 38 41 | |
| IRC | ICA | Mathematician | 51 50 | |
| IRC | IRE | Medical Technician | 26 33 | |
| IRC | IRC | Medical Technologist | 41 35 | |
| IR | IR | Optometrist | 42 39 | |
| ICR | ICE | Pharmacist | 46 33 | |
| IAR | IAR | Physician | 31 40 | |
| IRA | IRA | Physicist | 45 47 | |
| IA | IA | Psychologist | 33 33 | |
| IR | IRC | Research & Development Manager | 45 33 | |
| IRA | IRS | Respiratory Therapist | 34 37 | |
| IRS | IRS | Science Teacher | 42 39 | |
| IAR | (AI) | Sociologist | 28 (AI) | |
| IRA | IR | Veterinarian | 31 16 | |

CPP CONSULTING PSYCHOLOGISTS PRESS, INC. • 3803 E. Bayshore Road, Palo Alto, CA 94303

**Figure 1.** *Continued*

**STRONG INTEREST INVENTORY**™

Profile report for    **LESLIE**

ID:

7601

KEY (Sample Scores)

| THEME CODES | | | YOUR SCORES | | ◄——DISSIMILAR INTERESTS | | | SIMILAR INTERESTS ——► | | | |
|---|---|---|---|---|---|---|---|---|---|---|---|
| FEMALE | MALE | | FEMALE | MALE | 15 | 20 | 30—MID-RANGE— 40 | 50 | 55 | | |
| (IAR) | AI | Sociologist | (IAR) | 50 | | | | | • | | |
| S | * | Child Care Provider | 45 | * | | | | | | | |

( ) You can find your score compared to this gender under the Theme represented by the first letter of this code. For example, your score compared to female sociologists is shown under the I or Investigative Theme.

* The position of the dot shows how similar your interests are to those of individuals of your gender who say they are satisfied in their occupation.

* Not enough people of this gender who work in this occupation could be found to make a good comparison.

(R) I
C (A)
(S)

**OCCUPATIONAL SCALES** (continued)

NOTES

(A)
E

**ARTISTIC** (creating or enjoying art, drama, music, writing)

| THEME CODES | | | YOUR SCORES | | DISSIMILAR INTERESTS | | | SIMILAR INTERESTS | | |
|---|---|---|---|---|---|---|---|---|---|---|
| FEMALE | MALE | | FEMALE | MALE | 15 | 20 | 30—MID-RANGE— 40 | 50 | 55 | |
| AE | AE | Advertising Executive | 5 | 8 | • | | | | | |
| ARI | ARI | Architect | 12 | -1 | • | | | | | |
| ARI | A | Artist, Commercial | -19 | -3 | • | | | | | |
| AR | A | Artist, Fine | -3 | 16 | • | | | | | |
| ASE | AS | Art Teacher | -13 | -3 | • | | | | | |
| AE | AE | Broadcaster | 6 | 8 | • | | | | | |
| AES | AES | Corporate Trainer | 23 | 37 | | • | | | | |
| ASE | ASE | English Teacher | 17 | 20 | | • | | | | |
| (EA) | AE | Interior Decorator | (EA) | 15 | | | | | | |
| A | A | Lawyer | 15 | 23 | • | | | | | |
| A | A | Librarian | 32 | 42 | | | • | | | |
| AIR | AIR | Medical Illustrator | -9 | -14 | • | | | | | |
| A | A | Musician | -4 | 19 | • | | | | | |
| ARE | ARE | Photographer | 0 | 0 | • | | | | | |
| AER | ASE | Public Administrator | 10 | 19 | • | | | | | |
| AE | AE | Public Relations Director | -12 | 4 | • | | | | | |
| A | A | Reporter | -1 | 9 | • | | | | | |
| (IAR) | AI | Sociologist | (IAR) | 26 | | | | | | |
| AIR | AI | Technical Writer | 14 | 29 | • | | | | | |
| A | AI | Translator | 9 | 41 | • | | | | | |

(E)
S

**SOCIAL** (helping, instructing, caregiving)

| THEME CODES | | | YOUR SCORES | | DISSIMILAR INTERESTS | | | SIMILAR INTERESTS | | |
|---|---|---|---|---|---|---|---|---|---|---|
| FEMALE | MALE | | FEMALE | MALE | 15 | 20 | 30—MID-RANGE— 40 | 50 | 55 | |
| (RIS) | SIR | Athletic Trainer | (RIS) | 20 | | | | | | |
| S | * | Child Care Provider | 37 | * | | | • | | | |
| SE | SE | Community Service Organization Director | 29 | 34 | | | • | | | |
| (IES) | SEC | Dietitian | (IES) | 34 | | | | | | |
| S | S | Elementary School Teacher | 37 | 56 | | | • | | | |
| SAE | SA | Foreign Language Teacher | 26 | 36 | | • | | | | |
| SE | SE | High School Counselor | 30 | 45 | | | • | | | |
| SE | * | Home Economics Teacher | 26 | * | | • | | | | |
| SAR | SA | Minister | 13 | 29 | • | | | | | |
| SCE | SCE | Nurse, LPN | 23 | 35 | | • | | | | |
| SI | SAI | Nurse, RN | 37 | 39 | | | • | | | |
| SAR | SA | Occupational Therapist | 28 | 29 | | • | | | | |
| SE | SE | Parks and Recreation Coordinator | 23 | 22 | | • | | | | |
| SRC | SR | Physical Education Teacher | 17 | 12 | • | | | | | |
| SIR | SIR | Physical Therapist | 25 | 23 | | • | | | | |
| SEA | SEC | School Administrator | 30 | 31 | | • | | | | |
| SEA | SEA | Social Science Teacher | 25 | 30 | | • | | | | |
| SA | SA | Social Worker | 29 | 34 | | • | | | | |
| SE | SEA | Special Education Teacher | 44 | 55 | | | | • | | |
| SA | SA | Speech Pathologist | 41 | 39 | | | • | | | |

*CPP* CONSULTING PSYCHOLOGISTS PRESS, INC. • 3803 E. Bayshore Road, Palo Alto, CA 94303

**Figure 1.** *Continued*

*(continued)*

# STRONG INTEREST INVENTORY™

Profile report for  **LESLIE**
ID:

7601

Page **5** of 6

KEY (Sample Scores)

| THEME CODES FEMALE MALE | | YOUR SCORES FEMALE MALE | DISSIMILAR-INTERESTS 15  20  30—MID-RANGE—40  50  55  SIMILAR-INTERESTS |
|---|---|---|---|
| EA | (AE) | Interior Decorator | -46 | (AE) |
| CSE | * | Dental Assistant | 15 | * |

( ) You can find your score compared to this gender under the Theme represented by the first letter of this code. For example, your score compared to male interior decorators is shown under the A or Artistic Theme.

• The position of the dot shows how similar your interests are to those of individuals of your gender who say they are satisfied in their occupation.

* Not enough people of this gender who work in this occupation could be found to make a good comparison.

## OCCUPATIONAL SCALES (continued)

NOTES

### ENTERPRISING (selling, managing, persuading)

| THEME CODES FEMALE | MALE | | YOUR SCORES FEMALE | MALE | DISSIMILAR INTERESTS | | | SIMILAR INTERESTS | | |
|---|---|---|---|---|---|---|---|---|---|---|
| | | | | | 15 | 20 | 30—MID-RANGE—40 | 50 | 55 | |
| * | ECR | Agribusiness Manager | • | 14 | | | | | | |
| EC | EC | Buyer | 4 | 7 | • | | | | | |
| ERA | ER | Chef | -7 | 10 | • | | | | | |
| EIS | * | Dental Hygienist | 20 | • | | | • | | | |
| EAS | ESA | Elected Public Official | 8 | 13 | • | | | | | |
| EAS | EAS | Flight Attendant | 4 | 23 | • | | | | | |
| EAC | EAC | Florist | -3 | 15 | • | | | | | |
| EC | EA | Hair Stylist | 6 | 8 | • | | | | | |
| ECS | ECS | Housekeeping & Maintenance Supervisor | 22 | 21 | | | • | | | |
| EAS | ES | Human Resources Director | 28 | 32 | | | • | | | |
| EA | (AE) | Interior Decorator | -11 | (AE) | • | | | | | |
| EIR | ECI | Investments Manager | 30 | 30 | | | • | | | |
| E | E | Life Insurance Agent | 16 | 17 | | • | | | | |
| EA | EA | Marketing Executive | 28 | 40 | | | • | | | |
| ECR | ER | Optician | 23 | 17 | | • | | | | |
| ECR | ECR | Purchasing Agent | 15 | 21 | • | | | | | |
| E | E | Realtor | 10 | 15 | • | | | | | |
| ECR | ECR | Restaurant Manager | 15 | 7 | • | | | | | |
| ECA | ECS | Store Manager | 21 | 16 | | • | | | | |
| ECA | ECA | Travel Agent | 15 | 21 | • | | | | | |

### CONVENTIONAL (accounting, organizing, processing data)

| THEME CODES FEMALE | MALE | | YOUR SCORES FEMALE | MALE | DISSIMILAR INTERESTS | | | SIMILAR INTERESTS | | |
|---|---|---|---|---|---|---|---|---|---|---|
| | | | | | 15 | 20 | 30—MID-RANGE—40 | 50 | 55 | |
| CE | CE | Accountant | 49 | 50 | | | | | • | | |
| CI | CI | Actuary | 67 | 67 | | | | | | • | |
| CE | CE | Banker | 37 | 46 | | | • | | | | |
| C | C | Bookkeeper | 46 | 39 | | | | • | | | |
| CES | CES | Business Education Teacher | 37 | 34 | | | • | | | | |
| CE | CE | Credit Manager | 40 | 32 | | | • | | | | |
| CSE | * | Dental Assistant | 25 | • | | | • | | | | |
| CSE | (RC) | Farmer | 32 | (RC) | | | • | | | | |
| CES | CES | Food Service Manager | 27 | 26 | | | • | | | | |
| CIR | CIS | Mathematics Teacher | 52 | 53 | | | | | • | | |
| C | C | Medical Records Technician | 42 | 48 | | | | • | | | |
| CRE | (RCE) | Military Enlisted Personnel | 25 | (RCE) | | | • | | | | |
| CES | CES | Nursing Home Administrator | 29 | 45 | | | • | | | | |
| CE | CA | Paralegal | 27 | 20 | | | • | | | | |
| CES | * | Secretary | 19 | • | | • | | | | | |
| CE | (RE) | Small Business Owner | 26 | (RE) | | | • | | | | |

CPP CONSULTING PSYCHOLOGISTS PRESS, INC. • 3803 E. Bayshore Road, Palo Alto, CA 94303

**Figure 1.** *Continued*

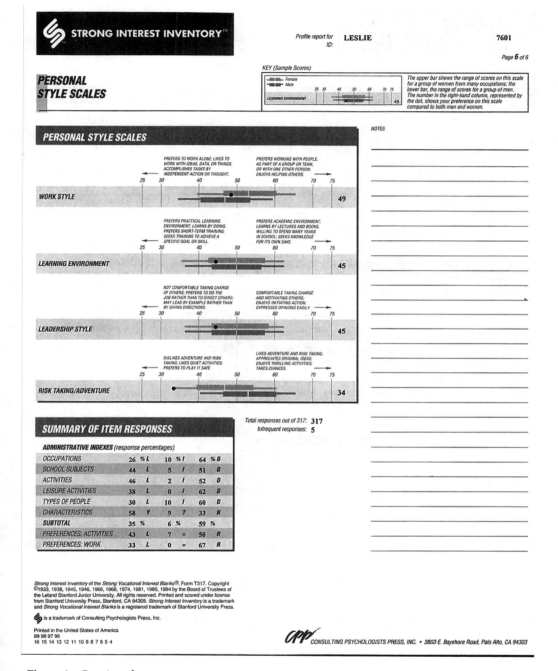

**Figure 1.** *Continued*

## SKILLSCONFIDENCE INVENTORY

BY NANCY E. BETZ • FRED H. BORGEN • LENORE W. HARMON

| | |
|---|---|
| Profile report for | |
| ID: | **LESLIE** |
| Age: | 0 |
| Gender: | Female |

7601

Date tested: 10/21/97
Date scored: 7/30/98

Skills page **1** of **1**

### LEVELS OF SKILLS CONFIDENCE BY THEME

Your *Skills Confidence Inventory* results describe how you perceive your own capabilities in performing activities related to six broad areas, the General Occupational Themes. Keep in mind that these results may not reflect your actual abilities; the results reflect how you rate yourself. Your own rating may influence what kinds of activities you try or avoid and may determine what occupations or educational programs you consider as possibilities for exploration.

Your confidence in each of the six areas is shown at the right in rank order. The Theme code below your results summarizes the areas in which you feel most confident performing particular activities.

| THEME CODE | THEME | SCORE (1–5) | VERY LITTLE CONFIDENCE | LITTLE CONFIDENCE | MODERATE CONFIDENCE | HIGH CONFIDENCE | VERY HIGH CONFIDENCE | TYPICAL SKILL AREAS |
|---|---|---|---|---|---|---|---|---|
| I | INVESTIGATIVE | 4.6 | ☐ | ☐ | ☐ | ☐ | ☑ | Research, math, science |
| S | SOCIAL | 3.7 | ☐ | ☐ | ☐ | ☑ | ☐ | Education, counseling, social service |
| C | CONVENTIONAL | 3.6 | ☐ | ☐ | ☐ | ☑ | ☐ | Finance, computers, organization |
| E | ENTERPRISING | 2.4 | ☐ | ☑ | ☐ | ☐ | ☐ | Sales, speaking, management |
| A | ARTISTIC | 1.6 | ☑ | ☐ | ☐ | ☐ | ☐ | Creative expression, music, design |
| R | REALISTIC | 1.2 | ☑ | ☐ | ☐ | ☐ | ☐ | Outdoor work, construction, repair |

Your Skills Confidence Theme code is ISC—(see explanation at left).

### COMPARISON OF LEVELS OF SKILLS CONFIDENCE AND INTEREST

See the back of this page for information on how to use this comparison of confidence in your skills and your interests to find satisfying career, educational, and leisure options.

Shown in rank order by confidence level.

Further exploration (if Moderate is highest level of confidence)

Further exploration

Priorities for career exploration

| THEME CODE | THEME | | |
|---|---|---|---|
| I | INVESTIGATIVE | Skills Confidence / Interest | High priority |
| S | SOCIAL | Skills Confidence / Interest | High priority |
| C | CONVENTIONAL | Skills Confidence / Interest | High priority |
| E | ENTERPRISING | Skills Confidence / Interest | Low priority |
| A | ARTISTIC | Skills Confidence / Interest | Low priority |
| R | REALISTIC | Skills Confidence / Interest | Good option if confidence in skills can be increased |

Your Skills Confidence Theme code is ISC. Your Interest Theme code is SCI. Consider both codes as you select the Themes you would like to explore further.

Total responses out of 60:  60

*CPP* CONSULTING PSYCHOLOGISTS PRESS, INC. • 3803 E. Bayshore Road, Palo Alto, CA 94303

**Figure 2.** Leslie's Skills Confidence Inventory Profile

SOURCE: Betz, Borgen, and Harmon (1996). Modified and reproduced by special permission of the Publisher, Consulting Psychologist Press, Inc., Palo Alto, CA 94303 from the **Skills Confidence Inventory, Leslie** ▮▮▮ **profile.** Copyright 1996 by Consulting Psychologists Press, Inc. All rights reserved. Further reproduction is prohibited without the Publisher's written consent.

## MINNESOTA IMPORTANCE QUESTIONNAIRE
### Ranked Form

Name: *LESLIE*
LCT score = 92%

Date: *12/09/97*

Score

**ACHIEVEMENT  1.5**

*Ability Utilization:* I could do something
that makes use of my abilities........................1.6
*Achievement:* The job could give me a
feeling of accomplishment ............................1.3

**COMFORT  −0.4**

*Activity:* I could be busy all the time................−0.7
*Independence:* I could work alone on the job...−0.9
*Variety:* I could do something different every
day .........................................................−0.6
*Compensation:* My pay would compare well
with that of other workers ...........................0.4
*Security:* The job would provide for steady
employment..............................................−0.3
*Working Conditions:* The job would have
good working conditions ...........................−0.2

**STATUS  −0.7**

*Advancement:* The job would provide an
opportunity for advancement........................0.3
*Recognition:* I could get recognition for the
work I do.................................................0.0
*Authority:* I could tell people what to do.........−1.9
*Social Status:* I could be "somebody" in the
community ...............................................0.7

**ALTRUISM  1.3**

*Co-workers:* My co-workers would be easy
to make friends with .....................................0.8
*Social Service:* I could do things for other
people ...........................................................1.1
*Moral Values:* I could do the work without
feeling that it is morally wrong ...................2.1

**SAFETY  −0.4**

*Company Policies:* The company would
administer its policies fairly........................0.9
*Supervision—Human Relations:* My boss
would back up the workers.........................0.0
*Supervision—Technical:* My boss would train
the workers well ....................................... -0.3

**AUTONOMY  0.7**

*Creativity:* I could try out some of my own
ideas..........................................................0.5
*Responsibility:* I could make decisions on my
own...........................................................0.8
*Autonomy:* I could plan my work with little
supervision ...................................................0.8

Score

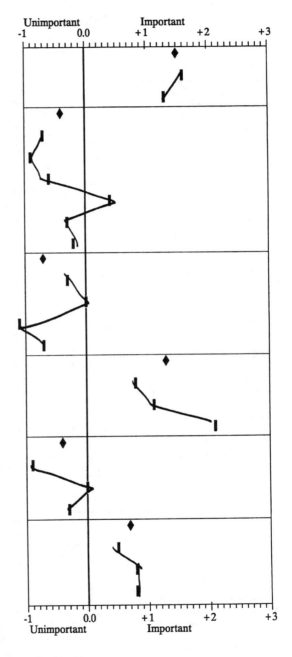

**Figure 3.** Leslie's Minnesota Importance Questionnaire Profile
SOURCE: Rounds, Henley, Dawis, Lofquist, and Weiss (1981). Used with permission.

## Minnesota Importance Questionnaire

Correspondence report for *LESLIE*                                          *12/09/97*

The MIQ profile is compared with Occupational Reinforcer Patterns (ORPS) for 90 representative occupations. Correspondence is indicated by the C index. A prediction of *Satisfied (S)* results from C values greater than .49, *Likely Satisfied (L)* for C values between .10 and .49, and *Not Satisfied (N)* for C values less than .10. Occupations are clustered by similarity of Occupational Reinforcer Patterns.

| | C Index | Pred. Sat. | | C Index | Pred. Sat. |
|---|---|---|---|---|---|
| **CLUSTER A (ACH-AUT-Alt)** | .68 | S | **CLUSTER B (ACH-Com)** | .51 | S |
| *Architect* | .62 | S | Bricklayer | .43 | L |
| *Dentist* | .58 | S | Carpenter | .31 | L |
| Family Practitioner (M.D.) | .45 | L | Cement Mason | .42 | L |
| *Interior Designer/Decorator* | .63 | S | Elevator Repairer | .31 | L |
| Lawyer | .48 | L | Heavy Equipment Operator | .48 | L |
| *Minister* | .52 | S | Landscape Gardener | .49 | L |
| *Nurse, Occupational Health* | .58 | S | *Lather* | .55 | S |
| *Occupational Therapist* | .68 | S | *Millwright* | .54 | S |
| *Optometrist* | .54 | S | Painter/Paperhanger | .38 | L |
| *Psychologist, Counseling* | .72 | S | Patternmaker, Metal | .33 | L |
| *Recreation Leader* | .63 | S | Pipefitter | .43 | L |
| *Speech Pathologist* | .67 | S | Plasterer | .37 | L |
| *Teacher, Elementary School* | .65 | S | Plumber | .54 | S |
| *Teacher, Secondary School* | .66 | S | Roofer | .46 | L |
| *Vocational Evaluator* | .60 | S | *Salesperson, Automobile* | .50 | S |
| **CLUSTER C (ACH-Aut-Com)** | .60 | S | **CLUSTER D (ACH-STA-Com)** | .48 | L |
| *Alteration Tailor* | .57 | S | Accountant, Certified Public | .49 | L |
| *Automobile Mechanic* | .47 | L | *Airplane Co-Pilot, Commercial* | .32 | L |
| *Barber* | .60 | S | Cook (Hotel-Restaurant) | .32 | L |
| *Beauty Operator* | .68 | S | Department Head, Supermarket | .19 | L |
| *Caseworker* | .66 | S | Drafter, Architectural | .46 | L |
| *Claim Adjuster* | .50 | S | Electrician | .44 | L |
| Commercial Artist, Illustrator | .46 | L | Engineer, Civil | .47 | L |
| Electronics Mechanic | .32 | L | *Engineer, Time Study* | .51 | S |
| Locksmith | .40 | L | Firm-Equipment Mechanic I | .33 | L |
| Maintenance Repairer, Factory | .40 | L | Line-Installer-Repairer (Telephone) | .08 | N |
| *Mechanical-Engineering Technician* | .60 | S | Machinist | .29 | L |
| Office-Machine Servicer | .41 | L | *Programmer (Business, Engineering, Science)* | .54 | S |
| Photoengraver (Stripper) | .42 | L | Sheet Metal Worker | .44 | L |
| *Sales Agent, Real Estate* | .70 | S | Statistical-Machine Servicer | .28 | L |
| Salesperson, General Hardware | .40 | L | Writer, Technical Publication | .57 | S |
| **CLUSTER E (COM)** | .24 | L | **CLUSTER F (Alt-Com)** | .54 | S |
| Assembler, Production | −.05 | N | *Airplane-Flight Attendant* | .57 | S |
| Baker | .18 | L | Clerk, General Office, Civil Service | .30 | L |
| Bookbinder | .22 | L | Dietitian | .40 | L |
| Bookkeeper I | .28 | L | Fire Fighter | .35 | L |
| Bus Driver | .22 | L | *Librarian* | .65 | S |
| Key-Punch Operator | .25 | L | *Medical Technologist* | .61 | S |
| Meat Cutter | .10 | L | Nurse, Professional | .46 | L |
| Post-Office Clerk | .19 | L | Orderly | .38 | L |
| Production Helper (Food) | .35 | L | *Physical Therapist* | .58 | S |
| Punch-Press Operator | .20 | L | Police Officer | .48 | L |
| Sales, General (Department Store) | .35 | L | Receptionist, Civil Service | .42 | L |
| Sewing-Machine Operator, Automatic | .23 | L | Secretary (General Office) | .46 | L |
| Solderer (Production Line) | .11 | L | Taxi Driver | .35 | L |
| Telephone Operator | .19 | L | Telephone Installer | .41 | L |
| Teller (Banking) | .24 | L | *Waiter-Waitress* | .51 | S |

Vocational Psychology Research, Department of Psychology
University of Minnesota, Minneapolis MN 55455

**Figure 3.**  Leslie's Minnesota Importance Questionnaire Profile *(continued)*

SOURCE: Rounds, Henley, Dawis, Lofquist, and Weiss (1981). Used with permission.

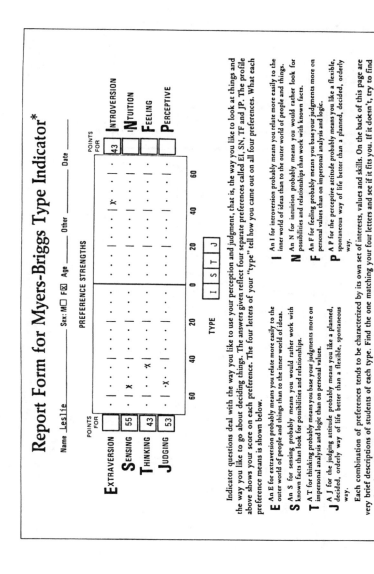

**Figure 4.** Leslie's Myers-Briggs Type Indicator Profile

SOURCE: Myers and McCaulley (1985). Modified and reproduced by special permission of the Publisher, Consulting Psychologists Press, Inc., Palo Alto, CA 94303 from the **Myers-Briggs Type Indicator® Report Form**. Copyright 1976 by Isabel Briggs Myers. All rights reserved. Further reproduction is prohibited without the Publisher's written consent. Myers-Briggs Type Indicator is a registered trademark of Consulting Psychologists Press, Inc.

243

# Individual Analysis of Career Concerns

Name  **Leslie**                    Age _____

Compared with _____              Date _____

**Consulting Psychologists Press, Inc.**
**Palo Alto, CA 94303**

The ACCI can be self-scored to yield a profile based on the clusters of career development tasks of most concern to you. The procedures for self-scoring and profile analysis are:

1. On the Career Concerns Chart below, enter the distribution of ratings for each of the groups of 5 items in each subtage. For example, if for items 1 to 5, you marked 1 for two items, 2 for two items, and 3 for one item, you would enter those numbers in the appropriate spaces on the Crystallization line.

2. Then compute the average score for the subtage by dividing the weighted sum by the number of items in the group. For the above example, the weighted sum would be 2+4+3=9, divided by 5, equals 1.8. Enter the weighted sum and average in the appropriate columns. Follow the same procedure for each subtage and stage.

3. Circle the number of the response you chose for item 61.

4. Plot your Career Stage and Subtage Profile below by marking with a capital X on the appropriate line the location of each of the four Stage averages, and with a small x each of the Subtage averages. Connect the small x's in each Stage to draw the four profiles of your current career concerns. Intraindividual interpretations of average Subtage scores are usually more insight-producing than are Stage scores because of present and future orientations and recycling.

5. Convert the raw scores (5-point ratings) into percentiles with the appropriate table in the Manual or from local norms. Percentiles make it possible to compare one person with a group of relevant people, and average ratings on the 5-point scale help when a person compares him or herself using the profile.

6. Record for each Subtage the number of items rated either 4 or 5 to show the clustering of major concerns and to help interpret Stage and Subtage averages in the Career Concerns Chart below.

## CAREER CONCERNS CHART

| Items | Career Concerns | None 1 | Little 2 | Some 3 | Cons. 4 | Great 5 | Weighted Sum | Average |
|---|---|---|---|---|---|---|---|---|
| | **A: EXPLORATION STAGE** | | | | | | | |
| 1–5 | Crystallization | | 1 | 1 | 3 | | 17 | 3.4 |
| 6–10 | Specification | | | 2 | | 3 | 21 | 4.2 |
| 11–15 | Implementation | | 2 | 3 | 3? | | 13 | 2.6 |
| 1–15 | TOTAL EXPLORATION | | 3 | 6 | 3? | 3 | 51 | 3.4 |
| | **B: ESTABLISHMENT STAGE** | | | | | | | |
| 16–20 | Stabilizing | 1 | 2 | | 1 | 1 | 14 | 2.8 |
| 21–25 | Consolidating | | 4 | 1 | | | 11 | 2.2 |
| 26–30 | Advancing | | 3 | 2 | | | 12 | 2.4 |
| 16–30 | TOTAL ESTABLISHMENT | 1 | 9 | 3 | 1 | 1 | 37 | 2.5 |
| | **C: MAINTENANCE STAGE** | | | | | | | |
| 31–35 | Holding | 1 | 4 | | | | 9 | 1.8 |
| 36–40 | Updating | 3 | 1 | 1 | | | 8 | 1.6 |
| 41–45 | Innovating | | 1 | 1 | 3 | | 17 | 3.4 |
| 31–45 | TOTAL MAINTENANCE | 4 | 6 | 2 | 3 | | 34 | 2.3 |
| | **D: DISENGAGEMENT STAGE** | | | | | | | |
| 46–50 | Deceleration | 5 | | | | | 5 | 1.0 |
| 51–55 | Retirement Planning | 5 | | | | | 5 | 1.0 |
| 56–60 | Retirement Living | 5 | | | | | 5 | 1.0 |
| 46–60 | TOTAL DISENGAGEMENT | 15 | | | | | 15 | 1.0 |
| 61 | CAREER CHANGE STATUS | 1 | 2 | ③ | 4 | 5 (Circle Response) | | |

## CAREER STAGE AND SUBSTAGE PROFILE

| | | %-ile | Amount of Current Concern — None 1.0 Little 2.0 Some 3.0 Cons. 4.0 Great 5.0 | Number of Concerns Rated 4 (Considerable) or 5 (Great) Substages |
|---|---|---|---|---|
| | Crystallization | | | 3 |
| | Specification | | | 3 |
| | Implementation | 79 | | – |
| | Stabilizing | | | 1 |
| | Consolidating | | | 1 |
| | Advancing | 25 | | – |
| | Holding | | | – |
| | Updating | | | – |
| | Innovating | 23 | | 3 |
| | Deceleration | | | – |
| | Retirement Planning | | | – |
| | Retirement Living | 1 | | – |

97  96  95  94                    13  12  11

Copyright © 1988 by Consulting Psychologists Press, Inc., 3803 E. Bayshore Road, Palo Alto, CA 94303. All rights reserved. Printed in the U.S.A.

0383

**Figure 5.** Leslie's Adult Career Concerns Inventory Profile

SOURCE: Super, Thompson, and Lindeman (1988). Modified and reproduced by special permission of the Publisher, Consulting Psychologists Press, Inc., Palo Alto, CA 94303 from the **Adult Career Concerns Inventory Report Form.** Copyright 1988 by Consulting Psychologists Press, Inc. All rights reserved. Further reproduction is prohibited without the Publisher's written consent.

244

## CBI
### Report Form

Name: **LESLIE** _____   Date: _____

This report summarizes the beliefs you reported on the *Career Beliefs Inventory* (CBI) into 25 scales. In general, the lower your score on a scale (39 or less), the more valuable it will be for you to determine whether the belief is blocking or facilitating your progress. Your beliefs are neither good nor bad; they are what you currently believe to be true for you. Examining the reasons for your beliefs on each scale and discussing them with others may open new possibilities. Use the CBI handscoring keys and the directions on the first page of this booklet to determine your scale scores.

| Scale | A Sum | B # | C A/B | Score C x 10 | | More Valuable to Explore | |
|---|---|---|---|---|---|---|---|

**My Current Career Situation**

| | Scale | A Sum | B # | C A/B | Score C x 10 | (left anchor) | Rating | (right anchor) |
|---|---|---|---|---|---|---|---|---|
| 1 | Employment Status | 10 | 2 | 5.0 | 50 | Unemployed | X (at 50) | Employed |
| 2 | Career Plans | 8 | 2 | 4.0 | 40 | Plans already decided | X (at 40) | Plans open to change |
| 3 | Acceptance of Uncertainty | 6 | 2 | 3.0 | 30 | Should have decided by now | X (at 30) | Indecision is understandable |
| 4 | Openness | 15 | 4 | 3.75 | 38 | Keep reasons for choices private | X (near 38) | Willing to disclose reasons for choices |

**What Seems Necessary for My Happiness**

| | Scale | A Sum | B # | C A/B | Score C x 10 | (left anchor) | Rating | (right anchor) |
|---|---|---|---|---|---|---|---|---|
| 5 | Achievement | 7 | 2 | 3.5 | 35 | Motivated by goals other than achievement | X (at 35) | Highly motivated to achieve |
| 6 | College Education | 6 | 2 | 3.0 | 30 | College is necessary for a good job | X (at 30) | College is only one of the routes to a good job |
| 7 | Intrinsic Satisfaction | 21 | 5 | 4.2 | 42 | Work is a means to other goals | X (at 42) | Work tasks must be satisfying |
| 8 | Peer Equality | 4 | 3 | 1.3 | 13 | Desire to excel others | X (at 13) | Need not excel others |
| 9 | Structured Work Environment | 7 | 2 | 3.5 | 35 | Prefer flexible work hours with no supervision | X (at 35) | Prefer standard work hours with supervision |

**Factors That Influence My Decisions**

| | Scale | A Sum | B # | C A/B | Score C x 10 | (left anchor) | Rating | (right anchor) |
|---|---|---|---|---|---|---|---|---|
| 10 | Control | 5 | 2 | 2.5 | 25 | Career path is influenced by others | X (at 25) | Career path is self-determined |
| 11 | Responsibility | 12 | 5 | 2.4 | 24 | Expert help can determine the best career choice | X (at 24) | A career choice is a personal one |
| 12 | Approval of Others | 2 | 2 | 1.0 | 10 | Approval is important | X (at 10) | Approval does not matter |
| 13 | Self-Other Comparisons | 14 | 4 | 3.5 | 35 | Compare self with others | X (at 35) | Avoid comparisons with others |

**Figure 6.** Leslie's Career Beliefs Inventory Profile

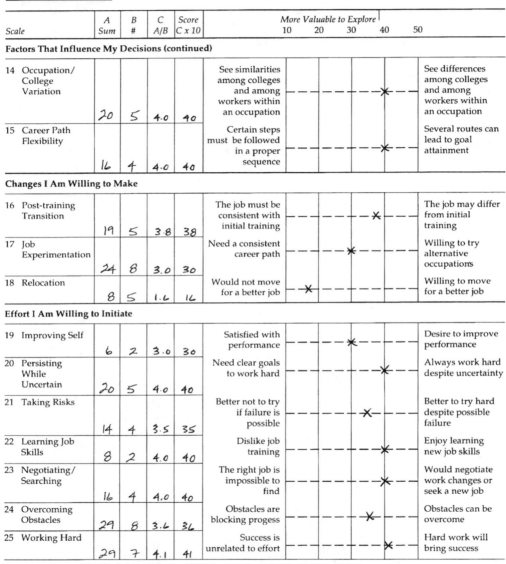

| Scale | A Sum | B # | C A/B | Score C x 10 | | More Valuable to Explore 10   20   30   40   50 | |
|---|---|---|---|---|---|---|---|

**Factors That Influence My Decisions (continued)**

14 Occupation/ College Variation — A: 20, B: 5, C: 4.0, Score: 40 — See similarities among colleges and among workers within an occupation ———X——— See differences among colleges and among workers within an occupation

15 Career Path Flexibility — A: 16, B: 4, C: 4.0, Score: 40 — Certain steps must be followed in a proper sequence ———X——— Several routes can lead to goal attainment

**Changes I Am Willing to Make**

16 Post-training Transition — A: 19, B: 5, C: 3.8, Score: 38 — The job must be consistent with initial training ——X——— The job may differ from initial training

17 Job Experimentation — A: 24, B: 8, C: 3.0, Score: 30 — Need a consistent career path ——X——— Willing to try alternative occupations

18 Relocation — A: 8, B: 5, C: 1.6, Score: 16 — Would not move for a better job X——— Willing to move for a better job

**Effort I Am Willing to Initiate**

19 Improving Self — A: 6, B: 2, C: 3.0, Score: 30 — Satisfied with performance ——X——— Desire to improve performance

20 Persisting While Uncertain — A: 20, B: 5, C: 4.0, Score: 40 — Need clear goals to work hard ———X——— Always work hard despite uncertainty

21 Taking Risks — A: 14, B: 4, C: 3.5, Score: 35 — Better not to try if failure is possible ———X——— Better to try hard despite possible failure

22 Learning Job Skills — A: 8, B: 2, C: 4.0, Score: 40 — Dislike job training ———X——— Enjoy learning new job skills

23 Negotiating/ Searching — A: 16, B: 4, C: 4.0, Score: 40 — The right job is impossible to find ———X——— Would negotiate work changes or seek a new job

24 Overcoming Obstacles — A: 29, B: 8, C: 3.6, Score: 36 — Obstacles are blocking progess ———X——— Obstacles can be overcome

25 Working Hard — A: 29, B: 7, C: 4.1, Score: 41 — Success is unrelated to effort ———X——— Hard work will bring success

**Figure 6.** *Continued*

# Index

# *About the Authors*

**Jane L. Swanson** is Professor of Psychology at Southern Illinois University at Carbondale. She received her Ph.D. from the University of Minnesota in 1986. She is a Fellow of the Division of Counseling Psychology (Division 17) of the American Psychological Association, serves on the Executive Board of Division 17, and is Chair-Elect of the Society for Vocational Psychology (a section within the division). She currently serves on several journal editorial boards and has served as Associate Editor of the *Journal of Vocational Behavior.* Her areas of research include career barriers, career counseling process, measurement of vocational interests, and career psychology of women.

**Nadya A. Fouad,** Ph.D., is Professor in the Department of Educational Psychology at the University of Wisconsin—Milwaukee. She has published numerous articles and chapters on cross-cultural vocational assessment, career development, interest measurement, and cross-cultural counseling. She is Coeditor of the series "Legacies and Traditions" in *The Counseling Psychologist* and served as Associate Editor of the *Journal of Vocational Behavior* from 1994 to 1997. She is Chair of the Strong Research Advisory Board, a Fellow of Division 17 of the American Psychological Association, and is serving Division 17 as Vice President for Diversity and Public Interest and as Chair of the Society for Vocational Psychology.